Stroud Sings

THE HISTORY OF STROUD CHORAL SOCIETY
1834–2000

Susan Freck

Dedicated to

Leonard Keck 1904–78
For his generous support, enthusiasm and vision for this choir

Sylvia Heymans 1936–99
Whose belief in this book gave us the courage to start

First published in the United Kingdom by Stroud Choral Society

© 2001 Stroud Choral Society
All rights reserved
Typeset in Goudy by Bookcraft Ltd, Stroud, Gloucestershire
Printed by Cromwell Press, Trowbridge, Wiltshire
ISBN 0–9541742–0–8

Cover and title page illustration

'The 1st Philharmonic Concert for the Season was held at the Subscription Rooms on Tuesday evening last – November 17th 1835 – and was attended by all the respectable families in the neighbourhood.' Mr Sapio, obviously singing 'Queen of my Soul', was 'repeatedly encored'. Note the trellis and paper flower decoration along the front of the 'orchestra'.

Back cover

Text: Sue Edwards. Painting: Brenda Dunn. Photography: Peckhams of Stroud.

Contents

Acknowledgements 4

Early beginnings 5

First concerts 9

The phoenix rises 22

'Chew's band' 30

'I dreamt that I dwelt in marble halls' 32

Sweet charity 39

Sammy's ascent 43

Dark days, post-war blues and an MBE 57

Winds of change 73

A new era 90

Anniversaries and celebrations 110

Let us now praise famous men – and women! 122
        Samuel William Underwood 125
        John Jacob 129
        Leonard Keck 131
        Claude Allen 131
        Gail Fearnley-Whittingstall 133
        Edward Garrard 134

Soloists of note 136

Unanswered questions, unsolved mysteries 142

Top of the Stroud Choral Pops 145

Concert lists 146

Membership lists 164

Bibliography 171

Index 173

Acknowledgements

We wish to express our gratitude to all present members, former members and friends of Stroud Choral Society, for their interest and help in the making of this book.

In particular our grateful thanks go to Ronald Nolan, whose extensive research and unpublished book on the life of Sammy Underwood, have been of invaluable help to the Society.

The Society's thanks go to the hard working 'book group'. Original idea, coordination and right-hand woman, Sue Edwards. Research, Elizabeth Akehurst, Pearl Foster and Alison Hesketh. Book title and index, Christine Headley. Our thanks also go to all members of the Choral Society Committee for their help and encouragement.

For the loan of photographs, documents, music, artwork and for additional information and ideas, we wish to thank Lesley Abraham, Sheila Adams, Betty Baker, Howard Beard, Freda Bishop, Anthony Boden, Peggy Bradshaw, Helen Briggs, Clive Burcher, Elisabeth and Cyril Campbell, John C Cant (London), Jackie Carpenter, Chalford Silver Band, William Chew (Glasgow), Brenda Dunn, Jenny Edwards, Neil Edwards, Gail Fearnley-Whittingstall, Mark Foster, John Gardiner, Eddie and Glennis Garrard, Marguerite Govier, Michael Gray, Carolyn Greet (Gloucester Choral Society), Adrian Harbridge, Pat Harbridge, Giles Harrison, Sue and Barry Harrison, Anita Hewitt-Jones, Peter Hillier (GCS), Sheila Hinder, Lorna Lane (Cirencester Choral Society), Joyce Longhurst, Susannah Mahler, Gwyneth and Eric Martin, Wilf Merrett, Hugh Morrison, Sheila Morrison, Glenys Nelmes, Tim Page (CCS), Eric Pankhurst, Reggie Price, John and Jenifer Ricketts, Kay Sandells, Rita Saville Stones, George Simner (Festival of Britain Society), Hilary Smith, Mo Smith, Jack Sollars, Tracy Spiers, Stroud District Council, Stroud Town Council, June Sturm, Barbara Thorley, Margery van Zyl.

For kind permission to reproduce printed material, we thank *The Citizen, Stroud News and Journal*, Gloucester Records Office, Gloucester Reference Library, Stroud Library, *Wilts and Gloucestershire Standard*, Peckhams Photography of Stroud.

The music *The Fire Kindled* is reprinted by permission of Roberton Publications. The poem *Maurice Broadbent: A Tribute* is reprinted by kind permision of Michael Holland.

Last but not least, special thanks go to my patient husband, daughters, family and friends, for putting up with my unavailability to come out to play during the preparation of this book.

The author wishes to apologise for any unknowing errors and omissions.

Sue Freck, August 2001

Working on the book: Sue Edwards and Sue Freck.

Early beginnings

Stroud prior to 1907

> *Stroudwater Green and Stroudwater Blue*
> *Red for the Guardsmen's Coats*
> *Preserves and Honey, Cakes and Milk*
> *Cheese from Cows and Goats*
> *Tools for Scything, tools for Digging*
> *Things for Work and Play*
> *Stuffs for Admiring; Staff for the Hiring*
> *It's Market Day today!*
>
> *Market Day*, Maurice Broadbent

Stroud in the nineteenth century: a busy, hustling, working town. Factories, mills, shops and workshops all jostled in amongst the stone cottages and the new red brick terraces which teetered up and down the steep hillsides and lined the lush valleys. A higgledy-piggledy town, full of noise and bustle and purpose. A manufacturing town, famous for its broadcloth and the invention of the lawnmower! Like other working towns, Stroud was making its mark on the nineteenth-century map and, like some other working towns, Stroud had a newly formed choral society.

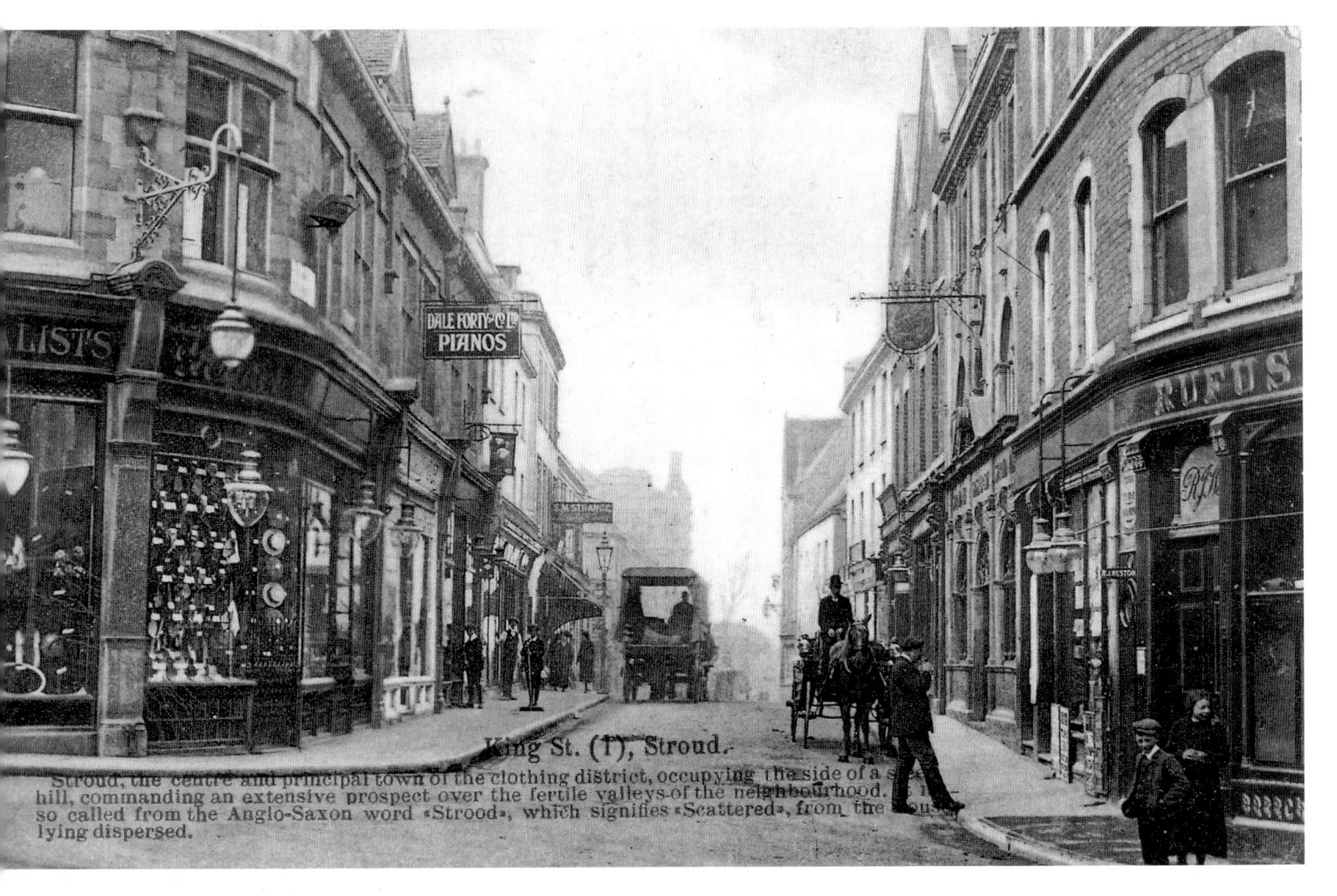

Stroud in the early years of the twentieth century. The name is now said to mean 'marshy ground overgrown with brushwood'.

Amid the great achievements of the nineteenth century, the rise and blossoming of the great choral societies does not spring readily to mind, but the growth of these choirs between 1834 and 1850 was unprecedented. Stroud was unusual, it was a small town in which to sustain a choral society, it was also one of the earlier choral societies to become established. What was it that enabled these societies to flourish at this time? What was it that was happening in Stroud? Almost certainly our Choral Society was not a chance occurrence but the result of a series of events that led to the Society's formation and continuation.

As early as 1757, Stroud had been described as 'a sort of capital of the clothing villages', and more industrial growth was stimulated by the completion of the canal links with the Severn in 1779 and the Thames in 1789. Communication and transport were further improved when in 1800 the new Bath to Cheltenham Road was finished, and in 1814, the London Road was completed. After 1830 travel was also made much easier by the rapid expansion of the railway system throughout Great Britain. As the railway network grew, the fares became cheaper, opening up another mode of transport to a greater number of people. Stroud was fortunate enough to have two railway stations. The Great Western opened in May 1845, having incorporated the Bristol and Gloucester Railway. The Midland Railway opened a station at Dudbridge in 1867. Later, a Midland link-line into Stroud, with a station near the Hill Paul building was opened in 1888. As transport improved in Stroud and work opportunities grew, there was, as in other places, some movement away from the countryside into the expanding town.

The importance of Stroud was acknowledged in 1832 when the Borough of Stroud was constituted and, in the same year, Stroud, and its adjoining district, was granted permission to return two Members of Parliament. Like other industrial towns, finding themselves newly fired with civic pride and wealthy enough to build themselves impressive town

EARLY BEGINNINGS

halls, Stroud also embarked on an imposing building to celebrate its new civic status. The Stroud Subscription Rooms, funded by 57 subscribers who between them purchased 61 £50 shares, were opened in 1834. The large ballroom of the Subscription Rooms was the venue for public meetings, concerts, lectures and other events.

Early in Victoria's reign education for all was beginning to be seen in a more important light. With the opening of the British School at Badbrook in 1840 and the National School (Blackboys) in 1844, Stroud was making its first fledging steps towards universal elementary education. It was at this time that the invention of a number of tonic 'sol-fa' systems made the reading of music more accessible and a Dr J P Kay's 'sol-fa' system was being introduced into the existing elementary schools.

Printing technology was improving and when the duty on paper and printing was abolished in the 1860s it led to a great increase in printing and publication. Cheaper printing meant more books of all kinds including music scores. Newspapers could now carry a wealth of advertisements including those for concerts. Local printers produced 'Books of Words' of the current work being performed. Because of improved road and rail networks distribution of all kinds of printed matter became easier.

During the eighteenth century, the Established Church had been happy to have music provided by the village bands and church musicians (now better known as West Gallery Musicians). But, during the nineteenth century, and in particular between 1840 and 1865, there was a systematic movement to remove these musicians in favour of organ-led, congregational hymns. In 1860 the desire to make church music more refined led to the birth of *Hymns Ancient and Modern*. The result was that in many places the church bands died out with perhaps only a residual revival at Christmas, when they could be found playing carols in the local public houses. Other bands looked for new opportunities and may well have become the nucleus of the players for the new Philharmonics and new choral societies.

A nationwide desire for education and knowledge led to the forming of many mutual benefit and improvement societies, clubs and classes. For perhaps the first time in history, and in spite of working long, hard days, the working man and woman had some time for leisure and some little money to spare to spend on it. A small item in the *Gloucester Journal* for December 26th 1835 spells out the economic situation in Stroud: 'We are happy to have it in our power to inform you that the manufacturers are doing more here than is

Stroud fruit sellers, early twentieth century.

normally the case at this season of the year and although the winter bids fair to be a hard one, yet as there is not a dearth of employment and provisions are cheap, we believe the labouring classes will have a tolerable season.' In 1839, it was reported that weavers in Stonehouse had fuller employment and better wages than many other weavers in Gloucestershire. Stroud, following the national trend for self-betterment, was simply bursting with clubs and societies throughout the second half of the nineteenth century.

This great enthusiasm for education and knowledge generated by the ordinary public found a ready home in amateur singing and the formation of choral societies. The first of these were founded in large industrial towns such as Halifax (1817) and Huddersfield (1836). The Stroud Choral Society has its early beginnings somewhere between 1834 and 1845. Its formation brought together the 'butchers, bakers and candlestick makers' of the town, with the 'gentry' taking the important role of the distinguished patrons and fashionable audience. Stroud's choral concerts held in the Subscription Rooms and accompanied by the legendary 'Chew's Band' were great social occasions. The lengthy descriptions of these concerts as given in the *Stroud Journal* dwelt as much on the people and manner of the audience as they do on the performances themselves. These reviews are perfect cameos of life in nineteenth-century Stroud.

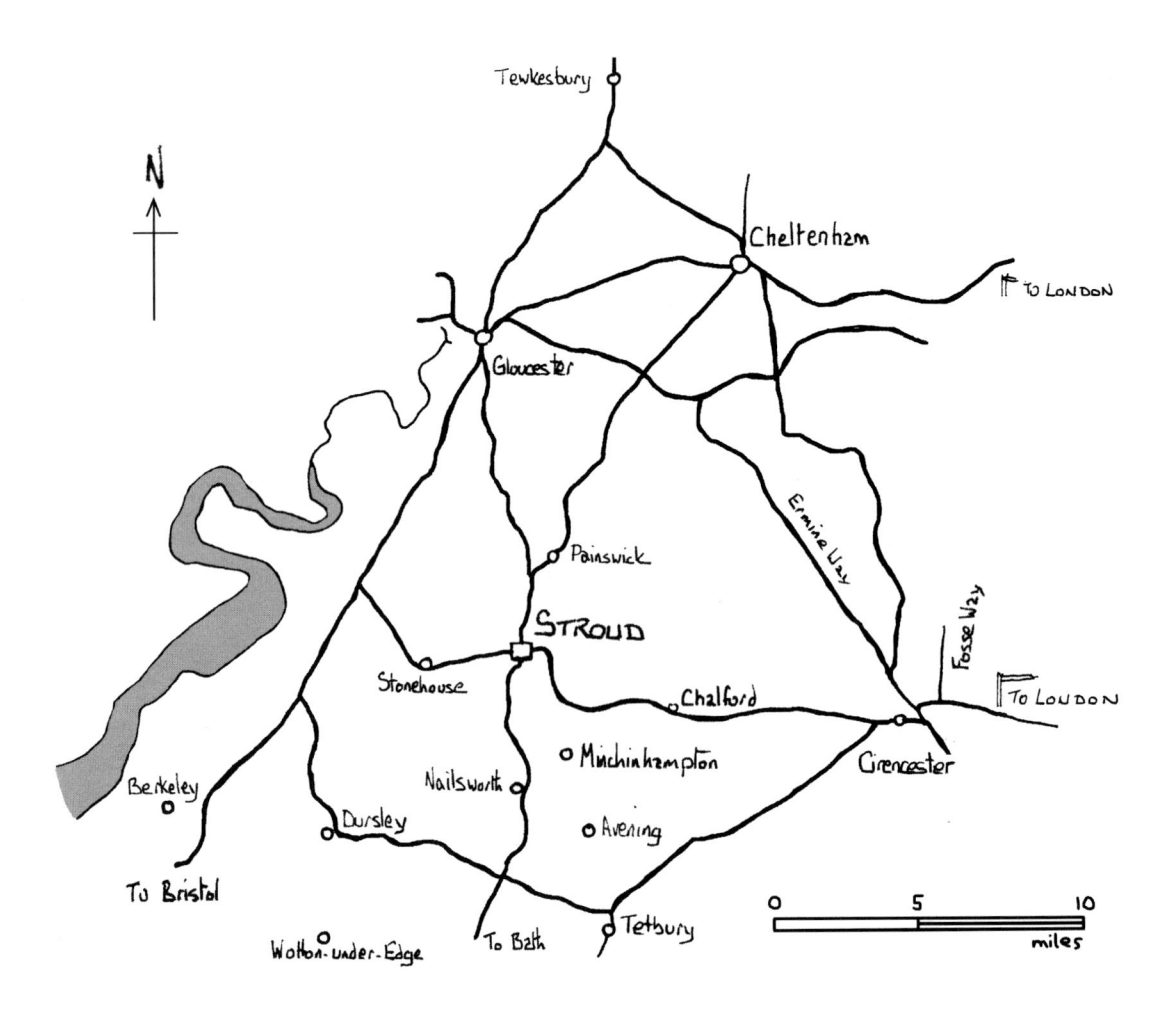

First concerts

About fifty members of the Choral Class established by the Athenaeum will assist in this performance.
Gloucester Journal, *November 18th 1848*

The exact date of the founding of Stroud Choral Society is not known, though we have sufficient clues to point to some time between 1834 and 1848. *The Victoria County History of Gloucester* (1972) baldly states, 'Stroud Choral Society was founded in or before 1835, being subsequently disbanded and reformed in the late nineteenth century'. We now know a great deal more about our history.

There were three items used as starting points for research: an old print dated 1835, a choral programme dated 1848 and an inscribed baton dated 1850.

In our choral archives we have a print showing an unknown artist's impression of a group of musicians playing *Queen of My Soul*, with the title 'Stroud 1st Philharmonic 1835'. The Stroud Philharmonic Society was founded in November 1834 and their inaugural concert was on November 26th in the newly opened Subscription Rooms.

The aims of the Philharmonic Society were ambitious. It was their intention to give a concert every three or four weeks at the Stroud Subscription Rooms. They intended to engage 'Performers of Eminence'. However, the number of concerts given and their individual excellence would have to depend on the extent of patronage bestowed on the Institution. Tickets would be by subscription only, 'money will not on any account be taken at the doors'. Subscribers were asked to forward their address to Mr Norris, Honorary Secretary, Frome Buildings, Stroud. Strangers (not residing within six miles of Stroud) could also apply for a Subscriber's Ticket. Subscription was £1 5s for the season which would give the subscriber three Tickets of Admission for each concert. The season would run from November to April. The old print entitled 'Stroud 1st Philharmonic 1835' is a reference to it being the first concert in the 1835 season and can now be dated as November 17th 1835. A subscription for the 1835 season now cost £1 11s 6d.

The concerts themselves were to be a mixture of orchestral items given by a small music group of about 20 players, interspersed with

Advert for the Birmingham Music Festival, Gloucester Journal, *July 18th 1846. The Misses Williams sang with Stroud Choral Society in 1848.*

Stroud Athenæum.

CHORAL CLASS.

The Directors have the pleasure to announce to the Subscribers, their Friends, and the Public
THAT THE SECOND

CHORAL MEETING,

For this Season, under the Patronage of
Sir. JOHN DEAN PAUL, BART., President of the Institution;
And
Wm. CAPEL, ESQ., High Sheriff of the County.
Will take place in the

SUBSCRIPTION ROOMS,

On *TUESDAY EVENING, NOVEMBER* 28th, 1848,
And that the

Misses Williams

Are engaged to sing on that occasion.

Tickets, Front Seats, 2s. 6d.; Back Seats, 1s. 6d.; Gallery, 1s.; and Books of the Words, 3d. each, may be had of the various Booksellers in Stroud, and of Mr. FOSTER, Nurseryman; Mr. HUMPHRYS, Auctioneer; and Mr. SPIRE, the Secretary.

Members of the Athenæum, and those Members of the Choral Class who do not assist in the Performance, will on production of their Tickets, be admitted to the respective seats at Half-price.

** *Doors open at a Quarter-past Seven, to commence at Eight o'Clock.*

The Directors of the Athenæum, earnestly hope that the Inhabitants of the Town and Neighbourhood, will by their attendance and support on this occasion, sanction and encourage the effort made to afford to Stroud, the same opportunities of instruction and amusement by means of a Choral Class, which have been so highly appreciated by most of the important Towns in the Empire, following the example of the Metropolis, where Mr. Hullah is now giving lessons to his *Eightieth* Class.

The Directors feel it due to their Friends, the Public, and themselves, to state that they had as early as September commenced preparations, and actually concluded their engagement with the *Misses Williams*, before the postponement of Mr. Willy's Concert was announced.

☞ The CHORAL CLASS will resume its weekly practice under the direction of Mr. W. HIGGS, on Thursday, January 19th, 1848.

THE PROGRAMME.

First Part.

CHORUS.—"Hail smiling morn"		Spofforth.
DUETT.—The Misses Williams—"Mid waving trees"		Benedict.
MADRIGAL.—"In these delightful pleasant Groves"		Purcell.
SONG.—Miss M. Williams—"Io l'tascio"		Mozart.
MADRIGAL.—"Come follow me"		Horsley.
DUETT.—The Misses Williams—"The Vision"		Mendelssohn.
GLEE.—"Here in cool grot"		Mornington.
QUARTETT and CHORUS.—"When winds breathe soft"		Webbe.

An Interval of Fifteen Minutes.

Second Part.

MADRIGAL.—"T'was on a bank"		Hullah.
DUETT.—The Misses Williams—"Swiss Maidens"		Holmes.
MADRIGAL.—"See the Chariot"		Horsley.
SONG.—Miss A. Williams—"I dare not sing"		Auber.
GLEE.—"Blow, Blow, thou winter wind"		Stevens.
BALLAD.—Miss M. Williams—"Fair Summer eve"		Maynard.
MADRIGAL.—"Now, O now, I needs must part"		Dowland.
GLEE.—"From Oberon in fairy land"		Stevens.
FINALE.—"God save the Queen"		

The earliest programme in our archives. Note the incorrect date for resumption of Choral Classes, which should read January 19th 1849

vocal items such as glees, madrigals, duets and quartets. The singing ranged from the simple well known folk songs and ballads to the operatic: 'Mr Sapio sung a piece from *Der Freischütz* but we confess we like him better in the simple ballad, or the sweet Scotch song full of sentiment and pathos' (*Gloucester Journal*, December 22nd 1835).

At the opening of the Subscription Rooms on October 13th 1834 we learn that between 600 and 700 people attended the opening concerts and that 'The Performances went off with immense eclat'. Amongst the notable soloists on that day were Miss Woodyatt, Mr Sapio and Mr Machin. These three people were professional singers. We have an old programme listing them amongst the principal singers at Exeter Hall, London, in April 1836, performing selections from Handel oratorios under the baton of Sir George Smart. Miss Woodyatt, Mr Sapio, and Mr Machin were to sing many times with the Stroud Philharmonic Society throughout the 1830s, with a last sighting of them at a grand Miscellaneous Concert on April 14th 1841. At this point we have no further information on the Philharmonic Society until we pick it up again in 1856 under the baton of Mr Chew.

At a Philharmonic Concert on April 2nd 1836 from a printed list of patrons, four names, P G Scrope Esq MP, W H Stanton, H Newman and J Watts, also appear as patrons on a Stroud Choral announcement for a concert in 1851. E G Hallewell, listed as a patron in 1836 could perhaps be the father of J W Hallewell listed as a patron in 1851. This would seem to show some further links between the Philharmonic Society and the Choral Society.

FIRST CONCERTS

The earliest concert programme in our possession, dated November 28th 1848, was for a concert given by the Choral Class of the Stroud Athenaeum. The Stroud Athenaeum had been formed in July 1847, and the aims of this Society were to promote many classes, predominantly in the arts. These classes were to include drawing, music and modern languages. The choral class was to be Hullah's course of lessons on vocal harmony. John Hullah (1812–1884) had studied G L Wilhelm's method of teaching singing in Paris between 1839 and 1840. On returning to England in 1841 he went to Exeter Hall, London, to train school masters on the technique of teaching singing in classes. This method was a form of tonic sol-fa and the idea that everyone could learn to sing with the right kind of training was somewhat revolutionary. Hullah's system later gave way to Curwen's Tonic Sol-fa which was widely advertised in the *Stroud Journal* in the 1860s.

One of the most intriguing clues to our date of origin comes from the inscription on a ceremonial baton presented to James Chew on Monday, October 7th 1850, which reads: 'Presented to Mr J Chew by the Stroud Choral Society, as a token of respect for his efficient and disinterested services, in the instruction and management of the Society. Oct 1850.' Although James Chew was only 27 in 1850, it does beg the question as to how many years he may have been conducting before he was presented with this baton. We know that James Chew was a prodigious early musician, an organist at the age of 14, and also in the same year, 1837, conducting or playing in a successful band for Queen Victoria's accession. We learn from the pages of the *Stroud Journal* that he was musically active in many ways in Stroud. We also know that at some time prior to 1850, Mr Chew was taking choral classes, and that 'he imparted the rudimentary knowledge of music to the pupils at 18 pence a quarter'. (Obituary, March 1899). The obituary also states that the original choral class existed for about twenty years under Mr Chew's conductorship and then was 'abandoned under regrettable circumstances which it is unnecessary to relate'. Unfortunately we have been unable to throw any light on these regrettable circumstances.

From the pages of the Stroud Subscription Rooms account ledgers, we learn that Mr

Music for the first concert, 1848.

> **STROUD CHORAL SOCIETY.**
>
> Under the Patronage of
> THE RIGHT HONORABLE THE EARL DUCIE.
> Sir John Dean Paul, Bart.
> G. P. Scrope, Esq., M.P.   W. H. Stanton, Esq., M.P.
>
> | Col. F. Abbott, C.B. | G. Edwards, Esq. | Rev. G. Hough. | T. W. Smith, Esq. |
> | J. G. Ball, Esq. | Captn. E. Fitzgerald. | J. W. Hallewell, Esq. | E. A. Uthwatt, Esq. |
> | John Biddle, Esq. | P. H. Fisher, Esq. | C. Hawker, Esq. | Joseph Watts, Esq. |
> | W. Capel, Esq. | C. H. Fisher, Esq. | S. S. Marling, Esq. | |
> | W. B. Cartwright, Esq. | C. Goddard, Esq. | H. W. Newman, Esq. | |
> | J. E. Dorrington, Esq. | G. S. Gregory, Esq. | T. A. Stoughton, Esq. | |
>
> The Committee respectfully announce that the Second
> **CHORAL AND INSTRUMENTAL CONCERT**
> For this Season, will take place in the
> **SUBSCRIPTION ROOMS; On THURSDAY EVENING, MARCH 13th, 1851:**
> **FOR THE BENEFIT OF THE CASUALTY HOSPITAL.**
>
> CONDUCTOR,—Mr. J. CHEW.
>
> Doors open at Half-past Seven.—To commence at Eight o'Clock.
> TICKETS.—First Seats, 2s. 6d.—Second Seats, 1s. 6d.—Gallery 1s.—May be had of the Booksellers, and of Mr. Spire the Secretary.

Advert in Stroud Journal, *February 28th 1851.*

Chew's first known concert in the Subscription Rooms was on February 10th 1846 and that the cost was one guinea for the hire of the large room. He again hired the room on July 21st 1847 and August 30th 1849. On December 15th 1849 he hired the 'small lecture room' at a charge of 5 shillings. Sometimes the small lecture room was hired at the same time as the large room, as in March 1851, when a concert was held for the Benefit of the Casualty Hospital. (Whether the small room was for refreshments, or for the personal effects of the performers, one can only guess.) As we have newspaper evidence for the concert in March 1851 and also Ledger evidence of a hiring fee of a guinea for the room, we may be able to assume that the other concerts with the same hiring fee are also choral concerts. Unfortunately for us, the Subscription Rooms' ledger stops itemising individual bookings around the mid 1850s. This would have been an ideal way to look for missing concerts in the nineteenth century!

Somewhere amongst these interweaving strands of music making and choral singing in Stroud, the Stroud Choral Society was born.

We found the first report of a concert given by the Society in the *Gloucester Journal* for December 2nd 1848. This was the concert that took place on November 28th 1848 and was the second Choral meeting of the season. 'Nothing could be more gratifying, and even astonishing, to those who were unacquainted with the usual results of Hullah's system when perseveringly followed out, than the ability and effect of the choral voices on this occasion … Only one piece during the evening betrayed any blemish, and that evidently arose from some inattention to the sound of the key-note given by the director. Every other piece was rendered not merely correctly, but with taste and energy. The singing of the Misses Williams, accompanied by Mr Morgan on the pianoforte, was received most enthusiastically; indeed, on one or two occasions, it seemed to take the company by surprise, and elicited very prolonged applause … The audience was both numerous and respectable, the side gallery being crowded to inconvenience.'

Our research has revealed that the soloists Miss A Williams, soprano, and Miss M Williams, contralto, were amongst the principal vocal performers at the Birmingham Music Festival of August 1846. The work was the first performance of *Elijah* and was conducted by the composer, Dr Felix Mendelssohn. At that concert the Misses Williams sang the original duet form of *Lift thine eyes*. (Mendelssohn died the following year in November 1847.) Knowing now the importance of the status of the Misses Williams, the note at the foot of the concert programme, November 28th 1848, can be better understood!

FIRST CONCERTS

The *Journal* goes on to make this following social observation: 'One other circumstance deserves notice: amongst the choristers in the orchestra we were happy to recognize the members of some very respectable families, and whose support and co-operation in such societies is almost indispensable to give them permanence and success. On the continent, the co-operation of professional and respectable persons is no doubt the chief cause of their great reputation; and we think were the fear of losing caste laid aside a little more in 'happy England', it would be greatly to the advantage and improvement of all classes.' (The 'orchestra' seems to have been a term applied to the erected staging put up for the choir and band to stand on.)

The conductor for this concert was Mr W Higgs and the programme notes go on to say that the choral class would resume its weekly practice, under his direction, on January 19th 1849. (The programme gives the date as 1848 but this is obviously a misprint.) After this we have no further information on Mr Higgs.

The patrons for this season of choral music, 1848–49, are listed as Sir John Dean Paul, Bart, and Wm Capel Esq, High Sheriff of the County. Later on, in a concert announcement for the Stroud Choral Society in March 1851, the Patronage is again listed as The Right Honourable The Earl Ducie, Sir John Dean Paul, Bart, and W Capel Esq – their names join a list of 22 other patrons.

After this concert in 1848, it now seems to fall to James Chew to continue with choral singing in Stroud where the Athenaeum left off. We can chart James Chew's conductorship from 1850 through to 1856 with the Stroud Choral Society. From 1857 into the 1890s James Chew conducts other Stroud concerts. For most of that time he was also Leader of the Band for Stroud Choral concerts. He was obviously a well-liked local personality and the reviews of his concerts were often liberal in their praise. After the concert on March 13th 1851 the reviewer tells the readers that it was the second concert for the Season and 'notwithstanding that towards the evening there was some indication of wet, there was a large and respectable attendance, the reserved seats being completely filled. The performance afforded a treat to those present.' After a choral concert for the Benevolent Society in December 1854 the writer comments: 'We would not undervalue the assistance of Mr Chew, and the members of his choral society, they contribute largely to the success which for years past, has attended the efforts of the Benevolent Society.'

STROUD CHORAL SOCIETY.

President:
J. E. DORINGTON, Esq.

Vice-Presidents:
Rev. T. H. TARLTON. | S. S. DICKINSON, Esq.

Musical Director:
Mr. FREDERICK HELMORE,
(Choir Master to his late R. H. the Prince Consort.)

THE FIRST CONCERT of the Society will take place in the SUBSCRIPTION ROOMS, STROUD, on TUESDAY EVENING, February 10.

Pianist:
MISS CLARK,
(Pupil of Miss Loder and Mr. W. C. Macfarren.)

To commence at Eight o'clock. Tickets—Reserved seats, 2s. 6d.; Unreserved, 2s.; Gallery 1s., (children half-price); to be had at Clark's Library, King Street, Stroud.

Programmes will shortly be issued. Books of the Words may also be obtained at Clark's Library, on the day of the Concert.

The proceeds of the Concert will be applied to the purchase of music for the use of the Society.

Concert advert, Stroud Journal, February 7th 1863.

13

In October 1856, again under the auspices of the Stroud Philharmonic, James Chew departed from the usual miscellaneous style of concert and embarked on an ambitious newly-written oratorio, *Moses*, by J M Capes. No mean feat – and one not undertaken by a weak conductor. In the nineteenth century, choral music was thought to develop through three stages or levels. New groups of small choirs would progress from part-songs to cantatas and then to oratorio. Capes' *Moses* would be seen as a defining moment in the Society's history. The critic(s) announce that: 'We are unwilling to make a single remark until we have congratulated with him on having kept a musical society of any kind together for so long a time as they have. Musical taste has been so little cultivated and the amount of musical knowledge is so small amongst us that any one who succeeds in stimulating the former and furnishing the latter deserves our warmest thanks and praise.'

In view of this statement it is strange that this seems to have been the last Stroud Choral Concert that Mr Chew conducted. There may be some clues in the following: 'The choruses are the best portions ... The little band of choristers sang them with precision and force for which we were entirely unprepared and which inspired us with high hopes of what they will do hereafter. The instrumental accompaniments were, however, very defective and badly executed – probably both.' It may be that at this point James Chew decided to concentrate on the Band and relinquish conducting the choir. The reviewer goes on to say: 'They were not implicitly obedient to the conductor's wand. Even a bad conductor should be obeyed, but Mr Chew is far from that. He has two of the most important qualifications of a good conductor – firmness and perseverance.' The writer(s) end by noting: 'The audience at the Subscription Rooms – one of the largest and most respectable ever assembled therein – gave it more than cordial welcome, testifying their gratification by loud applause and frequent encores.'

After this, there is a gap in our records until Mr Frederick Helmore advertises choral classes in September 1862. (In 1863 he also advertises choral classes in Cirencester.) These classes for the new choral season are to be held on Mondays commencing October 6th at 8 pm, at the Blackboy Schoolroom, terms 5s a quarter. Classes would also be held on Fridays at 3pm in the Subscription Rooms, terms 10s 6d per quarter (admitting to both classes). 'Ladies and Gentlemen wishing to join the classes of the Society are requested to enrol their names at their earliest convenience, that Mr Helmore may have an opportunity of trying individual voices before the first meeting.'

In the *Stroud Journal* advert for the concert on February 10th 1863, Mr Helmore is described as 'Choir Master to his late Royal Highness the Prince Consort'. Did Mr Helmore have family or relatives in Stroud to bring him west from London after the death of Prince Albert in December 1861? Or had he been a visiting choirmaster, attending the Prince Consort at intervals? Maybe this title should be taken 'with a pinch of salt'. Likewise, the title 'professor of music', that James Chew uses in his advertisement for his music shop.

Having established himself in Stroud, Mr Helmore launched the 1862–63 season with serious intent. There were two concerts within the first four months of 1863, with a third in December. The first, a miscellaneous concert on February 10th was well received and had been produced with the intention of using the profits from the concert to purchase music for the use of the Society. The Subscription Rooms' Ledger shows that Mr Helmore paid £6 0s 0d for the use of the large room.

Affording choral scores may well have been a problem for all choirs. It is difficult to assess whether the ordinary choral member could afford to buy music, or whether they were totally dependent on the Society's music library. Certainly, some choirs were taught solely by the sol-fa method, though, except for the short period in the late 1840s, this does not seem to have been the case in Stroud. Paradoxically, probably more people in the middle of the nineteenth century could read a music score than people a hundred years later in the middle of the twentieth century. In the *Stroud Journal*, with each concert notice there were adverts for 'Books of Words' that could be purchased at various printers and stationers. It seems that these were for the use of the audience. The *Stroud Journal* gives us some examples of the cost of music scores. For instance, in March 1853, *Novello's Cheap Music* has several pages of adverts, *The Messiah*, octavo, was 6s 6d, the folio, 10s, *Mozart 12th Mass*, 3s 6d, *Judas Maccabaeus*, 4s, *Beethoven's Mass in C*, 2s 6d. An average weekly wage in 1867 for skilled labourers, such as blacksmiths, hardware makers, paper workers, boot and shoe workers, tailors, bakers, butchers, rope and harness makers, was between 21s and 25s. So it can be seen that purchasing a choral score would represent a significant fraction of a weekly wage. The value of the pound remained relatively stable throughout Victoria's reign in spite of mini depressions in the 1870s and 1880s. You would require £42 in today's money (1999) to purchase £1 worth of goods in 1860.

The concert on April 18th 1863 was a landmark for the Society, being their first performance of Handel's *Messiah*. This was the third time it had been performed in Stroud, the first being in 1817 in the Parish Church where it apparently caused a great sensation. The second was in 1852 when the Gloucester Choral Society gave a performance in the Subscription Rooms. This third performance also received critical acclaim. The writer tells us that there were, with singers and orchestra, more than 250 performers and that there was nearly as large an audience in the square outside as there were 'crammed' inside: 'The singers were all young and with voices in the best possible condition, affording a marked contrast to the harshness of London choruses' and Mr Helmore 'led with fire and animation and had them most completely in hand'. We also have the first mention of James Chew as leader of The Band: 'The Band was a capitally selected one; in fact it would have been difficult to have got together a better one in the provinces. Among them were our accomplished townsman, Mr Chew, who in conjunction with Herr Pfeiffer, a celebrated solo violinist of Bristol, took the lead of the first violins.'

Miss Susanna Cole of London, soprano, and Miss Holroyd of Cheltenham, contralto, delighted the audience with their singing.
The audience was comprised of 'the rank, wealth and beauty of the district', together with the 'elite of the borough'. Messiah 1863, painting by Brenda Dunn.

Also amongst the accomplished townsmen and playing the harmonium was a visitor from Cheltenham, a Herr M von Holst. Gustavus Mattias von Holst was a noted pianist and composer who eleven years later would become Gustav Holst's eldest uncle. This concert was also special for another reason, as it was almost certainly part of the town's celebrations for the marriage of Prince Albert Edward to Princess Alexandra of Denmark, which had taken place on March 10th 1863. As part of the local festivities James Chew and Mr J Watts Hallewell, being the tallest men in the district, led the torchlight procession to Rodborough Fort prior to the lighting of a bonfire.

Mr Helmore finished the year with Mendelssohn's *Hymn of Praise* and the choral season 1863–64 drew to a close with a performance of Haydn's *Creation* in April 1864. Each of Mr Helmore's concerts was said to have been a financial success. However, it is intriguing to find a note in the Subscription Rooms' Ledgers (March 31st 1864) to the effect that 'Mr Elliot be instructed not to let the Room to the Choral Society until the arrears be paid'. The Society must have paid up!

ORATORIO.

STROUD CHORAL SOCIETY.

President:
J. E. DORINGTON, ESQ.

Vice-Presidents:
REV. T. H. TARLTON. | S. S. DICKINSON, ESQ.

Treasurer:
EDWARD WINTERBOTHAM, ESQ.

THE CONDUCTOR BEGS TO ANNOUNCE A PERFORMANCE OF

HANDEL'S MESSIAH,

IN THE

SUBSCRIPTION ROOMS, STROUD,

ON TUESDAY, THE 28TH OF APRIL, 1863.

The CHORUS will comprise the Members of the Society, who, with the BAND, will number

TWO HUNDRED PERFORMERS.

DOORS OPEN AT HALF-PAST SIX O'CLOCK, TO COMMENCE AT SEVEN.

TICKETS.—NUMBERED RESERVED SEATS, 5s.—FAMILY TICKETS to admit Five, £1 1s.; SECOND SEATS, 3s. 6d.—FAMILY TICKETS to admit Five, 15s.; GALLERY, 2s. 6d.—FAMILY TICKETS to admit Five, 10s. 6d., to be had at CLARK'S Library, STROUD; BAILY'S Library, CIRENCESTER; and NEST'S Library, GLOUCESTER, where Plans of the Room may be seen and Places secured.

RAILWAY ARRANGEMENTS.

RETURN TICKETS will be issued on April 28th, for Trains leaving CIRENCESTER at 1.30, 4.45, and 7.0, p.m.; TETBURY ROAD at 2.15 and 5.5, p.m.; and BRIMSCOMBE at 2.35 and 5.30, p.m.; returning from Stroud by Special Train a quarter of an hour after the close of the performance.

FARES FOR THE DOUBLE JOURNEY:—

	1st Class	2nd Class
	s. d.	s. d.
FROM CIRENCESTER	3 9	2 6
" TETBURY ROAD	3 0	2 0
" BRIMSCOMBE	1 0	0 9

For the accommodation of Visitors from Stonehouse and neighbourhood, arrangements are being made for the Down Mail Train to stop at Stonehouse Station.

[CLARK, PRINTER, STROUD.

PRINCIPAL VOCALISTS:

Soprano:
MISS SUSANNA COLE.

Contralto: Tenore:
MISS HOLROYD.   MR. HUNT.

Basso:
MR. F. MUGFORD.

INSTRUMENTALISTS:

VIOLINS:

1st.	2nd.
MR. CHEW.	MR. GROUTRIDGE.
HERR PFEIFFER.	— HIGGS.
MR. JACQUES.	— S. GRIST.
MASTER LANE.	— J. CLARK.

TENORS:
MR. WOODWARD.   MR. HERRING.   MR. J. SMITH.

BASSES:
MR. UGLOW.   MR. LOUIS WAITE.   MR. HEMMING.

DOUBLE BASSES:
MR. HATTON.   MR. PEAKE.   MR. WOOD.

FLUTES:
MR. POORE.   MR. JONES.

OBOE:
MR. TEAKEL.

CLARIONETTS:
HERR FORKET.   MR. FYFFE.

HORNS: TRUMPETS:
MR. DUNN. MR. NEATE.   MR. WOODCOCK. MR. HALE.

TROMBONE: SONOROPHONE:
MR. MORGAN.   MR. FOLEY.

DRUMS:
MR. TEWKESBURY GOODFELLOW.

HARMONIUM:
HERR M. VON HOLST.

CHORUS:
THE MEMBERS OF THE STROUD CHORAL SOCIETY.

Conductor, FREDERICK HELMORE.

Just as Stroud had got used to having a highly successful Choral Society in its midst, a notice in the *Journal* for September 24th 1864 tells us that as Mr Helmore had not returned it was desirable that a new society should be started and they would be earnestly looking for a new conductor. The meeting had been called to discuss the choral classes and society, and ended by producing seven firm resolutions:

That a Choral Society for the town of Stroud and its vicinity be established.

That it be under the charge and superintendence of a committee consisting of – Rev W Butlin, Mr W Grist, Mr Bragg, Mr Clark, Mr Hill, and Mr Webb, with power to add to their number.

That Mr Dorington be elected President, Rev T H Tarlton and Mr Dickinson, Vice-Presidents, Mr E Winterbotham Treasurer, and Mr Bragg, Secretary.

That the choice of conductor and the appointment of class meetings be left to the committee.

That the conductor receive all fees for attending the classes – paying all expenses of such classes.

That there be annually two concerts, and that the society take the receipts and pay all the expenses of such concerts – the committee and officers guaranteeing the society against all risk.

That Honorary Members (subscribers of £1 1s) be entitled to three tickets (reserved) to each of the two annual concerts.

The Committee must have worked quickly and efficiently, as the new conductor Mr Richard Mann successfully produced a Christmas Concert on December 20th 1864. Some special features of the concert were glees sung by the Stroud Glee Club and the 'instrumental gem of the evening' was Mr Chew's cornet solo. Mr Mann initially lived at 3 Albert Buildings, Stroud, until moving to Cirencester in September 1867.

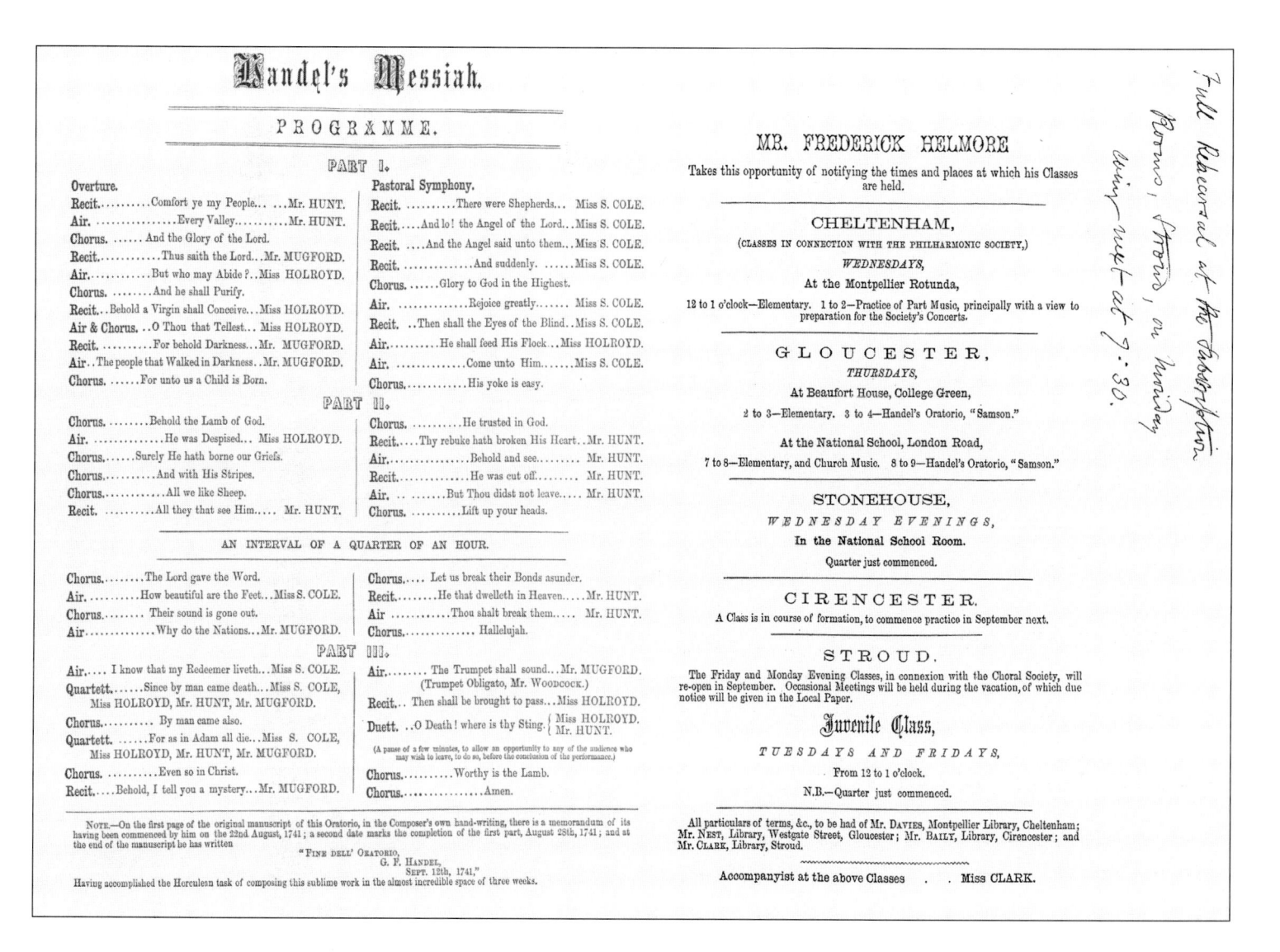

Handel's Messiah.

PROGRAMME.

PART I.

Overture.
Recit. .... Comfort ye my People ... ... Mr. HUNT.
Air. .... Every Valley .... Mr. HUNT.
Chorus. ...... And the Glory of the Lord.
Recit. .... Thus saith the Lord ... Mr. MUGFORD.
Air. .... But who may Abide? .. Miss HOLROYD.
Chorus. .... And he shall Purify.
Recit. ... Behold a Virgin shall Conceive ... Miss HOLROYD.
Air & Chorus. .. O Thou that Tellest ... Miss HOLROYD.
Recit. .... For behold Darkness ... Mr. MUGFORD.
Air .. The people that Walked in Darkness ... Mr. MUGFORD.
Chorus. ...... For unto us a Child is Born.

Pastoral Symphony.
Recit. .... There were Shepherds ... Miss S. COLE.
Recit. ..... And lo! the Angel of the Lord ... Miss S. COLE.
Recit. ..... And the Angel said unto them ... Miss S. COLE.
Recit. .... And suddenly. .... Miss S. COLE.
Chorus. ...... Glory to God in the Highest.
Air. .... Rejoice greatly .... Miss S. COLE.
Recit. ... Then shall the Eyes of the Blind .. Miss S. COLE.
Air. .... He shall feed His Flock ... Miss S. COLE.
Air. .... Come unto Him .... Miss S. COLE.
Chorus. .... His yoke is easy.

PART II.

Chorus. .... Behold the Lamb of God.
Air. .... He was Despised ... Miss HOLROYD.
Chorus. ...... Surely He hath borne our Griefs.
Chorus. .... And with His Stripes.
Chorus. .... All we like Sheep.
Recit. .... All they that see Him ..... Mr. HUNT.

Chorus. .... He trusted in God.
Recit. .... Thy rebuke hath broken His Heart .. Mr. HUNT.
Air. .... Behold and see .... Mr. HUNT.
Recit. .... He was cut off .... Mr. HUNT.
Air. .. .. But Thou didst not leave ..... Mr. HUNT.
Chorus. .... Lift up your heads.

AN INTERVAL OF A QUARTER OF AN HOUR.

Chorus. .... The Lord gave the Word.
Air. .... How beautiful are the Feet ... Miss S. COLE.
Chorus. .... Their sound is gone out.
Air. .... Why do the Nations ... Mr. MUGFORD.

Chorus. .... Let us break their Bonds asunder.
Recit. .... He that dwelleth in Heaven ..... Mr. HUNT.
Air .... Thou shalt break them ..... Mr. HUNT.
Chorus. .... Hallelujah.

PART III.

Air. .... I know that my Redeemer liveth ... Miss S. COLE.
Quartett. ...... Since by man came death ... Miss S. COLE,
Miss HOLROYD, Mr. HUNT, Mr. MUGFORD.
Chorus. .... By man came also.
Quartett. ...... For as in Adam all die ... Miss S. COLE,
Miss HOLROYD, Mr. HUNT, Mr. MUGFORD.
Chorus. .... Even so in Christ.
Recit. ..... Behold, I tell you a mystery ... Mr. MUGFORD.

Air. .... The Trumpet shall sound ... Mr. MUGFORD.
(Trumpet Obligato, Mr. WOODCOCK.)
Recit. .. Then shall be brought to pass ... Miss HOLROYD.
Duett. .. O Death! where is thy Sting. { Miss HOLROYD. Mr. HUNT.
(A pause of a few minutes, to allow an opportunity to any of the audience who may wish to leave, to do so, before the conclusion of the performance.)
Chorus. .... Worthy is the Lamb.
Chorus. .... Amen.

Note.—On the first page of the original manuscript of this Oratorio, in the Composer's own hand-writing, there is a memorandum of its having been commenced by him on the 22nd August, 1741; a second date marks the completion of the first part, August 28th, 1741; and at the end of the manuscript he has written

"FINE DELL' ORATORIO,
G. F. HANDEL,
SEPT. 12th, 1741."

Having accomplished the Herculean task of composing this sublime work in the almost incredible space of three weeks.

MR. FREDERICK HELMORE

Takes this opportunity of notifying the times and places at which his Classes are held.

CHELTENHAM,

(CLASSES IN CONNECTION WITH THE PHILHARMONIC SOCIETY,)
WEDNESDAYS,
At the Montpellier Rotunda,
12 to 1 o'clock—Elementary. 1 to 2—Practice of Part Music, principally with a view to preparation for the Society's Concerts.

GLOUCESTER,

THURSDAYS,
At Beaufort House, College Green,
2 to 3—Elementary. 3 to 4—Handel's Oratorio, "Samson."

At the National School, London Road,
7 to 8—Elementary, and Church Music. 8 to 9—Handel's Oratorio, "Samson."

STONEHOUSE,

WEDNESDAY EVENINGS,
In the National School Room.
Quarter just commenced.

CIRENCESTER.

A Class is in course of formation, to commence practice in September next.

STROUD.

The Friday and Monday Evening Classes, in connexion with the Choral Society, will re-open in September. Occasional Meetings will be held during the vacation, of which due notice will be given in the Local Paper.

Juvenile Class,

TUESDAYS AND FRIDAYS,
From 12 to 1 o'clock.
N.B.—Quarter just commenced.

All particulars of terms, &c., to be had of Mr. DAVIES, Montpellier Library, Cheltenham; Mr. NEST, Library, Westgate Street, Gloucester; Mr. BAILY, Library, Cirencester; and Mr. CLARK, Library, Stroud.

Accompanyist at the above Classes . . Miss CLARK.

May 1865 saw another successful concert, the first Society performance of *Judas Maccabaeus*. The reviewer of this concert tells us that he sees 'no reason why the Choral Society of this town should not in a few years be able to take a place in the foremost rank of musical amateur societies'. The concert programme gives detailed arrangements for transport to and from the Subscription Rooms. Carriages are asked to have the horses' heads facing the Casualty Hospital and to take up with the horses facing in the same direction after the concert ended at 11 o'clock. An omnibus would leave the King's Head Hotel, Cirencester for Stroud at 'Half-past Five o'clock', returning after the Oratorio. Fare for the double journey, 2s. Visitors from Cheltenham and Gloucester could conveniently come by the Evening Up-Train, leaving Cheltenham at 6.30 pm and return by the Mail leaving Stroud at 12.15 am. While every opportunity was made for performers and audience travelling from a distance to get safely to and from concerts, sometimes it was difficulties closer to home that caused problems. The review for *Judas Maccabaeus* ends with a damning comment on the state of the gas lighting in Stroud: 'The stupidity of the present lighting arrangements of the town were well illustrated in the Egyptian [sic] darkness which prevailed in the streets. Persons had to grope their way from The Rooms as if gaslight were a thing unknown, the only purpose served by the gas lamps being to run against in the dark. The state of things was disgraceful and calls loudly for a remedy.'

Mr Mann seems to have been an exceptionally pleasant person judging from the charmingly worded letter which appeared in the *Journal* following this concert. Everyone connected with the concert is thanked including the Stroud tradesmen for observing the 'early closing movement'.

At the Annual General Meeting in September 1865, with the President J E Dorington in the chair, the Society set out to put itself on an even firmer footing by establishing a new constitution. (John Edward Dorington senior, was President of the Society from 1862 until his death in 1874. His son, also John Edward Dorington, became a patron on his father's death and later President.) It was noted that the Choral Society had so far never made a loss and that the balance in hand was £2 13s 7d. It was proposed that, unlike previous years, the Society would not be dissolved at the end of each season and then re-started, but would be a permanent society. Nineteen rules were then agreed upon.

CHORAL SOCIETY
FOR STROUD AND NEIGHBOURHOOD.

THE

CHRISTMAS CONCERT

Of the Society will take place in the

SUBSCRIPTION ROOMS, STROUD,

On TUESDAY EVENING, December 20th, 1864,

TO COMMENCE AT EIGHT O'CLOCK (DOORS OPEN AT 7.30).

President:
J. E. DORINGTON, ESQ.

Vice-Presidents:
REV. T. H. TARLTON, | S. S. DICKINSON, ESQ.

Treasurer:
EDWARD WINTERBOTHAM, ESQ.

PIANISTE - - - - - - MISS CLARK.

PROGRAMME.

PART I.

A SELECTION FROM

"THE SEASONS" .. *Haydn.*

- No. 3. CHORUS,...... "Come gentle Spring,"......
- No. 4. RECIT...... "At last the bounteous Sun,"......
- No. 5. AIR...... "With joy the impatient Husbandman,"......
- No. 6. RECIT........... "Laborious Man,"......
- No. 7. TRIO & CHORUS,... "Be propitious."
- SONG,...... "My Mother bids me bind my Hair,"...... *Haydn.*
- GLEE,............ "Discord dire Sister,"...... *S. Webbe.*
- SOLO PIANOFORTE,... "Thème Italien,"...... *Leybach.*
- PART SONG,...... "The Sun shines fair,"...... *Macirone.*
- SONG,............ "She loves not me,"...... *Hullah.*
- PART SONG (by special request) "The Echo Song," *Neithardt.*

PART II.

- MADRIGAL,...... "Come again, sweet Love,"...... *Dowland.*
- SONG,......... "O would I were a Boy again,"...... *F. Romer.*
- QUARTETT,............... "Home,"............ *Benedict.*
- SOLO CORNET,...... "Lucia di Lammermoor,"
  Arranged by *T. Harper.*
- MADRIGAL,...... "Maidens, never go a wooing,"... *Macfarren.*
- SONG,............ "Sweet Love arise."............ *Henrion.*
- GLEE,......... "The Tiger couches in the Wood,"...... *Bishop.*
- SONG,............ "The Stirrup Cup,"............ *L. Arditi.*
- MADRIGAL,............ "The Silver Swan,"............ *Gibbons.*
- GOD SAVE THE QUEEN,............ *Leslie.*

AN INTERVAL OF TEN MINUTES BETWEEN THE PARTS.

Conductor, RICHARD MANN.

TICKETS:—Reserved Seats, 2s. 6d.; Unreserved, 1s. 6d.; Gallery, 1s.—to be had at Clark's Library, King Street, Stroud, where Books of the Words may be obtained on the day of the Concert.

Subscribers of £1 1s. are entitled to Three Reserved Tickets for this Concert, and for the Oratorio in the Spring. Subscribers' Names received by the Gloucestershire Banking Company, or by the Honorary Secretary.

CARRIAGES will enter by the Barrier adjoining Messrs. Libby and Pearce's Warehouse, and set down with the horses' heads towards the Hospital. The same arrangement will be observed in taking up after the Concert.

ROBERT BRAGG, Hon. Sec.

☞ *The Classes in connexion with this Society will meet during the ensuing Quarter at 8.0 p.m., at the Black Boy School Room, on Mondays, for Elementary Instruction and the Study of Psalmody; and on Tuesdays, for the practice of Part Music and Handel's Oratorio, "Judas Maccabæus."*
The Quarter commences Monday, February 6th, 1865.

Clark, Printer and Bookseller, King Street, Stroud.

These rules included having a guarantee fund of not less than £10 at the beginning of each season, that a season shall run from October 1st to September 30th the following year, that annual members' subscriptions shall be 17s payable in advance, and that a register shall be kept of attendance of classes. Annual members were to have free admittance to both classes (elementary and choral) and 'needful music' for their use provided by the Society.

SATURDAY, SEPTEMBER 28, 1867
EDWARD W. WINTERBOTHAM, TREASURER, IN ACCOUNT WITH
THE STROUD CHORAL SOCIETY
SESSION 1866–7

Dr.		RECEIPTS		PAYMENTS			Cr.
Balance of Last Year's Account	8	6	11	Expenses for Christmas Concert, viz:			
				Hire of Room, Gas, &c	3	10	6
Sixty-nine Honorary Members	72	8	0	Erection of Orchestra	3	5	0
				Decoration Expenses	3	10	0
Tickets Sold for Christmas Concert	18	3	0	Hire of Chairs	1	3	8
				Advertising and Posting	4	4	6
" " Spring Oratorio	31	8	9	Printing	4	18	11
				Professionals	7	6	0
Donations	2	2	0	Hire of Instruments	2	18	6
				Refreshments Contract	3	9	6
				Sundries	1	9	10
					£35	16	5
				Expenses of Spring Oratorio, viz:			
				Hire of Rooms, Gas, &c	5	17	0
				Erection of Orchestra	3	11	6
				Decoration Expenses	3	8	0
				Hire of Chairs	1	4	3
				Advertising, Printing & Posting	14	3	5
				Professionals	58	15	6
				Hire of Instruments	4	7	6
				Refreshments contract	3	16	0
				Sundries	0	10	0
					£93	13	2
				Balance in hand	£0	19	1
	£132	8	8		£132	8	8

Richard Mann also advertised Choral Classes in Cirencester during October 1865. They were to be held in the Corn Hall on Tuesdays at 8 pm: 'A Quarter of an Hour at the end of each meeting will be devoted to the practice of Sight Singing, on Mr Mann's system of instruction, just published by Novello & Co.'

Things continue very happily with the Society, but in the May 1866 concert review of Handel's *Samson* a note of warning is sounded: 'Mr Mann, whom we congratulate upon his restoration to health, after a recent and severe illness, was the conductor, and most efficiently wielded the baton.'

The end of this concert, however, was marked by a lack of concert etiquette. The reviewer reports: 'Notwithstanding the pause of a few minutes allowed before the last song to afford an opportunity to any of the audience who wished to leave before the conclusion to do so, a great number walked out during the performance of the last two pieces. This was as great a violation of a tacit agreement as it was of good taste and had the effect of utterly spoiling the final chorus. The principals, too, followed the bad example; but we hope on the next occasion those who wish to retire before the conclusion will do so in the interval for that purpose.'

At the Christmas Concert, December 20th 1866, a successful performance of Mozart's *Twelfth Mass* was given. Again the concert reviewer was unhappy about the way the concert was conducted: 'We must, however, protest very earnestly against the practice indulged in on Thursday to an unreasonable extent, of encoring nearly everything sung. It is of course a compliment to the singers, but it is a tax upon them to which they ought not to be subjected, and has the effect of prolonging the concert to an inconveniently late hour. It was after eleven o'clock on this occasion when "God Save the Queen" was sung.' The Stroud public was obviously enjoying itself!

The good citizens of Stroud may well have been enjoying themselves inside the Subscription Rooms but once outside their exasperation with the state of Stroud's gas lighting was still running high. In a letter in the *Stroud Journal* next to the review of Mozart's *Mass*, a Stroud citizen complains about the positioning of the town lamps: 'Why in some parts are the lamps close together, and at others as far removed as angel visits?' The writer goes on to say: 'I refer to a lamp about the middle of Nelson-street, which at present lights a cabbage garden and darkens the road. Ingeniously placed behind a privet hedge it throws heavy shadow over twenty or thirty yards of road. Anyone driving up or down the street after the lamp is lit must plunge in speculation into the abyss of darkness, trusting to good luck to avoid collision with any other vehicle passing through this 'valley of shadow'. It may, perhaps, be too much to ask the Board of Health to pay attention to so small a matter as altering the position of the lamp, but at all events, can they not be induced to order the lamp lighter not to light a lamp which only serves as a source of danger?' It was signed, 'A sufferer from the inconvenience' (*Stroud Journal* December 15th 1866).

In the following May 1867, we read that Mr Edward Brind, who was the organist of Highnam Church, was *in locum tenens* for Mr Mann during his illness and absence. This concert was an interesting departure from the usual choral work. Mr Mann had chosen the complete programme that had been sung by the London Handel Festival Choir in 1862 at the Crystal Palace. This must have been an ambitious departure from the norm and says much about the skill of the Society and the ability of its conductors. Again, the critic is fulsome in his praise. The concert, which had commenced at 7.45 pm, terminated exactly at 11 pm: 'There was but one opinion as to this having been the most successful of all performances of the Choral Society.'

Conductor Richard Mann began the 1867–68 season with a Christmas Concert on December 17th. This was a miscellaneous concert, a mixture of songs, glees and musical items with one Christmas item, '*Let us now go even unto Bethlehem*'. The conductor wished to save the choir's best efforts for the forthcoming concert of *Elijah* in the Spring. Perhaps this is why the review concludes with a well-meant suggestion that the choir should rehearse their positions beforehand: 'None of the gentlemen knew where to stand or what had become of their music.'

The run up to *Elijah* was marked by a flurry of correspondence in the *Stroud Journal* about the choice of soloists. Someone writing as 'Ex-Impresario' on March 18th 1868 used over 2,500 words to point out that it was the duty of one of experience to share this knowledge with others. He felt that the solo parts in *Elijah* were so important that only soloists of the highest order should be employed and he suggested that a Mr Santley, a Signor Foli and Mlle Lancia should be engaged. He hoped that his remarks would be received in the spirit given. (In 1886, Mr Santley was a soloist at the Three Choirs, Gloucester for a fee of 200 guineas!)

The following week there was a much shorter reply from Mr Mann to say that he could not comply as he had already engaged Miss Cecilia Westbrook and Mr Brandon and also that he would feel uncomfortable engaging such a 'Queen of Song' as Mlle Lancia with the small band that he had at his command. He pointed out that the committee had to expend a large sum in addition to the ordinary concert expenses such as printing, advertising, and in making the room look decent, in building an orchestra (staging), and in hiring seats for the audience. Mr Mann finished his letter by explaining that he had not approached *Elijah* without some knowledge of the needs of this particular oratorio. His knowledge was learnt under Mendelssohn's own baton. As one of the children of Her Majesty's Chapels Royal, he had attended all the rehearsals and performances of *Elijah* during Mendelssohn's last visit to England. (Mendelssohn's last visit to England was in April 1847. He conducted four performances of his revised *Elijah* in London during that month. Richard Mann would have been 11.)

On April 6th 1868, a letter from C Holmes of Paganhill was printed in which he praised Mr Mann's excellent communication respecting the judicious engagements already made. The writer had been to many concerts in Gloucester, Worcester, Hereford and at Exeter Hall, London. He had also heard Miss Westbrook and Mr Brandon and was in no doubt that they would be fully equal to their task.

Ex-Impresario was back on April 23rd (over 1,000 words) to inform the Stroud public that it was not true that Mr Mann viewed his letter with contempt. He had been in communication with Mr Mann who had, on his advice, agreed to a Miss E Foote of Bath, 'a contralto of much promise', being engaged. He again urged the committee to review the policy of engaging principals of a higher ability. He had spoken to many people who, unaware of who he was, had said that they were willing to pay an extra half-crown to ensure the engagements of artists of this calibre. Also, he had heard Miss Westbrook and Mr Brandon and held them in high regard, though he does regret that soloists in provincial productions use a loud voice to cover a multitude of sins. He looked forward to further discussions of the means whereby the Stroud Choral Society may attain a higher position amongst musical associations.

Unable to leave the subject, on May 5th 1868, Ex-Impresario (with 1,640 words) was still trying to educate Stroud on the need for good music. Although pressed, he was unable to reveal his real identity, having now reverted, in retirement, to his original name. He was sad that there was a lack of good musical entertainment in Stroud, and in England generally he felt that we lagged behind the Continent. He saw this as an age for educating the masses and not pandering to their love of 'nigger melodies and comic songs'. He feared that English audiences would frantically applaud a performance which, in Italy, would be brought to an ignominious end. He finished by apologising for the length of the letter.

The critic for the *Elijah* concert began by stating that the Choral Society was one of the best-trained and most efficient provincial choirs for its size. Despite the 'croakings of hostile critics and predictions of failure', they had worthily presented 'one of the most magnificent and perfect of orchestral works'. He continued: 'When it is remembered that the members are subjected to no process of selection, but consist of all comers who choose to purchase a member's ticket and, further, the choir is without the advantage of practising with the Band (a matter of no small importance), it must be admitted that the results achieved by the conductor with the material at his command are highly creditable.'

Unsurprisingly, Ex-Impresario, in order to have the last word hijacked the end of the review. After a fulsome wander through *Elijahs* he had known in Paris, Milan, London and Berlin he was happy to announce that the predictions of the 'croakers' that the oratorio would be 'murdered' were unfounded. As he was not taken to extravagant adulation and knew that it would be distasteful to the Society, he wanted to express his opinion that 'taken as a whole, it reflects great credit on all concerned'. Also, in a friendly spirit, he wished to point out that the strength of the strings was 'inadequate' and some important instruments were 'conspicuous by their absence'. He was aware that the 'question d'argent' was the sole cause. He purposely avoided all mention of the principal soloists but was anxious to express his satisfaction of the kind reception accorded to Miss Foote, 'that the touching quality of her voice, her true musical feelings, and her careful, correct, and unobtrusive style warranted my recommendation.' With this final fling, Ex-Impresario disappeared from the pages of the *Stroud Journal* and from the life of the Choral Society.

The phoenix rises

Less than twenty persons attended to perform the sad but necessary rites, and all was over within half an hour.
Annual General Meeting, September 1870

For the Choral Society, two events, the death of Richard Mann and the closure of the Subscription Rooms for extensive renovations, marked the end of the 1860s.

Richard Mann died on April 29th 1869 aged 34. Not only was Richard Mann the conductor at Stroud but he also conducted the Cirencester Choral Society and his death would have affected both societies. From the report of Richard Mann's death and account of his funeral in the *Wilts & Gloucestershire Standard* we learn that he had been suffering from consumption for at least four years. This was attributed, according to the *Standard*, to sleeping in a damp bed. Not only that, but 'the recent cold windy weather' had played a significant role in his death. Mr Mann was much respected for his musical abilities. He had been educated at St Michael's College Tenbury, under Sir F A Gore Ouseley and titled himself 'professor of music'. During his last illness, members of the Cirencester Choral Society wrote to him to express their grief at his severe illness and to offer heartfelt sympathy: 'It may afford you a moment's gratification if we also take this opportunity of saying how much we feel indebted to you for your kind instruction and your unvarying good tempered and patient perseverance with us. That your sufferings may be tempered as far as possible is the earnest prayer of your sincere friends.' Ill as he was, Richard Mann was still able to reply: 'How can I thank you properly for the kind expressions of sympathy? God has been very good to me and I suffer little pain. The periodic meeting of the Cirencester Choral Society has always been one of the bright spots in my week's work – you know that better than I can tell you. When the pain has held me, bright faces have made me forget all. I shall think of you on Thursday – you must do better than you have ever done before. With all best wishes and a request that you will give me your prayers. Richard Mann, Cirencester Market Place, April 13th 1869.'

At his funeral a composition by Mr Helmore was most impressively sung and a large number of his friends from Stroud were present in the church and in the funeral procession. The concert on May 13th, Mendelssohn's *St Paul*, had been chosen by Mr Mann but again

Richard Mann's grave in the churchyard of Cirencester Parish Church. The inscription on the stone reads 'In memory of Richard Mann, Organist of this Parish Church and conductor of the Stroud and Cirencester Choral Societies. Who died the 29th April 1869 in the 34th year of his life.'

conducted by Mr Brind. The reviewer commented on the choir having to adjust quickly to the differing styles of conductors. The choir appeared in half-mourning as a token of respect for the death of their conductor.

In the summer of 1869, Stroud Subscription Rooms were closed to allow major renovations to take place. By a curious coincidence, the first performance in the Subscription Rooms after their present major renovations (2000) was Mendelssohn's *St Paul*, 131 years on from its first performance in Stroud.

On December 20th 1869 at an unknown venue, the Choral Society gave a musical evening. We are told that it was in the way of being an innovation as it was an 'open night' and that it was 'a quiet, fresh and extremely enjoyable evening'.

Surprisingly enough, the concert to open the newly renovated Subscription Rooms on December 30th 1869 was arranged and conducted by none other than our old friend James Chew. During 1868 and 1869, Mr Chew had not appeared in any of the Stroud Choral concerts. One can only make a guess as to the reasons. Perhaps, simply, he was just too busy with his own charitable concerts during this period. He was of course still organist and choirmaster at Stroud Parish Church.

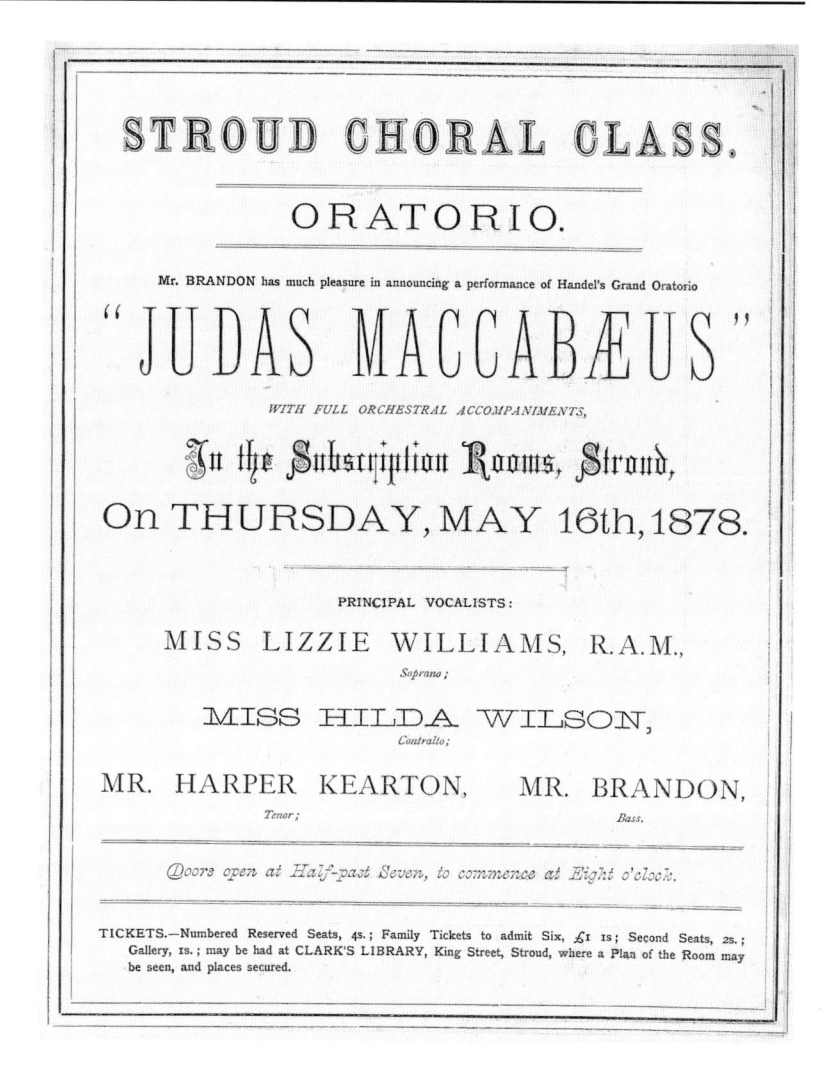

There was a good start to 1870 with a performance of *Messiah* on March 24th, under the conductorship of Mr Brind and again with James Chew as Leader of the Band. As usual, the reviewer enjoyed the concert, noting that it was the third time *Messiah* had been sung by the Society. It had been chosen as the oratorio most likely to prove pecuniarily successful as it never failed to attract a large audience. The newly renovated and decorated Subscription Rooms were described and praised. The only harsh words were saved for the tenor, a Mr Alfred Baylis, who, although having been 'engaged upon high recommendation, it was obvious that the committee had been unfortunate in their selection. Mr Baylis had no qualifications whatever for the task undertaken and was conspicuously and increasingly inefficient throughout'!

From the pages of the *Wilts and Gloucestershire Standard* we learn that the Society held a private soirée on April 25th 1870: 'Admission was by invitation only, and the affair was a really enjoyable evening party.' Between the musical items the company promenaded and refreshments were served. There was also a 'small museum of objects of interest' and a 'remarkable collection of ancient missals of extreme rarity' contributed by Mr W Bragge of Sheffield. Sadly, we also learn that this social event was a farewell evening as due to lack of public support the Society was to be dissolved.

The September 1870 Annual General Meeting was convened with the express purpose of formally registering the demise of the Society: 'Less than twenty persons attended to perform the sad but necessary rites, and all was over within half an hour.' The main reasons given were the falling off of both singers and audience and the Society being in deficit to the tune of £3 5s 6d. In spite of the gravity of the occasion, the meeting seems to have been held in a light-hearted manner, with laughter greeting some statements. The Secretary, Mr Bragg, gave his report and ended by giving this 'curious and remarkable' fact. The minutes book which he had used to enter all the proceedings of the Society 'would just hold the records of this meeting, and then it would be full'. He could not conceive of a more conclusive argument than that for the dissolution of the Society. This statement was met with laughter from the members present.

Mr Brind, however, had other thoughts. He could not understand the meeting. Many people had told him that they wanted the Society to continue and he could rely on their support. He proposed that if the Society ceased to exist he would start a singing class which he would hold at the Corn Hall every Monday, from 5.15 to 9.30. The season would consist of twenty practices, and there would be one or two concerts, depending on support. He proposed to start with Mendelssohn's *As Pants the Hart* and Sterndale Bennett's *May Queen*. The first practice would be on October 3rd with the music to be supplied either by Clark's Library or at the Corn Hall. Members' tickets for the whole season would be 10s, payable in two instalments. Mr Brind would be happy to collect names of anyone interested in the classes at this meeting.

At the resolution for closing the Society, three or four hands only were raised and as there were no dissenting hands the motion was declared carried. At this point, in spite of Mr Brind's best efforts, the Society seems to have disappeared from public record for the next two and a half years.

We do, however, know a little more of what happened to Edward Brind. During Richard Mann's bouts of illness he had also conducted Cirencester Choral Society. In the *History of Cirencester* by Kenneth J Beecham 1886, we learn that 'The Choral Society holds meetings for practice under the leadership of Mr Brind, and gives a sacred concert twice a year'. We also know that he gave a concert, Sullivan's *Prodigal Son* and Gounod's *Messe Solonelle*, on April 17th 1890. Edward Brind was Organist at Highnam Church for sixteen years and later Organist at Cirencester Parish Church for nineteen years. He died on December 18th 1903 aged 64. From his Obituary, in the *Wilts and Gloucestershire Standard* for December 26th 1903, we are told that he was Conductor of the Stroud Choral Society for 10 years. Our records show that he conducted for two years in Stroud, 1869 and 1870, after the death of Richard Mann. Edward Brind was buried at Highnam and Sir Hubert Parry attended his funeral. It seems that Stroud's loss became Cirencester's gain!

The next appearance of the Stroud Choral Society (Stroud Choral Choir) was in May 1873 with a performance of 'Handel's Sublime Oratorio *Samson*'. Mr Chew was Leader of the 'orchestra', Miss Clark was at the piano and a new conductor wielded the baton. He is Mr Thomas Brandon, 'Professor of Music', residing at 10 Brunswick Square, Gloucester, previously appointed Supernumerary Lay Clerk of Gloucester Cathedral in 1864. Mr Brandon was no newcomer to the Choral Society. He had sung bass solo at all the Society concerts since his first appearance at the performance of *The Creation* on April 12th 1864. The *Journal* notes that it has been some time since they had had the pleasure of listening to a Stroud Choral Society concert 'as for the last year or two it had been extinct'. It praises Mr Brandon's talent and enterprise in bringing the Society a new lease of life. In this concert, as well as conducting, Mr Brandon sang the tenor solo *Honour and Arms* and was 'very well received'.

Two years later, in 1875, we find the Choral Society taking part in the Stroud Music Festival. Their contribution to the event is two concerts, *Messiah* on 14th April and a secular concert the following day. We learn that the alto soloist, Miss Margaret Hancock, was the winner of the Contralto Prize at the National Music Meeting at the Crystal Palace in 1873. In spite of this, the reviewer reported that her early solos were not so successful. Mr Brandon won praise for his 'baton wielding' and his solos, and Mr Chew as Leader and Miss Clark for her accompaniment: 'Altogether the interpretation of Handel's masterpiece was a gratifying success.'

Again, there is a gap of two years before the next mention of the Society in the press, with a notice for choral class practices in November 1877, the work to be *Judas Maccabaeus*. This concert takes place on May 16th 1878. Unfortunately, according to the reviewer, the weather was wretched and this affected the attendance: 'the second seats presented a beggarly array of empty benches'. The oratorio was said to have been fairly and creditably interpreted with fresh and vigorous choruses. The duet *O lovely peace* was a gem and much enjoyed. In spite of the 'want of general support' it was noted that 'a guarantee fund will prevent loss falling on the promoters'.

On the same pages of the *Stroud Journal* there is a review of a successful performance of *Joshua*, given the previous week by the Stonehouse Choral Society to a large audience comprised of the 'elite of the neighbourhood'. Several of the same soloists from the Stroud Choral Society, including Miss Williams and Mr Brandon, are listed. One could speculate that too many choral societies in a small neighbourhood could cause problems. In spite of advertisements in the *Journal* for choral classes in February and September 1879, and the printing of concert programmes for a December production of *Joshua*, this concert was later cancelled with no reason being given.

Fortunately, the decade of the 80s shows the Choral Society in much better heart and voice with at least one concert given every year after 1880. Sterndale Bennett's pastoral *The May Queen*, 'a charming little composition of no very great pretensions', according to the reviewer, was performed on May 21st 1881. Much praise was given to the choir, its conductor Mr Brandon and to Mr Chew for his 'thoroughly efficient' training of the Band: 'The Choral Society is formed of ample and good material and ought to prove a perennial institution.'

'Mr Brandon, the able and popular instructor of the Stroud Choral Class, wound up the season with a grand concert.' This was *Acis and Galatea* in April 1882. Mr Brandon was loudly cheered for his bass solo *Oh ruddier than the cherry* and the reviewer concluded the report by expressing the hope 'that the class is now a permanent institution'. The 1883 season ends with 'a highly meritorious' production of *Messiah*, 'reflecting the greatest credit upon Mr Brandon and the Stroud Choral Class'. No doubt the audience also appreciated the extra comfort of the second seats (price 2s); these had recently been provided with back rests.

In the May 1st 1884 concert *Elijah*, Mr Brandon becomes the principal bass soloist, singing the part of Elijah. The conductor's baton is taken by Mr J Hunt of Gloucester. The chorus numbered between 80 and 100 and sang with 'great precision and spirit'. The Band was 'well drilled' and 'effectively sustained their part except for the want of precision on the part of the trombones'. The reviewer notes that the interest of the audience increased as the evening wore on. Again the unpropitious weather was thought to have affected the receipts.

The Creation, due to be performed on April 28th 1885, was unexpectedly postponed. Mr Brandon, in the announcement in the *Journal*, states that it was 'from unavoidable circumstances'. This may have been a mark of respect for the Dowager Lady Marling who had died on April 13th, though one feels the notice would have stated this. There had been a Marling connection with the Society since 1851, when S S Marling was listed as a patron. Later, in 1864, William H Marling was also listed as a patron. On the programme for February 1888 he is shown as Sir W H Marling, Bart.

The Creation was finally performed on December 9th 1886, being the third time it had been sung by the Society. The reviewer states that in view of the postponement of the previous year, Mr Brandon intended to give two concerts this season. For *The Creation* the choir comprised 21 sopranos, 16 altos, 11 tenors and 14 basses and was 'fairly well balanced'. Mr Brandon is again the bass soloist and sang in spite of 'a very severe cold'. We are told that the concert was such a success that the Society would be able to pay the expenses of the postponed concert as well as the present one and still have a balance in hand. On the concert programme, the President, Sir John Dorington, Bt, is now listed as an MP.

Cowen's 'beautiful' cantata *The Rose Maiden* concluded the season on April 28th 1887. This was its initial performance in Stroud, though it had been heard recently in Stonehouse and some members of that choral society joined in with the performance. Instrumentalists from Gloucester and Cheltenham also attended. In a departure from normal practice, Mr Brandon conducted but did not sing. The bass solos were sung by a Mr Ineson from Hereford Cathedral. The choir consisted of 31 sopranos, 19 altos, 13 tenors and 17 basses. The report concluded that it is disheartening to find the Subscription Rooms only partially filled especially when Mr Brandon and the committee had gone to such lengths to procure the 'crème de la crème' of professional artistes. The hire of the Subscription Rooms for this concert cost the Society £30 16s 6d.

An innovation for the Society in 1887 was to propose a Promenade Concert to be held at Stratford Park on August 25th. This was to be a light-hearted programme of solos, part-songs and glees. The Band of the 2nd Volunteer Battalion, Gloucestershire Regiment would also be in attendance. (Admission to the Park from Four to Six o'clock, 1s. After Six, 3d.) Unfortunately, the weather was 'unfavourable' and the concert was postponed at first to September 1st and then in resignation and at very short notice into the Subscription Rooms for the evening of Friday September 2nd. (Reserved seats 1s, Promenade 6d, Gallery 3d.) The attendance was modest but 'the various performances were excellent and highly appreciated'. The reviewer felt that postponed events seldom prove satisfactory and that 'few people take kindly to indoor pursuits until the summer and autumn have both disappeared.'

STROUD SINGS

Due in part to the poor weather, and in part to the late notice given to the concert being held in the Subscription Rooms, the event was a financial upset. From the Subscription Rooms Minutes, September 30th 1887, we learn that the Choral Society's secretary E Northam Witchell had written requesting a concession on the hiring charge. The Society was in an impecunious position due to the poor attendance at the Promenade Concert. The Subscription Rooms committee considered that 'to reduce the fee in this instance would be creating an undesirable precedent and therefore they could not comply'.

It may have taken some time to recover financially as the next concert was not until February 1888. The Subscription Rooms Ledger shows that Mr Brandon paid £31 14s 0d on December 31st 1887. Was this payment in advance or arrears? A grand performance of *Messiah*, with full Band and chorus of 120 performers took place on February 7th 1888.

The concert was 'proof positive of the perennial freshness of this great work and the choral class acquitted themselves admirably'. The bass solos were again taken by Mr Brandon. Unfortunately, during the solos 'the band gallantly struggled to keep time without the guidance of the conductor's baton and Mr Chew had to step in and conduct in order to pull the band together'. Around this time, James Chew's musical activities began to take second place as he became increasingly more involved in public life. In 1884, he had been appointed to the local Board of Health and in 1889 became chairman of the newly constituted Urban District Council. He was made a JP in 1895.

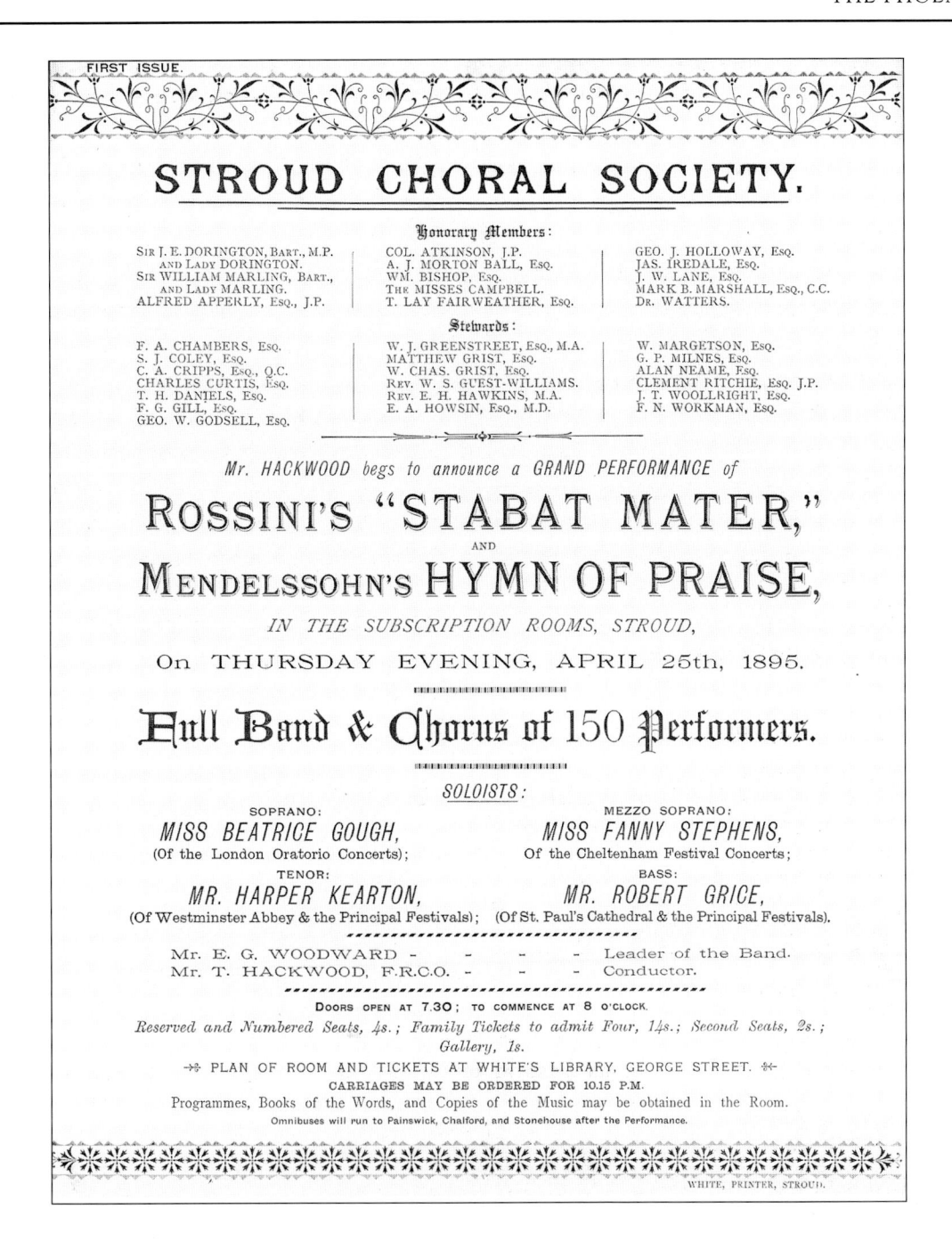

> **FIRST ISSUE**
>
> # STROUD CHORAL SOCIETY.
>
> **Honorary Members:**
>
> Sir J. E. Dorington, Bart., M.P. and Lady Dorington.
> Sir William Marling, Bart., and Lady Marling.
> Alfred Apperly, Esq., J.P.
> Col. Atkinson, J.P.
> A. J. Morton Ball, Esq.
> Wm. Bishop, Esq.
> The Misses Campbell.
> T. Lay Fairweather, Esq.
> Geo. J. Holloway, Esq.
> Jas. Iredale, Esq.
> J. W. Lane, Esq.
> Mark B. Marshall, Esq., C.C.
> Dr. Watters.
>
> **Stewards:**
>
> F. A. Chambers, Esq.
> S. J. Coley, Esq.
> C. A. Cripps, Esq., Q.C.
> Charles Curtis, Esq.
> T. H. Daniels, Esq.
> F. G. Gill, Esq.
> Geo. W. Godsell, Esq.
> W. J. Greenstreet, Esq., M.A.
> Matthew Grist, Esq.
> W. Chas. Grist, Esq.
> Rev. W. S. Guest-Williams.
> Rev. E. H. Hawkins, M.A.
> E. A. Howsin, Esq., M.D.
> W. Margetson, Esq.
> G. P. Milnes, Esq.
> Alan Neame, Esq.
> Clement Ritchie, Esq. J.P.
> J. T. Woollright, Esq.
> F. N. Workman, Esq.
>
> Mr. HACKWOOD begs to announce a GRAND PERFORMANCE of
>
> ## ROSSINI'S "STABAT MATER,"
> AND
> ## MENDELSSOHN'S HYMN OF PRAISE,
>
> *IN THE SUBSCRIPTION ROOMS, STROUD,*
>
> On THURSDAY EVENING, APRIL 25th, 1895.
>
> ### Full Band & Chorus of 150 Performers.
>
> **SOLOISTS:**
>
> SOPRANO: **MISS BEATRICE GOUGH,** (Of the London Oratorio Concerts);
> MEZZO SOPRANO: **MISS FANNY STEPHENS,** Of the Cheltenham Festival Concerts;
> TENOR: **MR. HARPER KEARTON,** (Of Westminster Abbey & the Principal Festivals);
> BASS: **MR. ROBERT GRICE,** (Of St. Paul's Cathedral & the Principal Festivals).
>
> Mr. E. G. WOODWARD - Leader of the Band.
> Mr. T. HACKWOOD, F.R.C.O. - Conductor.
>
> Doors open at 7.30; to commence at 8 o'clock.
> Reserved and Numbered Seats, 4s.; Family Tickets to admit Four, 14s.; Second Seats, 2s.; Gallery, 1s.
> PLAN OF ROOM AND TICKETS AT WHITE'S LIBRARY, GEORGE STREET.
> CARRIAGES MAY BE ORDERED FOR 10.15 P.M.
> Programmes, Books of the Words, and Copies of the Music may be obtained in the Room.
> Omnibuses will run to Painswick, Chalford, and Stonehouse after the Performance.
>
> WHITE, PRINTER, STROUD.

In December 1889, the Stroud Choral Class performed sections of Mendelssohn's *St Paul* and Cowen's *Sleeping Beauty*. The reviewer is moved to comment that 'it seems a pity that the Stroud public do not give Mr Brandon the support he is so worthy of ... the attendance was really miserable, the second seats (still at 2s) being practically empty'. Mr Brandon is reported as being 'fired with perpetual youth'. (An ominous statement, as it always seems to precede the imminent demise or disappearance of the person named!) The concert from a musical point of view was said to be a success, though financially 'we fear it otherwise'.

A notice in the *Stroud Journal* in January 1890 announces the commencement of practices for *Messiah* to be performed in March that year. We can find no confirmation of this concert and it is not until April 1892 that we find the next concert, J F Barnett's *The Ancient Mariner* and this time the conductor is Mr T Hackwood, FRCO. There is no mention in the concert write-up that gives any clue as to what happened to Mr Brandon. On the programme, the title Choral Class has now become Choral Society and the *Journal* reviewer is full of enthusiasm for the new conductor Mr Hackwood and the 'thoroughly trained' choir and band, which together numbered 150 performers. The new leader of the band was Mr W E Butland. 'This was the most successful and excellent concert ever given in Stroud by a choral society.'

The *Stroud Journal* reviewer was equally captivated by Smart's cantata *The Bride of Dunkerron* in April 1893, claiming it to be 'an unqualified success'. He felt that rarely had such a cantata of fine music been more pleasingly or correctly performed.

The following year, in April 1894, *Elijah* was played to a full house. The reviewer felt that choral societies generally earn their fair share of ridicule but this could not be said of the Stroud 'class'. Mr Hackwood's choir had created a reputation to be envied by societies in larger and more important towns than Stroud. 'It was apparent throughout that members were animated with a desire to excel' and had been 'well trained and thoroughly practised.'

Rossini's *Stabat Mater* and Mendelssohn's *Hymn of Praise* were performed in April 1895. Mr Hackwood's choir was unusually good and 'showed if possible increased signs of vitality'. 'Choral societies as a rule are not long-lived, the Stroud Society is one of the fortunate few and has been in existence a long number of years.' The only jarring note in the review was to castigate the tenor soloist, Mr Harper Kearton, for yet again failing to fulfil his engagement. His place was taken by Mr Hirwen Jones (of the Hereford Three Choirs and principal London concerts).

In the following year, 1896, the April concert was postponed to November due to a smallpox epidemic at Gloucester. (There were also smallpox outbreaks in Stroud during the 1890s, in particular in 1894, though the concert for that year seems to have gone ahead.) This concert was Spohr's *Last Judgement*, a very popular Victorian work, though it would now be regarded as somewhat turgid and dreary. The reviewer felt that the opportunity the postponement gave for extra practice had been useful! Again, it was a commendable performance, although some choruses showed 'a slight hesitancy to join in the general attack'.

In the Spring of 1897 there were many activities in Stroud to celebrate Queen Victoria's 60th year on the throne. There was no sign of a choral concert, although James Chew, JP, and his Band produced a magnificent effort on May 14th in the Subscription Rooms. James Chew had requested the free use of the large hall as the concert was in aid of the poor on the occasion of the Queen's Diamond Jubilee. The Subscription Rooms committee refused but voted to donate two guineas to the fund! A national hymn *Victoria* with words by Sidney Cubitt and set to music by Thomas Hackwood, FRCO was sung throughout the district on Sunday 20th June.

> Victoria reigns!
> Let heart and voice acclaim
> The priceless blessing of her gracious sway.
> Victoria Reigns!
> Do honour to her name
> And thank the Lord for this all happy day.

The November concert, 1897, was Mendelssohn's *Elijah* and the 'music lovers' of the neighbourhood were there in force. The choir consisted of 38 trebles plus choirboys, 23 altos, 16 tenors and 21 basses. This formed an admirable and evenly balanced choir'. The critic observed that to those who had heard a Leeds, Birmingham or London choir it would have been easy to point out blemishes in the performance. Recognising that Mr Hackwood had drawn all his performers from local amateur circles and, apart from a few tenors or basses who were 'too full of ardour', the whole chorus was a 'credit to their conductor'. The chorus *He slumbers not* was said to have given 'the most pleasure' to everyone. As well as soloists from Exeter Cathedral and Christchurch College, Oxford, a Mrs John Lane from Cainscross was singled out for considerable praise, the reviewer stating that 'we have certainly heard no singer who has excelled and few to equal her reading of the music'.

This concert seems to have been the last that we can find for the nineteenth century. Again, it seems strange that the Society disappears from sight after a memorable and well-supported concert. We know that Mr Hackwood was still in the district. In March 1899 reference is made in James Chew's Obituary to the effect that 'the Choral Society is now conducted by Mr T Hackwood FRCO'. In July 1899 he was appointed by the Rev Cannon Fox to the post of organist at Stroud Parish Church; this was to fill the vacancy left by the death of James Chew. In September 1899, there were presentations made to him at Holy Trinity Church and he expressed 'greatest grief at leaving Holy Trinity and its choirmen'. Mr Hackwood's indifferent health may have been the reason for no Society concerts during the last three years of the century.

The late Mr. James Chew, J.P.,
Chairman of the Stroud Urban District Council.

James Chew's gravestone, Stroud Old Cemetery, May 2000.

Photograph from the Stroud Journal, *March 1899.*

James Chew, after a long life full of music, good causes and service to the Stroud public, died aged 75 on March 6th 1899. It seems very fitting that at his funeral it was Mr S W Underwood of Gloucester who played the organ voluntary *I know that my Redeemer liveth*.

The *Stroud Journal* in its 50 years Jubilee issue of May 3rd 1904 looked back on the nineteenth century and had the following to say about Stroud Choral Society: 'After an existence of some years the Stroud Choral Society came to an end. To a very great extent the Society has DIED OF AMBITION. A small town can hardly be expected to maintain an unbroken succession of oratorio performances which involve an outlay of close on £100. The wonder is the Society was able to keep it up so long.' How wrong they were!

The twenty-first century Choral Society can look back to its early beginnings with wonder and humble affection for those fellow singers who kept faith in a choral presence in this 'small town' of Stroud.

'Chew's band'

The Band will be full and efficient, and to render the Performance in every respect complete.
Programme notes, May 11th, 1867

There could have been very few people living in nineteenth-century Stroud who had not heard of 'Chew's Band'. They were prolific performers, playing not just for the Choral Society but for many other organisations and occasions, in particular for fund-raising events. James Chew was born on July 14th 1823 into what could be described as a local family of modest musical accomplishment. His father, Richard Chew, was a blacksmith who played the violin and also conducted the Chalford Band. James' half-brother Richard was a gifted trombonist. Another brother, although it could have been the trombonist, was said to have been a member of the band touring with Wombwell's celebrated Menagerie. His grandfather and great-uncle both played in the Chalford Band. James became organist of Chalford Church at the age of fourteen and held this post for at least six years. In 1843, at the age of nineteen he was presented with an inscribed family Bible from the teachers and children of the National schools and other friends at Chalford for 'the trouble which he has taken to instruct them in Psalmody.'

In 1847, when he was 23, he moved from Chalford to Beard's Wharf, London Road, Stroud where he took over the established business of a coal merchant. Ambrose Beard, an uncle of James' first wife Ann, had bequeathed this position to him. Within a few years, he had given up coal-trading and devoted himself entirely to music. His first music shop was in Union Street. Later, he bought premises in Russell Street, where he opened a music shop and built his home, Meldon House.

James Chew was married twice: his first wife Ann died in February 1868 aged 43. Later he married Miss Lawrence of Bracknell, Berkshire, who he had met at the home of his friend Mr Henry Holloway. They were to have four sons and three daughters.

James Chew officiated at both the Old Chapel and Bedford Street Chapel before his appointment as organist of Stroud Parish Church on Christmas Day 1851. For many years he was also a music instructor 'at nearly all the schools in the neighbourhood'.

In connection with the Volunteer movement, which was formed in 1852, James Chew was sworn up as a member of the Stroud Volunteer Rifle Corps on October 26th 1859. 'He immediately organised a Band which he conducted with great skill.'

In his obituary in 1899, the Stroud Journal says that he was not what might be described as a brilliant musician but rather a clever 'all round man'. He was said to have acquired a practical knowledge of many reed and cup instruments, his best instrument being the cornet. However, it was as

> **PIANO-FORTES,**
> And other MUSICAL INSTRUMENTS for SALE or HIRE, at
> **JAMES CHEW'S,**
> *Professor of Music,*
> 1, UNION BUILDINGS, STROUD.
>
> *₊*₊* INSTRUMENTS TUNED AND REPAIRED.
>
> **MR. JAMES CHEW,**
> *Professor of Music,*
> BEGS to inform his Pupils and Friends that he will RESUME his DUTIES on MONDAY NEXT, July 27.

Advert for James Chew's shop, July 25th 1857, Stroud Journal.

The surviving timpani from Chew's Band. October 2000.

first violin that he led the Band for many of the Stroud Choral Society concerts. A close musical friend, quoted in the obituary, stated that James Chew was the quickest reader of music that he had ever known. 'He was not a brilliant executant, but as a practical musician it was questionable whether he could be touched, and he will be very much missed.'

On March 23rd 1959, a Mr Reginald Cox of The Bumps, Edge, Stroud, presented to the Society the set of three timpani that were in his possession. The timpani had been made originally for a group of musicians that were operating in a room off Russell Street, Stroud, in the 1890s. They called themselves 'Chew's Band' and he was the last surviving member of that Band. Mr Cox was a cellist and played in many of the Society's performances from 1901 onwards. On other occasions he also sang with the bass section. The timpani were reputed to have been made by Chew, the local blacksmith, and were said to be a fine example of the local craftsman's art. The timpani may have been made by a T L Chew and Sons, who advertised their ironworks in King Street, Stroud, through the second half of the nineteenth century. These timpani look to be late Victorian in date and seem more likely to be the work of a blacksmith than a professional instrument maker. At some time the timpani were stored in the Parish Church and then loaned to the New Stroud Orchestra, formed by Claude Allen, in the 1960s. Adrian Harbidge, who was playing in the New Stroud Orchestra in the 1960s, reported that by 1965 there were only two timpani in existence. In more recent times, the Chalford Silver Band have kindly stored these ancient instruments.

James Chew's engraved ebony presentation baton, given to him in October 1850 by the Stroud Choral Society, was discovered in a Minchinhampton antique shop in 1970 by Howard Beard, a local historian. Mr Beard purchased the baton and it was given to Frank Miller, the Society's President. This baton was later presented to the then Choral conductor, Tony Hewitt-Jones, as a mark of esteem. Unfortunately, some years ago the baton appears to have been stolen, along with other silver items from the Hewitt-Jones' family home. It would be a fitting tribute to James Chew and his long association with music making in Stroud, if this baton could be found and returned to Stroud. Then, perhaps together with the timpani, the baton could find a permanent home in the new Museum in the Park.

'I dreamt that I dwelt in marble halls'

At Stroud they have beautiful rooms, built by subscription for the purposes of the arts and literature as well as public amusement, whilst nothing of the kind exists either here or at Cheltenham.

Gloucester Journal, 1842

The disgruntled writer of the above statement goes on to say, 'No artist of talent comes to this county without an invitation to display his powers at Stroud.' When Stroud became a Borough in 1832 it was no doubt felt that a large imposing building was needed to reflect Stroud's new status. Prior to this, meetings had been held in the Victoria Rooms (now the present site of Woolworths' forecourt) and these rooms went into decline with the opening of the Subscription Rooms in 1834. It was in the Victoria Rooms that James Chew set up choral classes in the early days of the Society.

The official opening of the Subscription Rooms on Monday October 27th 1834 was a very grand affair. There was a concert of sacred music in the morning, followed by an evening concert of secular music. The principal soloists were well-known London singers and, if not resident in Stroud, would have travelled there by stagecoach. It cost £54 8s 0d to engage the soloists and £41 5s 0d for the instrumentalists. The price of admission was 4s for the morning concert (beginning at 12 noon, as was the custom), 5s for the evening concert at 7.30pm and 8s for a ticket for both. The concerts were an immense success and thought of as a 'great event for Stroud'. These concerts inspired the formation of the Stroud Philharmonic, which exactly three weeks later, on 17th November, gave its first ever performance in the Stroud Subscription Rooms. The inhabitants of Stroud took to these concerts with great enthusiasm. It was no doubt the equivalent of radio, television, CDs and tapes all rolled into one! The concerts were great social occasions, a time to see and be seen in Stroud.

For the Choral Society concerts, the local traders were encouraged to support the 'early closing scheme' so that their employees could attend the concerts either as part of the audience or to assist the chorus. 'All the traders of the town with few insignificant exceptions, closed their shops at six o'clock' (April 1863). On the front page of the *Stroud Journal* for Saturday, December 15th 1866, under Early Closing, is a notice that is a variation on this request. 'As the Christmas Concert of the Society will be held this year on a Thursday, the evening on which so many tradespeople close their Establishments at Five O'clock, the Committee think it unnecessary to make their usual personal request, and express a hope that all will second their efforts for the success of the concert by kindly closing their shops at Six O'clock, or as early as convenient, in order that those in their employ may have the opportunity of attending the performance. 13th December 1866, Robert Bragg, Hon. Sec.' If, in the early 1860s, early closing was at five o'clock, it does beg the question, what time was normal closing time?

By the 1860s the Society concerts were being reported on at great length in the Stroud Journal. In particular, as well as commenting on the performance, the soloists, and the background to the music, many column inches were devoted to describing the decoration of the Ballroom. This large room was 70 feet long by 43 feet wide and 25 feet high. There was a raised platform, often referred to as the 'orchestra', which was 26 feet long and 14 feet wide. This 'orchestra' was always reported as being enlarged (built over the existing platform) for the concerts. Sometimes it had raised sections and on some occasions extended as high as, and into, the gallery. For some concerts an additional 'orchestra' was raised at the back of the room. The staging was usually draped with scarlet broadcloth, no doubt in plentiful supply in the Stroud area. Along the front of the 'orchestra' was amassed a profusion of hothouse flowers, shrubs and ferns of 'the finest growth'. These flowers and shrubs came from the greenhouses and 'stove rooms' of some well-known Stroud personages, the Stantons, Winterbothams, Dickinsons, Doringtons, Hallewells, Gregorys

T. L. Chew and Son's shop, late nineteenth century. Opened in January 1869, it was situated on the corner of King Street and Bath Street.

and Fosters. Some plants got a specific mention, 'two bigonias (sic) sent by Mr. Kingdom being remarkably fine specimens' (December 1866). Trelliswork was also intertwined with laurels (April 1864).

From our old print dated 1835, the drawing shows what appears to be trelliswork, studded with artificial flowers. This trelliswork runs along the front of the 'orchestra' and seems to be standing on this platform and not on the floor. Not content with the 'greenhouse plants and ornamental foliage' along the front of the orchestra, there were added to this collection statues or carved shields. Sometimes these statues were draped to represent classical figures and the shields carved with inscriptions: 'We praise thee, O God' (May 1867). Mr. Joshua Wall was a local sculptor and most concerts were graced by his work. As well as statues, ornamental busts were used. A gilt bust of Handel was lent by a Mr Woodward of Cheltenham, for the *Messiah* Concert (April 1863). For Christmas concerts 'a figure of Old Father Christmas with flowing white locks, jolly countenance and scarlet robe' stood in the centre at the front of the 'orchestra'.

Mirrors and large pier glasses were used to glittering effect, arranged so that they reflected gas burners. Between the mirrors, busts or figures were placed with more greenery draped across linking them and the mirrors. The gas chandeliers were hung with wreaths 'studded with capitally made artificial flowers'. Evergreen pendants hung from the walls and the windows were 'tastefully draped'. According to the season, or concert choice, large inscriptions on banners were hung across the walls or behind the choir: 'A huge motto in Antique writing, The Earth is the Lord's and the fullness thereof' (*Creation*, April 1864). For the Mozart *12th Mass* in December 1866, the salutation 'A Merry Christmas and a Happy New Year' had been worked by the ladies in laurel leaves and hung on a red banner behind the orchestra. Last but not least, some concerts were graced with working fountains, 'a small fountain amid the floral grove played during the evening with charming effect' (May 1867).

As can be imagined, it took several days of work to decorate the room in readiness for a performance. During the 1860s, this seems to have been masterminded by a Mr Rouse, who is often mentioned in the reviews as planning the designs and supervising the erection of staging and decoration. Towards the end of the 1860s, there are references made to the extreme shabbiness of the room and 'how decorated with taste and skill it is transformed into a bright and brilliant salon'.

The newspaper report after the Christmas concert in December 1868 (*Creation*) seems to suggest that some alterations to the Subscription Rooms had been carried out in advance of the main renovation to start in May the following year. 'It may be mentioned that an unexplained arrangement caused considerable confusion to the company leaving the hall. It had been very judiciously arranged to let the occupants of the front seats depart by the usual front entrance, and those of the back seats and gallery by the new back entrance. A barrier was accordingly erected to ensure this division, which would have ensured greater comfort and rapidity of exit; but, unfortunately, the new staircase was unlighted, its presence was not known, and for some time people were crowding and struggling against the barrier, and using language more vigorous than polite at the idea of being shut in.'

In the spring of 1869, shortly after the May production of Mendelssohn's *St Paul*, the Subscription Rooms, now 35 years old, were closed for extensive renovation. The Stroud Journal comments that 'The Building was not "put into dock" before it was absolutely necessary, for the dingy appearance and dilapidated condition of the large room had become notorious.' The planning, drawings and work of decorating the Ballroom had been given to a Mr Leonard Collman of 70 Grosvenor Street, London, and was carried out under his personal supervision.

During the renovations the stairs to the front entrance were removed and replaced by a portico and covered carriageway. Inside the hall the floor was lowered and the old pavement replaced by mosaic tiles by Maw & Sons of Benthall, Edge. The staircase was improved with slate slabs substituted for the 'old much worn stone steps'. The alteration to the front wall meant that the entrance doors to the two front rooms had to be closed off and resited inside the hall. The main entrance was to be lit by a star burner. An additional entrance to the rear of the building was made by a broad flight of steps from Threadneedle Street behind the Subscription Rooms and this led to the first floor.

In the main room the 'old orchestra' was removed and in its place a convenient moveable platform was provided. The new platform could be made to any size or placed in any part of the room and consisted of 'several pieces' so that it could be converted into a row of dining tables 'sufficient to dine 500 persons'. The front of the gallery, originally made of chest-high solid wood, was lowered and filled in with ornamental ironwork including gilt standards. This lightened the look of the gallery and gave better vision to its occupants. This work was done by T L Chew & Sons of King Street, Stroud. (We are unable to verify that T L Chew and James Chew were related though this seems a strong possibility.)

The lighting in the room was from a large 'sunburner' in the middle and four handsome 'starburners' around it. The ventilation of the room, through the ceiling, was improved. Elegantly designed pilasters were placed between the windows and at the ends of the room and a dado of glazed tiles went round the room. This had the 'special advantage that it cannot be chipped and broken like paint or plaster and any amount of lounging, or rubbing against it will do it no injury'. The architraves of the windows and massive chimneypieces were in Italian pink marble and the woodwork of the windows and entrance door in grained oak. The ceiling was painted light fawn with purple ornaments, the inner panels a violet tint with purple round the central 'sunlight'. The beams were white on a pink ground and the cornice was deepened with a frieze marbled in Italian pink. There was a fine line of vermilion above and below the frieze. In contrast to this, the walls were painted a 'delicate tone of grey' and the skirting was 'a band of black'.

All the work had been carried out by local tradesmen: the principal building work by Mr English, the stonework by Mr Joshua Wall, the painting and decoration by Mr John Hewlett, the gas-fittings and ironwork by Mr Butt and the decorative ironwork by T L Chew & Sons. As in more recent times, complaints were made of the slowness of the progress of the renovations as 'during which time there was no place for public meetings or entertainments of any

Stroud Subscription Rooms prior to 1902. The cannons from Sebastopol c 1855 were still in place.

kind'. Just as today, the *Journal* reporter observed 'but those who make the complaint have no idea of the labour and the amount of details involved, and the time necessarily consumed in such very delicate decorative work'.

Much praise was given to the newly refurbished rooms at the first concerts given after the re-opening. James Chew, giving a Stroud Hospital charity concert on 30th December 1869, led the formal re-opening of the Subscription Rooms. 'The beautiful appearance of the room was a theme of general comment and admiration. The substitution of a convenient and elegantly draped platform, constructed of the moveable flats provided for that purpose, in lieu of the old orchestra, was a striking improvement, and its height from the ground was remarked as preferable to the old arrangement. The convenience of the new entrances was put to the test on this occasion in consequence of the inclemency of the weather, and the arrangement by which carriages can take up and set down under a portico was greatly appreciated. The new entrance at the back was also largely used and found to be a great convenience, and to afford a marked facility for emptying the building.'

The renovated Subscription Rooms with its new elegant Ballroom seemed to take away the need for elaborate decoration for the concerts and there is hardly any mention in further reports other than a short sentence such as 'decorated in a chaste and highly effective way'. By the time the twentieth century dawns the decorating habit seems to have died out.

STROUD SINGS

The Choral society continued to sing in the Subscription Rooms until 1939 when, with war threatening and the Rooms requisitioned for other uses, the concert venue was changed to Stroud Parish Church. It was not until June 1975 that concerts were again held there.

The twentieth century has had its own Subscription Rooms stories. Sometimes it was too cold to sing in, as reported on December 16th 1920. 'A happy idea to include Christmas music, as it was certainly peculiarly suited to the Arctic atmosphere of the Subscription Rooms, for the most weather-hardened concert-goer could scarcely have appreciated songs about gardens of roses with chattering teeth.' Again in the 1920s, an irate letter in the *Journal* asked if there was any truth in the rumour that the Trustees of the Rooms intended burning the benches used for the cheaper seats at the Choral Society concert held the previous week.

When not too cold, the Rooms can often be too hot. If the temperature is right, the noise from outside can sometimes spoil the quieter pieces being sung inside. Sometimes the noise inside the Rooms can hold a concert to ransom. May 1990: 'Alas, the performance verged on disaster ... The main problem was the thunderous noise of the Subscription Rooms' fan conducted air conditioning.' Fortunately, just as the second half of the concert started, a brave member of the audience leapt up and called out to ask for it to be switched off. Dim lighting, or lighting that was too bright, spot lights that fought each other causing a foggy haze, to say nothing of the restrictions on the numbers in the audience, thanks to fire regulations and the surveyor's safety reports, have all brought their own particular difficulties to the production of concerts in the Subscription Rooms.

Whatever the pros and cons of the Rooms, they continue to be a favourite venue, acoustically very good, in fact, the only Stroud venue halfway big enough to house the choir. Now we look forward to singing in the twenty-first century in the Subscription Rooms and our *St Paul* concert opened the newly renovated Rooms in December 2000.

The custom of elaborately decorating the ballroom for the Society's concerts has long since gone. Instead, the choral members have taken their decorative skills to the shop windows of Stroud to advertise the coming concerts to a wider public. So successful was the three-window display depicting scenes from *Carmina Burana* (March 1998) that the window dressers were inundated by requests from passers by wanting to know when the shop was opening and could they buy goods in advance! A more simple design of arum lilies against a backdrop of pictures of Kosovan refugees (Verdi's *Requiem* May 1999) moved some members of the Stroud public to attend a concert for the first time.

From 1920, Stroud Parish Church had occasionally been used as a concert venue, but when war broke in 1939 it became the only venue. Of all the unusual practices and activities indulged in by choral societies, singing with their backs to the audience must surely rank amongst the strangest! This practice must have started from the very first times of singing in the church, because as early as 1922 a concert reviewer makes the following request: 'If at the Gloucester Festival it is possible for singers and instrumen-

Stroud Parish Church c 1919. Most of the twentieth century SCS rehearsals took place in the Church Institute on the left.

36

Stroud Subscription Rooms in 1955. The buildings to the left of the Subscription Rooms show (left to right) the site of the Stroud Dispensary, the Casualty Hospital 1835–1875 and Bedford Street Chapel.

talists to face the congregation and be well in view … then it should be possible to effect a similar arrangement in our own church.' It is not too difficult to speculate how this practice may have come about. The gentlemen occupied the choir stalls and the layout of the church allowed no room for the ladies other than in the front pews of the nave. The 'perks' for the ladies in the front pews were an uninhibited view of the soloists and an obscured view of the conductor. Very few of the lady singers enjoyed this situation and there were frequent requests at committee meetings and AGMs to be allowed to face the audience. It did not seem to be the idiosyncrasy of one particular conductor as the practice spanned the tenure of at least four. Questioned about this at the AGM in 1944, Sammy Underwood said it would be impossible to give their performances from the west end of the church (presumably because it was too far from the organ and the audience would have their backs to the choir). B W, reviewing after the Christmas concert in 1951, says 'it would be a great improvement if on these occasions, arrangements could be made for the choir to face the congregation, rather than at present, having to sing with their audience in the background'. In December 1954 the reviewer was complaining that 'the choir was in good form but probably because they were facing away from the congregation the words were almost unrecognisable'. It was not until the late 1960s, by dint of the simple act of asking the ladies to turn round in the pews to sing and placing the conductor down the aisle, that the problem was solved. In later years some restructuring of the church layout and new forms of heating have been a great help to the Society.

One endearing characteristic of Stroud Parish Church is its name, which can be spelt either St Lawrence or St Laurence. The debate as to which is correct, the 'w' or the 'u', has engaged the Stroud public for a long time. The Choral Society has chosen to play safe by nearly always printing Stroud Parish Church on their programmes. The only exceptions throughout the twentieth century were in 1979 and 1980 when they bravely chose St Lawrence, and in 1995 and 1998 when they thought St Laurence would make a change. The Society has always been made welcome at the Parish Church by its officers.

From time to time throughout the twentieth century there have been requests from members of the Stroud public for a larger concert and entertainment venue in Stroud. At the Society's 125th Anniversary dinner in 1960, the then President, Mr Frank Miller, called for a suitable hall for the Choral Society and other associations. Although the Subscription Rooms are a much appreciated venue the size of the ballroom restricts audience numbers which in turn limits the revenue raised to finance concerts. Since the building of the Stratford Park Leisure Centre in 1976 the Society has used the large sports hall for major concerts to celebrate specific anniversaries of the choir. In April 1985 the Society celebrated 150 years of music making in Stroud with a grand performance of Verdi's *Requiem*. Following the success of the Verdi concert the Leisure Centre was used in 1986 for the production of Beethoven's *Missa Solemnis*. The next important anniversary celebrated was the Society's 150th when Mendelssohn's *Elijah* was performed in May 1995. In 1999, to close the twentieth century and to celebrate the conductor Eddie Garrard's twentieth year with the Society, Verdi's *Requiem* was once again sung. We celebrated the new millennium in style in May 2000 with 'The Last Night of the Proms'. The Leisure Centre has excellent audience and car parking facilities. Unfortunately, it is not the best of performance halls acoustically and we have also been known to share rehearsal time with the roller skating club!

Other venues have been happy to welcome the Choral Society, such as: All Saints, Uplands; the Church of the Immaculate Conception, Beeches Green; Holy Trinity, Stroud; Malmesbury Abbey; Tewkesbury Abbey; the Priory, Leonard Stanley; St Barnabas, Gloucester; St Mary's, Painswick; St Mary's, Wotton-under-Edge; St Matthews, Cainscross; Sibley Hall, Wycliffe College; and Gloucester Cathedral.

Sweet charity

We are happy to state that upwards of five pounds have been handed over in aid of the funds for the Casualty Hospital.

Stroud Free Press *report, March 13th 1851*

The pleasure of singing and performing and the love of music were not the only reasons for the existence of a choral society, often they served the important purpose of raising money for good causes. As well as for philanthropic reasons, charitable activities were also socially acceptable occupations for the nineteenth-century woman. For some of the lady members of the choir, working for a charitable cause would have given them greater access to the outside world. Like other choral societies, Stroud also has a long tradition of supporting charitable needs.

Stroud Hospital 1885.

One of our early programmes for March 13th 1851, under the baton of Mr Chew, clearly states that the concert would be for the 'Benefit of the Casualty Hospital'. At this performance, in spite of it being a wet night, 'there was a large and respectable attendance, the reserved seats being completely filled'. The seats in question cost 3s 6d each.

Stroud had been fortunate enough to have a Dispensary since 1755 and this was situated in a brick building at the corner of George and Bedford Street. But by the 1830s the Dispensary was regarded as inadequate and public money had been subscribed to build a casualty ward next to it. A casualty ward in Stroud would save the badly injured having to travel to the Infirmary at Gloucester. In 1836, the Dispensary was extended and a Doctor and a Nurse were employed to run the new ward. So successful was the new casualty ward that there were reports of patients being reluctant to leave once restored to health!

Unfortunately, by the early 1840s, not only was expenditure exceeding income but a succession of serious accidents in the Sapperton Tunnel and on the Great Western Railway put the Dispensary and Casualty Hospital under great pressure. Considerable local efforts were made to raise more money to extend the Hospital.

By 1856, it was reported that the Hospital 'now had a fourteen bed ward, a physician's room, a patients' waiting room, a kitchen, a pantry, a wash house, a nurses' sleeping room and accommodation, a properly lighted operating room, a dead room and water closets'. Some of this was provided by money raised by the Choral Society. The Casualty Hospital is still standing and adjoins the Bedford Street Chapel.

By the 1870s, the need for a larger hospital in Stroud had been recognised and the present Stroud General Hospital was built on land next to Trinity Church. From 1873, a 'Hospital Sunday' was held each year: collections, and later carnivals, were staged to make money for the new hospital. Stroud General Hospital was opened in 1875. It was estimated that in his lifetime, James Chew had raised more than £700 for hospital funds.

On November 9th 1854, the Society, again with Mr Chew conducting, sang 'for the Benefit of Widows and Orphans of the soldiers in the present war with Russia'. The British Army had suffered great losses in the Crimean War. News of the disastrous Charge of the Light Brigade at Balaclava on October 25th must have reached Stroud quickly. As the awful situation in the Crimea went from bad to worse we again find the Society singing for war relief. At a December concert in 1854, given at the Christmas festivities of the Stroud Benevolent Society, Mr Chew and the Choral Society were warmly thanked for giving their services gratuitously on behalf of the Patriotic Fund. The fund had been raised 'for the widows and orphans of the bravest and noblest of our country and age'.

James Chew was an inveterate supporter of good causes and his concerts litter a vast track of the nineteenth century, somewhat muddying the ground where researching the Choral Society is concerned. The pages of the Stroud Journal chart these concerts, sometimes small, with a few instrumentalists and soloists, sometimes much larger, with the addition of a small or medium-sized choir. Sometimes these choirs are called the Stroud Choral Society and sometimes not. Soloists overlap, the same names appearing in Stroud choral concerts and sometimes as solo performers in the smaller 'Chew' concerts. As well as for the hospital, other Chew concerts raised money for the Stroud Baths, which had been damaged by fire (April 1877), and for the 'Aged Poor' of the district (January 1880).

Charity collections in the twentieth century began in December 1915 with a special performance of *Messiah*. This concert was held in aid of the Stroud Hospital. Concerts then ceased until after the end of the First World War when they were resumed in 1920.

In 1935, the concert programmes start to list the chosen charity for the retiring collection. The choice of charities would have reflected the work or interests of the committee members. Netlam Bigg, for instance, would have suggested the scouting charities. Without a doubt the following list is a historical record of the times in which we lived.

Dec. 1935	Dr. Barnardo's Homes and The Waifs and Strays Society
Dec. 1937	Stroud Social Services, Stroud District Nursing Association, The Waifs and Strays Society
March 1939	Stroud District Nursing Association, Stroud Social Services
Dec. 1939	Polish Relief Fund
March 1940	Stroud & District YMCA hut, Missions to Seamen, Finnish Relief Fund

Dec. 1940	Stroud and District Branch for the Care of Cripples
Jan. 1941	Duke of Gloucester's Red Cross and St John Fund
Feb. 1941	Gloucestershire Deaf and Dumb Society
Dec. 1941	Waifs and Strays Society, Dr. Barnardo's Homes
Jan. 1942	RAF Benevolent Fund
March 1942	Stroud Nursing Association
Dec. 1942	Baden-Powell Memorial Home
March 1943	Hospital for Sick Children, Great Ormond Street
Dec. 1943	Stroud District Nursing Association, Children's Hospital
March 1944	The Association for Moral Welfare
Dec. 1944	The Waifs and Strays Society
March 1945	The Stroud Branch, Council for the Care of Cripples
Dec. 1945	Aid to China Fund
April 1946	Gloucestershire Deaf and Dumb Association
Dec. 1946	The Children's Society, Dr. Barnardo's Homes
March 1947	Stroud and District Cripples Association
Dec. 1947	Handicapped Scouts of Gloucestershire
March 1948	Gloucestershire Deaf and Dumb Association
Dec. 1948	The Children's Society, Dr. Barnardo's Homes
March 1949	The Association for Moral Welfare
Dec. 1949	Restoration of the Parish Church Organ
March 1950	Restoration of the Parish Church Organ
Dec. 1950	Restoration of the Parish Church Organ
March 1951	Restoration of the Parish Church Organ
Dec. 1951	Friends of the Stroud Hospital Fund
March 1952	Gloucestershire Deaf and Dumb Association
Dec. 1952	The Children's Society
March 1953	Gloucestershire Cathedral Restoration Fund
Dec. 1953	Refurbishing seating in the Outpatients Department, Stroud Hospital
March 1954	Stroud Committee for the Care of the Physically Handicapped
Dec. 1954	The Save the Children Fund
March 1955	The Association for Moral Welfare
Dec. 1955	The Guild of Physically Handicapped
March 1956	For social and religious activities in the new Gloucestershire Housing Estates (This concert was *The Dream of Gerontius* and was a celebration of Sammy Underwood's 50 years of conducting the Society.)

Other notable charities mentioned during the 50s and 60s were The Gyde House, St Rose's Special School, Ebley Children's Home, St George's School, Eastington and, further away from home, The Mary Lovell School for Blind Girls, Jerusalem.

It is interesting to reflect on the different terminology and of our changed attitudes to some of the charities mentioned here. Within the twenty years of the list, the term 'cripples' had already become the 'physically handicapped' but not yet 'the disabled'. Dr Barnado and the Church of England Children's Society are still in operation though it is with a changed remit from that of 50 years ago. No longer do we have an Association for Moral Welfare. Charities concerned with the care of teenagers and young adults are now involved with housing, training and job opportunities. Extra finances for the Stroud Hospitals are now more likely to be raised in conjunction with the League of Friends. Such money would be spent on special beds and baths and large medical equipment, rather than on refurbishing seating in the outpatients department. During the latter part of the twentieth century there has been a trend on the Society's part to support the Hospice Movement. In general the Hospices are not part of the National Health Service, and their need for funds parallel the circumstances that were in existence at the end of the nineteenth century when the Society sang for the benefit of the new Stroud Hospital.

As well as supporting local charities, the choir has been involved in national charity events. Many of the choir sang Haydn's *Creation* in the Royal Albert Hall in March 1989, together with the BBC Symphony Chorus and the Orchestra of St John's Smith Square. The concert was on behalf of the Royal Marsden Hospital Cancer Appeal.

In March 1990, the choir had an open invitation to come to sing *Messiah* at St Mary's, Painswick, in aid of the Stroud and District Mencap Homes Foundation. This concert raised £426 for Mencap. In December of that year, the Society sang Bach's *Christmas Oratorio* in Gloucester Cathedral. It was the Society's first ever performance at the Cathedral and £825 was raised for the Cotswold Care Hospice at Burleigh, Stroud. The Society continued to support Cotswold Care with the proceeds of carol concerts through the 1990s.

On October 8th 1994, the Society sang *Messiah* in Gloucester Cathedral as part of the nationwide B T 'Hallelujah for Hospices' event. This was a simultaneous performance starting at 7.30 and was sung nationwide in 151 venues. The concert was broadcast live by Radio 2, tuning in and out of many of the performances, producing a more or less complete *Messiah*! Many countries abroad also took part in this charity concert.

A repeat of BT 'Voices for Hospices' took place at Holy Trinity Church, Minchinhampton, in October 1997, when The Beacon Singers and the Choral Society shared the concert programme. The Choral Society sang excerpts from Mozart, Haydn, Bach and Handel. By now, 40 countries were taking part, with New Zealand starting the chain of continuous singing thirteen hours ahead of the British. Again, BBC TV, Radio 2 and the World Service covered the event.

Members from the Choral society joined with 70 other choirs to take part in the 'Really Big Chorus' in aid of the Leukaemia Research Fund at the Royal Albert Hall in July 1998. The concert was billed as 'The most awesome Verdi *Requiem* in the Universe!'

On October 14th 2000, at Stroud Parish Church the Society took part in another international BT 'Voices for Hospices' concert. This was one of 500 concerts in more than 40 countries that took part on that day. A lively programme with excerpts from Mozart, Haydn, Mendelssohn and Handel was much enjoyed, and the final singing of the *Hallelujah Chorus* by both choir and audience was a fitting end to the concert. At this event more than £1000 was raised for the Cotswold Care Hospice at Burleigh. Stroud Choral Society has now entered its third century of supporting charities.

Sammy's ascent

And they say that Stroud is not musical!
Concert Advert for a Popular Concert, 'The Treat Of The Season,' Stroud News April 1906.

The twentieth century dawned bright and clear for the inhabitants of Stroud but there was no sign of any Choral Society activity, until a small notice appeared in the Stroud News and Gloucester County Advertiser for January 25th 1901. The notice stated that in view of the death of her Majesty the Queen on Tuesday January 22nd, 'there would be no practice of the Stroud Choral Class on Monday next' (January 28th 1901). The Choral Class were rehearsing *The May Queen*, which was given at the Subscription Rooms on April 18th 1901. (*The May Queen* was composed by the Yorkshire musician William Sterndale Bennett for the inauguration of Leeds Town Hall in 1858. Queen Victoria officiated at the opening ceremony.) This was the first concert performed since *Elijah* in 1897 and strangely there was nothing in the concert review that explains the gap of four years. We learn that the Choir was a well-balanced combination of about 70 voices with a band of 30 instrumentalists who were entirely drawn from the neighbourhood. Mr E M Chaundy the organist at Holy Trinity Church, Stroud, had trained the Band. The Conductor was Thomas Hackwood. Unfortunately this was Mr Hackwood's last concert as he died early the following year on March 13th, aged 39. He had been ill for some while and at one point had spent several months at the Smedley's Hydropathic establishment at Buxton. His death was attributed to 'emphysema and gangrene of the lung'. As he had no relatives in Stroud he had been cared for by a Mr and Mrs A H Cox of Bisley Road (these were the parents of R H Cox, a member of Chew's Band). Thomas Hackwood had been born in Durham and like James Chew had shown early musical ability. At eleven years old he had been appointed organist of St Paul's, Jarrow-on-Tyne, and had held this position for six or seven years. At eighteen he had come to Gloucester as a pupil of Dr Lloyd, organist of Gloucester Cathedral. Thomas Hackwood was held in great affection by the Choral Society. He is buried in Stroud Cemetery and the inscription on his gravestone reads 'Erected by members and friends of the above Society as a tribute of their love and esteem.'

Sammy Underwood awarded FRCO, July 1905. This photograph accompanied a long article about Underwood's appointment to Stroud in the Stroud News on October 6th 1906.

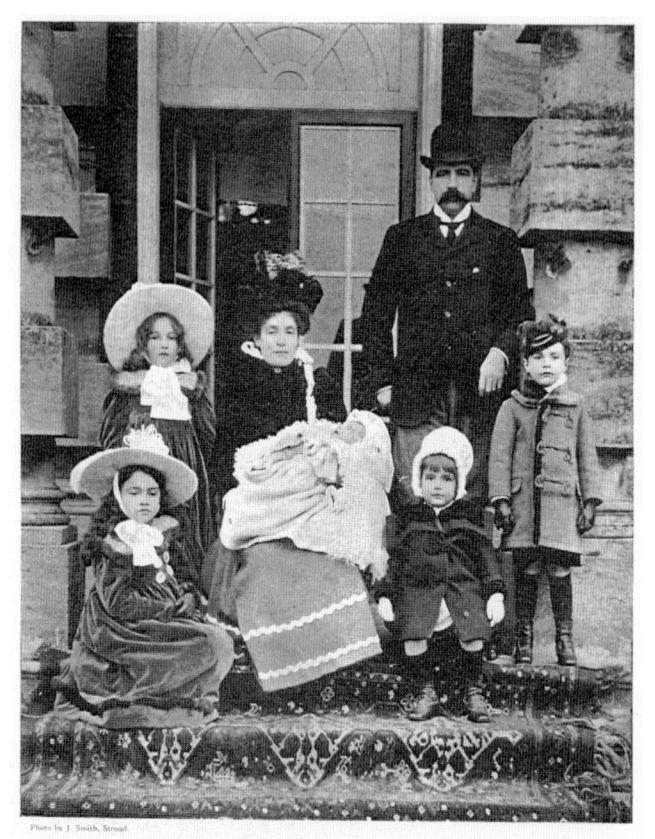

C P Allen was elected Liberal MP for Stroud in 1900. This photo dates from 1900 or 1906 when he was re-elected. The family are shown in the doorway of Farmhill Park House, now the site of Archway School. Charles Allen remained in Parliament until 1918. During the first decade of the twentieth century he is listed as Patron or Vice President of SCS. The Society enjoyed cross-party support as its President, up until his death in 1911, was the Right Hon Sir John E Dorington Bart MP, Conservative Member for Tewkesbury (living at Lypiatt Park, Stroud).

C. P. Allen, Esq., M.P., and Family.

Once more the Society was left without a conductor – but not for long. A notice in the Stroud News and Gloucester County Advertiser for September 1902 states that 'Mr J E Tidman, the organist of the Stroud Parish Church is anxious to resuscitate the Choral Society and to establish an orchestral branch.' *Messiah* was to be put into practice within a few weeks. The culmination of this work was two concerts on February 19th 1903. The afternoon concert was mainly orchestral with some part-songs. The Choir sang Henry Leslie's *The Lullaby of Life*. The evening concert was Handel's *Messiah*. There were 97 Choral singers and 55 members of the Band. The reviewer states that the concerts were most beneficial to the musical reputation of the locality and he expressed the sincere hope that they would become annual events as they had been in Mr Chew's and Mr Hackwood's times.

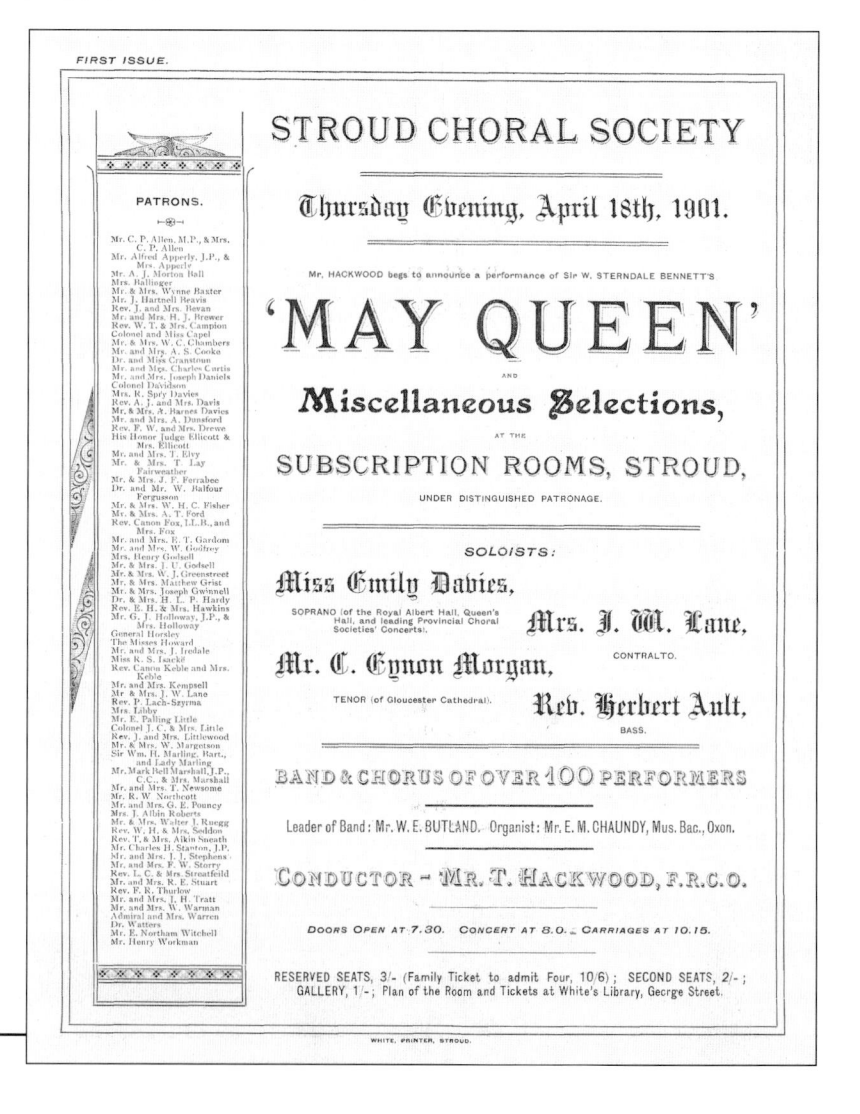

FIRST ISSUE.

STROUD CHORAL SOCIETY

Thursday Evening, April 18th, 1901.

Mr. HACKWOOD begs to announce a performance of Sir W. STERNDALE BENNETT'S

'MAY QUEEN'

AND

Miscellaneous Selections,

AT THE

SUBSCRIPTION ROOMS, STROUD,

UNDER DISTINGUISHED PATRONAGE.

SOLOISTS:

Miss Emily Davies,
SOPRANO (of the Royal Albert Hall, Queen's Hall, and leading Provincial Choral Societies' Concerts).

Mrs. J. W. Lane,
CONTRALTO.

Mr. C. Eynon Morgan,
TENOR (of Gloucester Cathedral).

Rev. Herbert Ault,
BASS.

BAND & CHORUS OF OVER 100 PERFORMERS

Leader of Band: Mr. W. E. BUTLAND. Organist: Mr. E. M. CHAUNDY, Mus. Bac., Oxon.

CONDUCTOR – MR. T. HACKWOOD, F.R.C.O.

DOORS OPEN AT 7.30. CONCERT AT 8.0. CARRIAGES AT 10.15.

RESERVED SEATS, 3/- (Family Ticket to admit Four, 10/6); SECOND SEATS, 2/-; GALLERY, 1/-; Plan of the Room and Tickets at White's Library, George Street.

WHITE, PRINTER, STROUD.

PATRONS.

Mr. C. P. Allen, M.P., & Mrs. C. P. Allen
Mr. Alfred Apperly, J.P., & Mrs. Apperly
Mr. A. J. Morton Ball
Mrs. Ballinger
Mr. & Mrs. Wynne Baxter
Mr. J. Hartnell Beavis
Rev. J. and Mrs. Bevan
Mr. and Mrs. H. J. Brewer
Rev. W. T. & Mrs. Campion
Colonel and Miss Capel
Mr. & Mrs. W. C. Chambers
Mr. and Mrs. A. S. Cooke
Dr. and Miss Cranstoun
Mr. and Miss Charles Curtis
Mr. and Mrs. Joseph Daniels
Colonel Davidson
Mrs. R. Spry Davies
Rev. A. J. and Mrs. Davis
Mr. & Mrs. Æ Barnes Davies
Mr. and Mrs. A. Dunsford
Rev. F. W. and Mrs. Drewe
His Honor Judge Ellicott & Mrs. Ellicott
Mr. and Mrs. T. Elvy
Mr. & Mrs. T. Lay Fairweather
Mr. & Mrs. J. F. Ferrabee
Dr. and Mr. W. Balfour Ferguson
Mr. & Mrs. W. H. C. Fisher
Mr. & Mrs. A. T. Ford
Rev. Canon Fox, LL.B., and Mrs. Fox
Mr. and Mrs. E. T. Gardom
Mr. and Mrs. W. Godfrey
Mrs. Henry Godsell
Mr. & Mrs. J. U. Godsell
Mr. & Mrs. W. J. Greenstreet
Mr. & Mrs. Matthew Grist
Mr. & Mrs. Joseph Gwinnell
Dr. & Mrs. H. L. P. Hardy
Rev. E. H. & Mrs. Hawkins
Mr. G. J. Holloway, J.P., & Mrs. Holloway
General Horsley
The Misses Howard
Mr. and Mrs. J. Iredale
Miss K. S. Isacké
Rev. Canon Keble and Mrs. Keble
Mr. and Mrs. Kempsell
Mr. & Mrs. J. W. Lane
Rev. P. Lach-Szyrma
Mrs. Libby
Mr. E. Palling Little
Colonel J. C. & Mrs. Little
Rev. J. and Mrs. Littlewood
Mr. & Mrs. W. Margetson
Sir Wm. H. Marling, Bart., and Lady Marling
Mr. Mark Bell Marshall, J.P., C.C., & Mrs. Marshall
Mr. and Mrs. T. Newsome
Mr. R. W. Northcott
Mr. and Mrs. G. E. Pouncy
Mrs. J. Albin Roberts
Mr. & Mrs. Walter J. Ruegg
Rev. W. H. & Mrs. Seddon
Rev. T. & Mrs. Alkin Sneath
Mr. Charles H. Stanton, J.P.
Mr. and Mrs. J. J. Stephens
Mr. and Mrs. F. W. Storry
Rev. L. C. & Mrs. Streatfeild
Mr. and Mrs. R. E. Stuart
Rev. F. R. Thurlow
Mr. and Mrs. J. H. Tratt
Mr. and Mrs. W. Warman
Admiral and Mrs. Warren
Dr. Watters
Mr. E. Northam Witchell
Mr. Henry Workman

44

The Late
MR. THOS. HACKWOOD, F.R.C.O.

Thomas Hackwood's gravestone in Stroud Old Cemetery was erected by members of the Society.

Thomas Hackwood conducted Stroud Choral Society from 1892 to 1901. Born in 1862, he died in March 1902, aged 39.

The concert on December 10th 1903 was a special event for both the Society and the town. Sir Hubert Parry had been invited to conduct his newly composed work *Voces Clemantium* (The voices of them that cry). This work had been composed for the 1903 Hereford Festival. The inhabitants of Stroud flocked to the concert and there was barely any standing room left for latecomers (obviously there were no fire or safety regulations to worry about in 1903). The whole concert and in particular Sir Hubert Parry's *Voces Clemantium* was received with great warmth and enthusiasm, 'A capital performance.' Sir Hubert Parry complimented Mr Tidman, the chorus and the Band, and said that he felt proud of his country in being able to bring music to such a state of perfection. The reporter tells us that Sir Hubert Parry was the guest of the Right Hon Sir J E Dorington, Bart, MP, at Lypiatt Park.

In the following year 1904, the April concert was *The Golden Legend*. Originally a poem by Longfellow, it had been set to music by the Rev H E Hodson who lived at Churchdown. Mr Hodson had begun the cantata in 1865 and had completed it in 1880. The first performance had been in London at the Kennington Assembly Rooms. During the interval the composer was called to the platform and was greeted with enthusiastic applause. Mr Hodson then addressed the company saying that the performance had touched his heart and he gave them many thanks.

The year 1904 was completed with Mendelssohn's *Hymn of Praise* and a miscellaneous selection. The reviewer makes some interesting comments about the Choir and the Band. Previously they had been separate entities coming together for the annual concert. But at Mr J Edis Tidman's suggestion there had been an amalgamation, which simplified the working arrangements. The Society was larger than at any other time with the chorus and Band numbering about 150. The chorus was especially strong in tenors and basses. At the concert on March 3rd 1905, the

Sir Hubert Parry's First Visit to Stroud.

Season 1903-1904.

Stroud Choral and... Orchestral Societies.

MADAME EMILY SQUIRE.

PRESIDENT:
The Rt. Hon. Sir J. E. Dorington, Bart., M.P.

VICE-PRESIDENTS:
Mr. C. P. Allen, M.P.
Mr. Alfred Apperly
Mr. H. Apperly
Mr. A. J. Morton Ball
Rev. G. Barrett
Mr. St. Clair Baddeley
Rev. J. Bevan
Mr. William Bishop
Mr. A. Herbert Brewer, Mus. Bac.
Rev. W. H. Butlin
Mr. F. A. Chambers
Mr. T. C. Colledge
Mr. Charles Curtis
Mr. E. C. Davis
Mr. Arthur Dunsford
His Honour Judge Ellicott
Rev. Canon Fox
Mr. George Godsell
Mr. W. J. Greenstreet
Dr. Hardy
Rev. E. H. Hawkins
Mr. G. J. Holloway
Mr. S. Gilbert Jones
Mr. J. W. Lane
Mr. W. Margetson
Sir William Marling, Bart.
Mr. W. J. P. Marling
Mr. Mark Bell Marshall
Mr. G. P. Milnes
Mr. R. O. P. Paddison
Mr. Charles Stanton
Mr. W. Warman
Dr. Watters

Programme of a Grand....

Choral and Orchestral Concert

TO BE GIVEN AT THE
SUBSCRIPTION ROOMS, STROUD, ON THURSDAY, DEC. 10, 1903.

BAND AND CHORUS OF 180.

ARTISTES:
Madame Emily Squire, Of the Handel, Worcester and Hereford Festivals, and all the principal Festivals.
Mr. F. Lightowler, Of Worcester Cathedral.
Mr. H. Wilde, Of the Queen's Hall Ballad Concerts, etc.

Hon. Conductor - - Mr. J. Edis Tidnam, F.R.C.O.

DOORS OPEN AT 7.30; COMMENCE AT 8.
Carriages at 10.15.
Tickets and Plan of Room at WHITE'S LIBRARY, George Street, Stroud.

ADMISSION:— Reserved Seats, 4/- (Family Tickets, four for 14/-);
Second Seats, 2/-; Gallery, 1/-.

WHITE, PRINTER, STROUD.

Flag of England, the choral numbers were put at 120 and the Band at 60. With 180 performers in the Subscription Rooms, one wonders if there was room for an audience!

The reviewer for the February 1906 performance of *Hiawatha*, amusingly describes the members of the chorus: 'On the brilliantly lighted rostrum was marshalled a bevy of ladies attired in pleasing, smart and fashionable toilette, embodying the latest "creations", flanked on either side by the "frail and weak" thing, man, in the more sombre garb of evening dress.' He waxes lyrical about the concert, 'a brilliant gathering,' 'inspiring music,' 'red letter events in the annals of local entertainment'. He points out how indebted the music-loving public of the time should be to Mr White (secretary to the Society since 1892) and the four Conductors. We think this must be a reference to Tidman, Hackwood, Brandon and Chew with whom they have been associated, 'for the standards of excellence and popularity, which today are cherished assets of the Society'. In April 1906 *Messiah* was given to another large audience, with every seat occupied, giving further proof that the inhabitants of Stroud were truly music-loving people. Highlights of that evening included Mr J Edis Tidman and the Band's brilliant interpretation of Schubert's *Unfinished Symphony* and Mr Reginald Cox's 'beautiful cello solo'.

By autumn of 1906 Mr Tidman had accepted the post of organist and music master at Dover College and Stroud was getting ready to welcome Mr S W Underwood to the position of organist and choirmaster at Stroud Parish Church. A tiny paragraph at the end of the newspaper column (October 12th 1906) states: 'It is also understood that Mr Underwood will succeed as a matter of course to the Conductorship of the Stroud Choral Society, and it is quite likely that the rehearsals for *Elijah* will be mostly under his direction.' Thus began the tenure of a Conductor whose extraordinary musical ability would shape and influence the Society for the next 52 years.

Along the top of a pale green programme for the spring concert of Mendelssohn's *Elijah*, 1907, in a firm pencil hand are the words, 'My first Choral Concert at Stroud, SWU.' The reviewer was under the opinion that 'We venture to assert that few of those present expected to hear such a really fine presentation of this grand oratorio as was given under Mr S W Underwood's direction. It was undoubtedly the most inspiring and impressive choral concert ever heard in Stroud, and we hasten to offer our heartiest congratulations to the talented Conductor upon the undoubted triumph he achieved.' Sammy Underwood had arrived! Many years later, speaking in May 1947, Sammy Underwood related an amusing anecdote about this concert. One of the gentlemen soloists (the tenor, Mr Ben Ivor) was unable to reach his top notes. In order to overcome the difficulty, Sammy had sung a vigorous 'shine' throughout the solo 'Then shall the righteous shine', leaving the soloist to continue singing the notes that he could reach.

Young Mr Underwood (aged 25 when he joined the Society) decided that his next concert would be an open-air performance in Stratford Park on Thursday July 4th 1907. History lost no time in repeating itself and the concert was postponed due to adverse weather conditions and the date changed to the 18th. The letter in the Stroud News apologising for the cancellation tells us that on the Wednesday rehearsal 'the turf was so sodden that we hardly liked our lady members to stand on it'. After another night of tempestuous rain they had no alternative but to cancel. The Society had no desire to 'run the risk of an

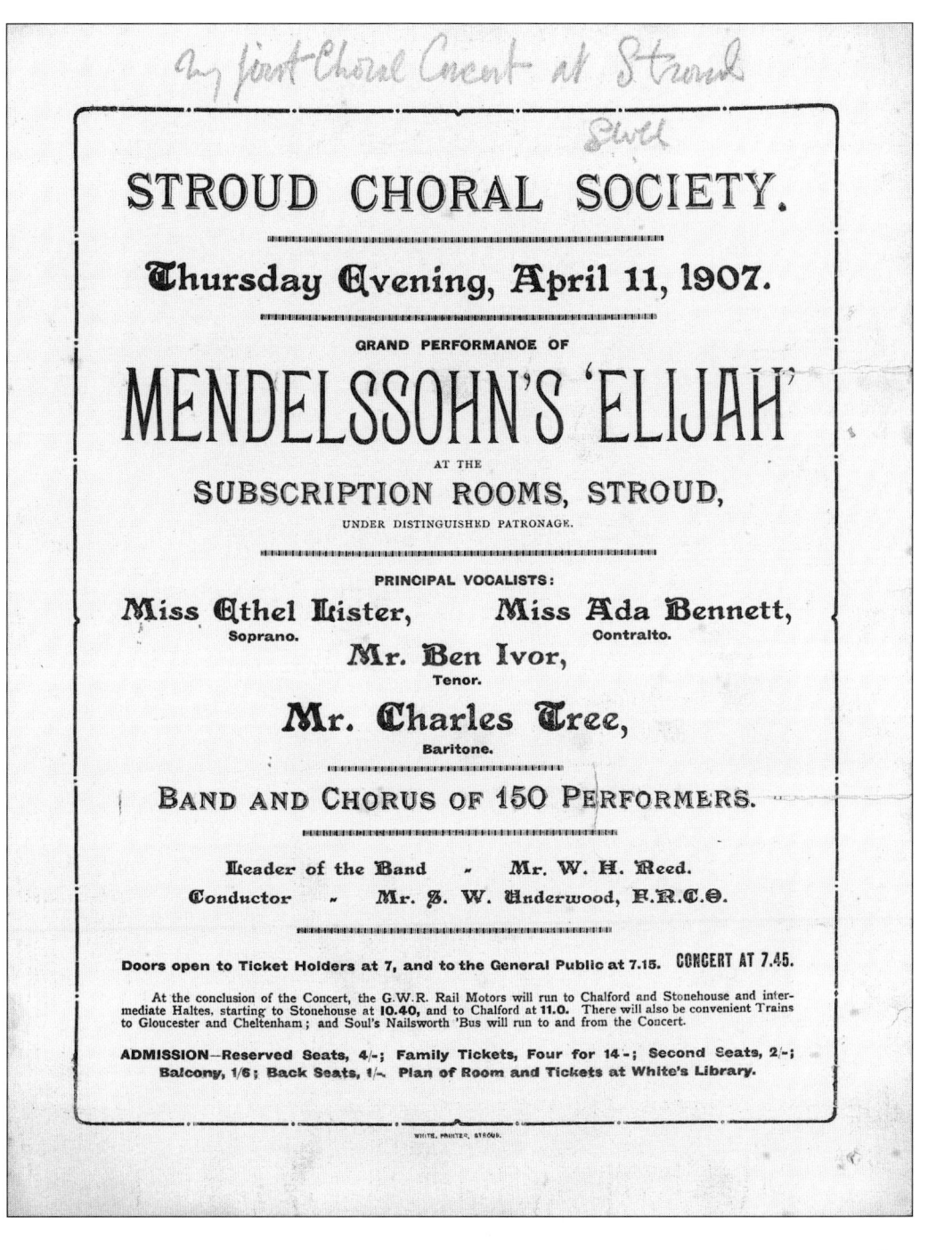

Sammy Underwood marks his first Stroud performance 'My first Choral Concert at Stroud, SWU'.

infinitum of discomfort and a series of heavy doctor's bills'. It was a change for the better as 'arctic conditions gave way to tropical' and it had been a delight to wander through the beautiful grounds of Stratford Park that Mrs Lort Phillips had placed at their disposal. There is a delightful photograph of the Choir taken by Mr Stone, a photographer of London Road, showing a very youthful Mr Underwood almost drowned in a sea of big hats and big blouses. Only twelve gentlemen singers are shown on the photograph. Although it was a Thursday afternoon and Stroud's half-day closing, it is possible that some members of the choir worked elsewhere and were not free to attend. The gentleman fourth from the left at the back, who looks so like Mr Underwood, could in fact be his brother Percy, who although living in Gloucester sang with the Choir on many occasions. Could it be Mrs Lort Phillips herself, seated in black, in the foreground of the photo?

The open-air concert in Stratford Park, Thursday, 18th July 1907

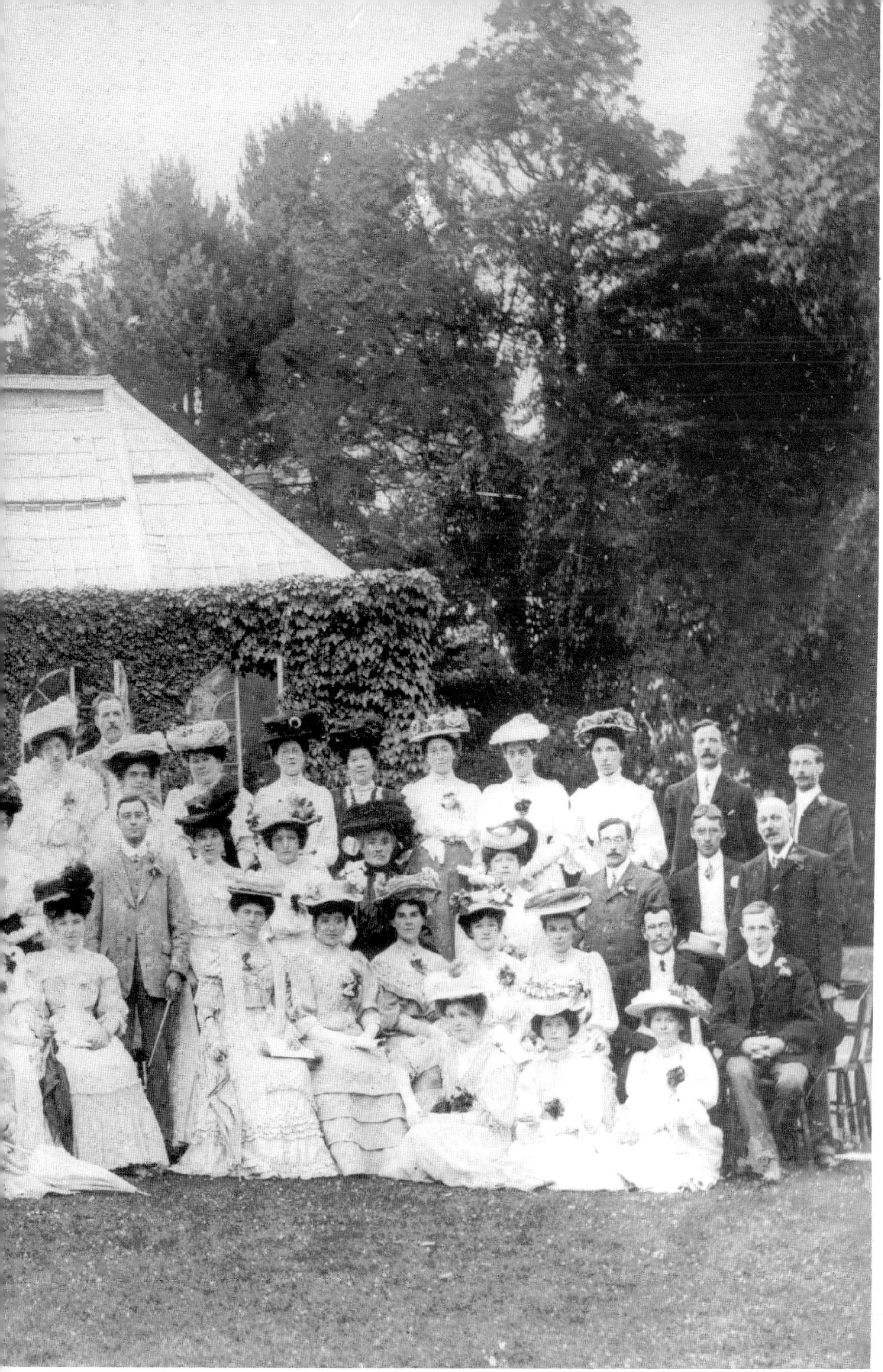

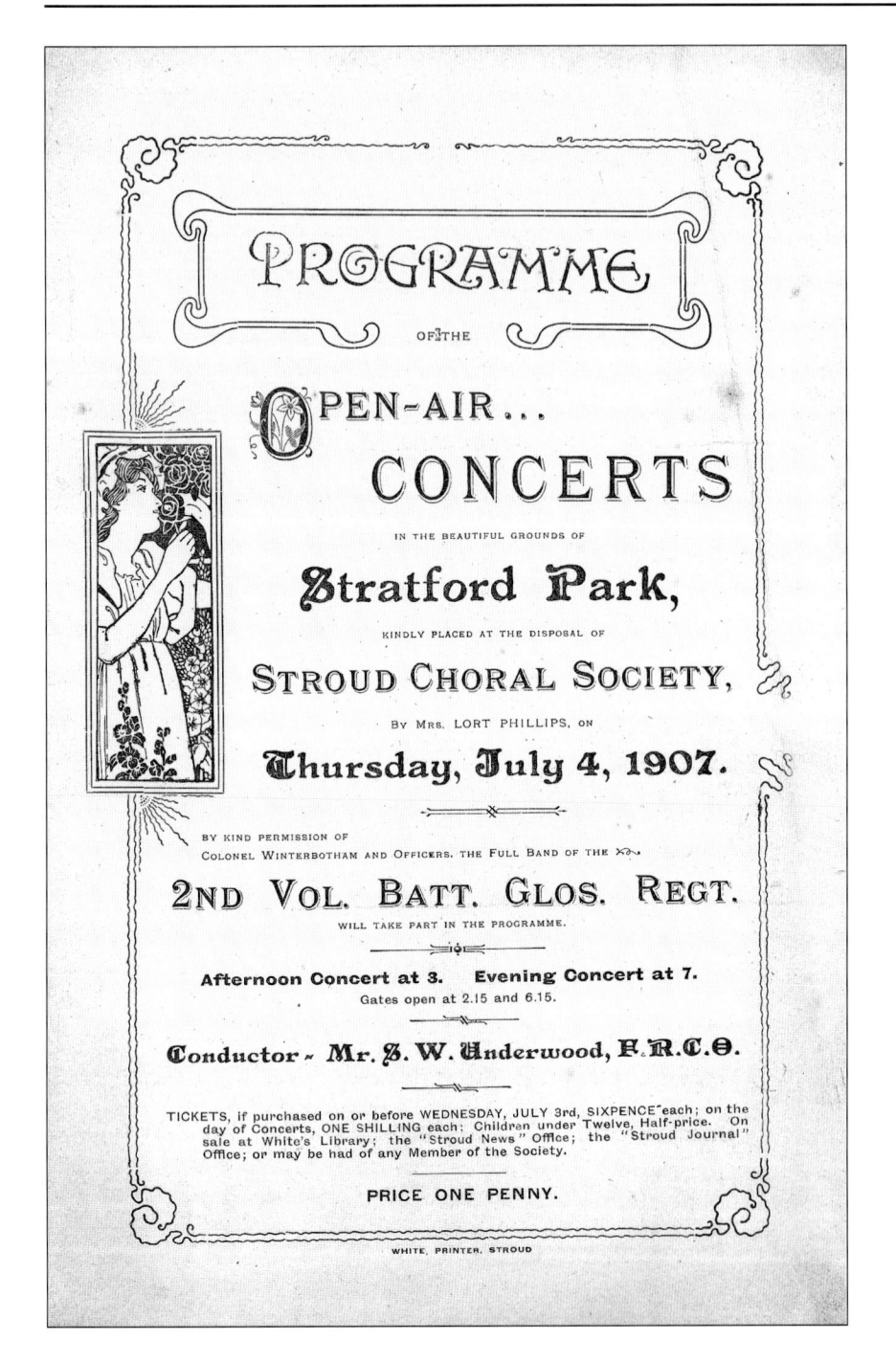

From 1909 to 1913 the Society produced one annual concert. In 1914 and 1915 the Society went back to two concerts a year. In spite of it being the war years it was felt that it would be a good thing to carry through the concert plans as the result could help to lift the morale of the local people. 'Some associations have temporarily ceased to exist, but amongst those who have kept their flag flying despite all difficulties, may be honourably mentioned the Stroud Choral Society' (December 1915). One can appreciate the sentiment of trying to carry on as normal for the sake of others, but probably the choir was facing difficulties. The programme for the April 1915 concert of *Elijah* quotes Band and Chorus numbers of 150, which by the December concert of *Messiah* are down to 100. This particular concert was a grand effort, especially performed to raise money for the Stroud Hospital. After 1915 there was a break in concerts until February 1920.

On March 20th 1916, Mr Underwood left Stroud to join the Gloucestershire and Worcestershire Yeomanry, at some later date he was attached to the 5th Gloucestershire Regiment. During the first two years of the war, signing up for active service had been voluntary. Early in 1916 it became compulsory for all men under the age of 41 to report for duty. Unfortunately the official Gloucestershire Regiment war records were destroyed by enemy action during the Second World War and we are unable to report Trooper Underwood's wartime activities with great accuracy. We understand that the Regiment was based in England for some time and later saw active service in France and Italy. Certainly we know for a fact that Trooper Underwood was in England and took part in the Cathedral Carol Concert in December 1916. We also understand that he contributed to musical activities in his regimental band by playing timpani and the horn. At some later stage he conducted the band of the 12th Gloucestershire Regiment, (Bristol's Own). Records show that this regiment served in Italy between 1917 and 1918, returning to France in 1918. The Underwood family recollected a story of Sammy conducting an army band on the beaches of Gallipoli! Trooper Underwood was able to visit Stroud on October 26th 1918, shortly before the Armistice of November 1918. He attended Stroud Parish Church and commented that the choir 'was not singing too badly'. He was released from the army sometime in 1919.

At some time in late 1919 or early 1920 Mr H W Carter, headmaster of Marling School, (1919–44) asked Mr Underwood to collaborate on a new school song. This song, with words by H W Carter and music by S W Underwood, was first sung in Marling School Hall on 27th March 1920. It was to prove a very popular school song, not just in school, but reportedly sung by old Marlingtonians far from home. In Oliver Wick's book *Marling School 1887–1987* he tells of a letter to the school from five old boys serving in the same regiment during the second world war, which quoted excerpts from the song. Also, 'Bevin Boys', W J Plank and K J Shilham, sang the school song to keep their spirits up whilst working down coal mines in South Wales. Even though by the mid 1950s the school song had slipped from use, Oliver Wicks tells of a 'spontaneous and enthusiastic outburst of singing of the first verse and chorus of the song' at an Old Marlingtonians' Annual Dinner in 1985.

The Choral concerts resumed in February 1920. At a miscellaneous concert the reviewer observes 'the annual concert of the Stroud Choral Society was one of the joys of which the latter years of the war deprived the public, and perhaps, until this year saw the revival of the Society, few people realised how much they had missed'. He goes on to refer to Mr Underwood who 'having beaten his sword into a more peaceful implement, has returned with vigour to his old musical pursuits'. Since the end of the First World War the Society has had an unbroken record of concert performances.

The choice of music during the 1920s was mostly kept to the traditional well-known oratorios. Handel, Mendelssohn, Bach, Mozart and Haydn were lightened with touches of Coleridge-Taylor, Holst and Elgar. The reviewer of the 1922 performance of Brahms' *German Requiem* pointed out that a few years ago it would have been impossible to have given this work such was the animosity to anything German. During this time there was a subtle change to the listings on the Society's concert programmes. On the concert programme for April 1924 is printed the following, 'Leader of the Band – Mrs Tregenza'. The following year in March 1925 at a concert of Bach, Holst and Purcell, Mr Maurice Alexander is listed as the 'Leader of the Orchestra'. From

Trooper Underwood in the uniform of the Gloucestershire and Worcestershire Yeomanry, 1916.

Marling School Song.

Words by H. W. Carter.
Music by S. W. Underwood.
In march time.

THE song that we sing is the song of our School,
  We will sing it with might and with main;
For it tells of the School of whose name we are proud,
  We will sing it again and again.
    There is no other school in the land of our birth,
    There is no other school on the face of the earth,
    That to us will be ever of quite the same worth,
      As the good old Marling School!

From the day when we first became sons of the School,
  It has cared for our wants everyone.
It has taught us in ways we shall never forget
  How the battle of life may be won.
    There is no other school, etc.

We have fought in the class with the problems of work,
  We have fought and we've many times won.
We have fought on the fields in a sportsmanlike way;
  It is thus that life's battle's begun.
    There is no other school, etc.

We must all pull together in work and in play,
  'Tis the good of the School that we seek.
For the goal that is scored and the scholarship won
  Of the School and its fame ever speak.
    There is no other school, etc.

Be it Cricket or Football, or drill with the Corps,
  Be it work for Matric. or a Schol.,
In Debate or the Mag., or in acting or song,
  The fair name of the School we extol.
    There is no other school, etc.

In the years that are coming, when school days are o'er,
  We will think of the grand days we passed
In the School that will ever be dearest to us;
  May its fame through the centuries last!
    There is no other school, etc.

The Marling School Song. A collaboration between the Headmaster H W Carter and S W Underwood c. 1919.

that time on, the Choral Society was always accompanied by 'the Orchestra' and the last link with Victorian times and 'Chew's Band' had been severed. Mr Alexander was to lead the orchestra for the next nineteen years.

As well as consolidating his position in Stroud, Mr Underwood was also in demand elsewhere. In 1928 the Three Choirs Festival Committee had asked him to train the Festival Choirs. In September 1929 he was appointed as Conductor of the Bristol Choral Society with a starting salary of £2 2s 0d per rehearsal. This was of course in addition to his duties as organist and choirmaster at Stroud Parish Church.

Finances were difficult and the committee was anxious to give a yearly honorarium to their conductor to show their grateful appreciation. In 1926 they were able to award him an honorarium of four guineas. But in 1927 the finances were in such a poor state that they were unable to offer anything. In 1928, very aware of this debt to Mr Underwood, they proposed that any balance of money left in the account after paying off debts should be given to the conductor. It seems that Mr Underwood was also unlucky in this year too. In October 1929 the President Mr Sidney Allen asked the membership to guarantee that in future Mr Underwood would have a 'more satisfactory financial recognition than hitherto'. Unfortunately this was still not possible. By the General Meeting of April 14th 1930 it was reported that there was a deficit of £12. The Society was urged to pay off its debts and to give the conductor a proper honorarium. To this effect, Mr Allen promptly put £10 into the kitty to start the ball rolling. Mr Underwood, ever the gentleman, replied that 'he looked on the Society as his own hobby and did not look for any remuneration. He felt amply repaid by the loyalty and the enthusiasm of the members.' At the end of this meeting, a small committee of ladies was set up to decide what line of action should be taken to address the deficit. Fundraising was discussed but seemingly the only outcome of the ladies' activities was to ask the secretary to write to all members asking them to make a small donation towards the outstanding debt. In October 1931 it was resolved that Mr Underwood should receive an honorarium of five guineas, but it was to be some years before the conductor's honorarium became an annual certainty.

It is also known at this time, that as well as his church and choral work in Stroud, Sammy Underwood taught at two local schools. Between 1929 and 1931 he taught singing and choir (part time) at Marling School. It was reported that he did not enjoy this particular teaching experience (Ronald Nolan's biographical research on Underwood). Between 1928 and 1933 he taught at Bussage House Boarding School. During the 1920s this school was run by Miss Dorothea M Beale, formerly Headmistress of Stroud High School and niece of the famous Miss Dorothea M Beale of Cheltenham Ladies College. We are not told if Mr Underwood enjoyed this latter experience!

In March 1928 when Sir Herbert Brewer (organist at Gloucester cathedral) died, there were many supporters of Sammy Underwood who wanted to see him fill this post. Sammy had been helping at Gloucester because of Brewer's illness. As Brewer lay dying Sammy Underwood was deputising for him and conducting the Gloucestershire Orchestral Society in Mozart's *Symphony No. 39 in E flat*. Brewer's last words were 'I feel as if I were conducting the Symphony.' Brewer had made it clear that he wanted Herbert Sumsion to succeed him. Unfortunately at that time Sumsion was in America and due to take up his position as organist at Coventry Cathedral later in the year. Because the Three Choirs Festival was due to be held in Gloucester that summer, Sammy Underwood was asked to help with the rehearsal preparations. It was Underwood who conducted the opening work of the Festival, then as Sumsion arrived, (relieved of his Coventry commitment) Sammy Underwood sang with the bass section for the remainder of the Festival.

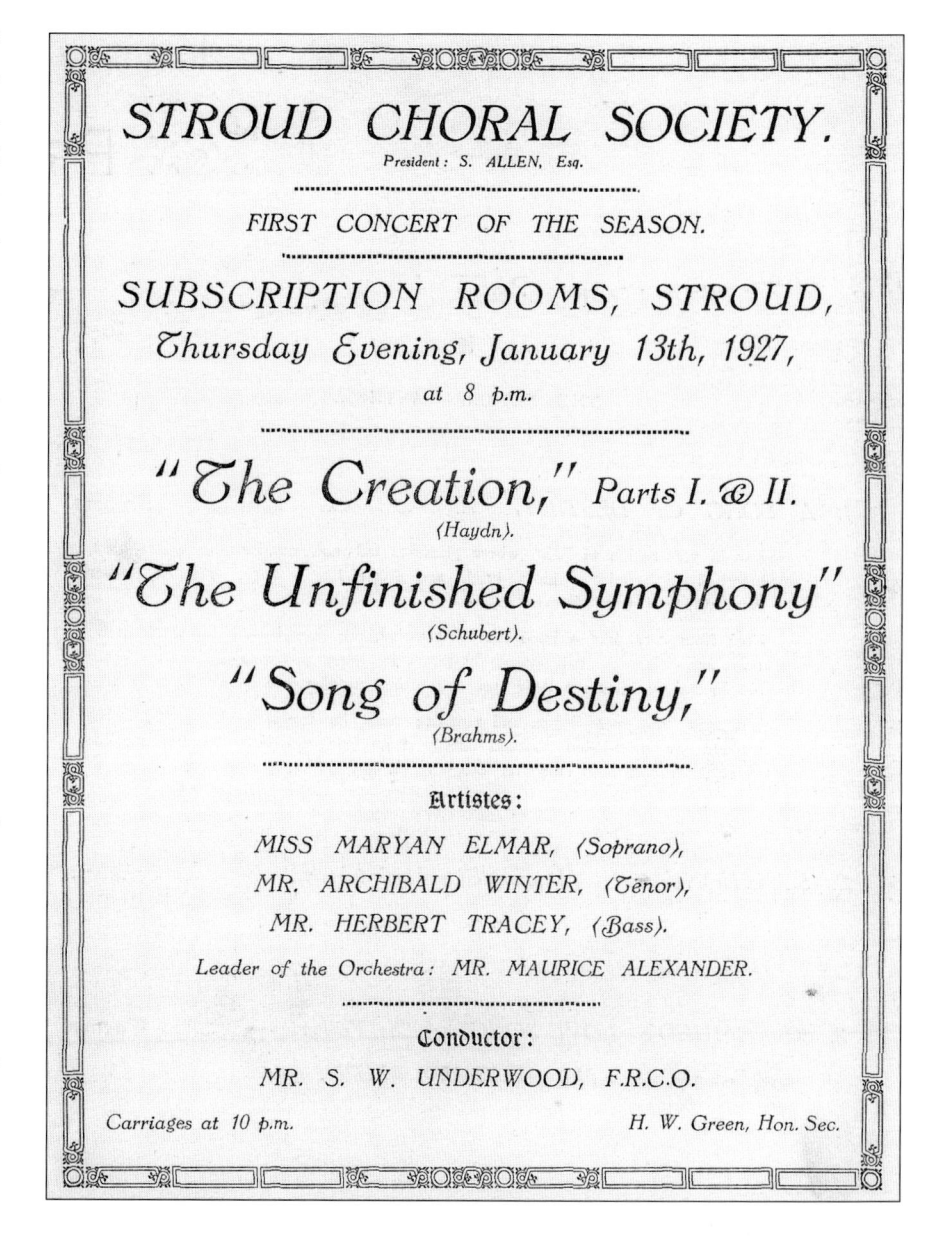

During the 1920s and 1930s the economic depression made life very difficult for most people. There was no doubt that this was reflected in the Society's problems with money and in some years the Society could only afford to fund one concert. At times both choral and audience numbers were down. At the concert in May 1926 it was remarked that the General Strike was a 'disturbing element' though it was thought that this alone would scarcely explain the noticeable falling off in attendance. (At this particular concert the soprano soloist Miss Hilda Blake, in spite of a cold, was highly praised and was said to be most reminiscent of Madame Albani.) An effort was made to counter lower audience numbers by staging popular 'crowd pullers.' *Messiah*, April 1924, was one such concert. At this concert local soloists were also engaged to encourage added local involvement. These were Miss Marjorie Kiddle, soprano, Miss Elsie Chambers, contralto, Mr Denys Erlam, tenor and Mr Kenneth Ellis, bass with Mrs Tregenza the leader of the Band.

STROUD CHORAL SOCIETY.

President: S. ALLEN, Esq.

FIRST CONCERT OF THE SEASON.

SUBSCRIPTION ROOMS, STROUD,

Thursday Evening, January 13th, 1927,

at 8 p.m.

"*The Creation,*" Parts I. & II.
(Haydn).

"*The Unfinished Symphony*"
(Schubert).

"*Song of Destiny,*"
(Brahms).

Artistes:

MISS MARYAN ELMAR, (Soprano),
MR. ARCHIBALD WINTER, (Tenor),
MR. HERBERT TRACEY, (Bass).

Leader of the Orchestra: MR. MAURICE ALEXANDER.

Conductor:

MR. S. W. UNDERWOOD, F.R.C.O.

Carriages at 10 p.m.   H. W. Green, Hon. Sec.

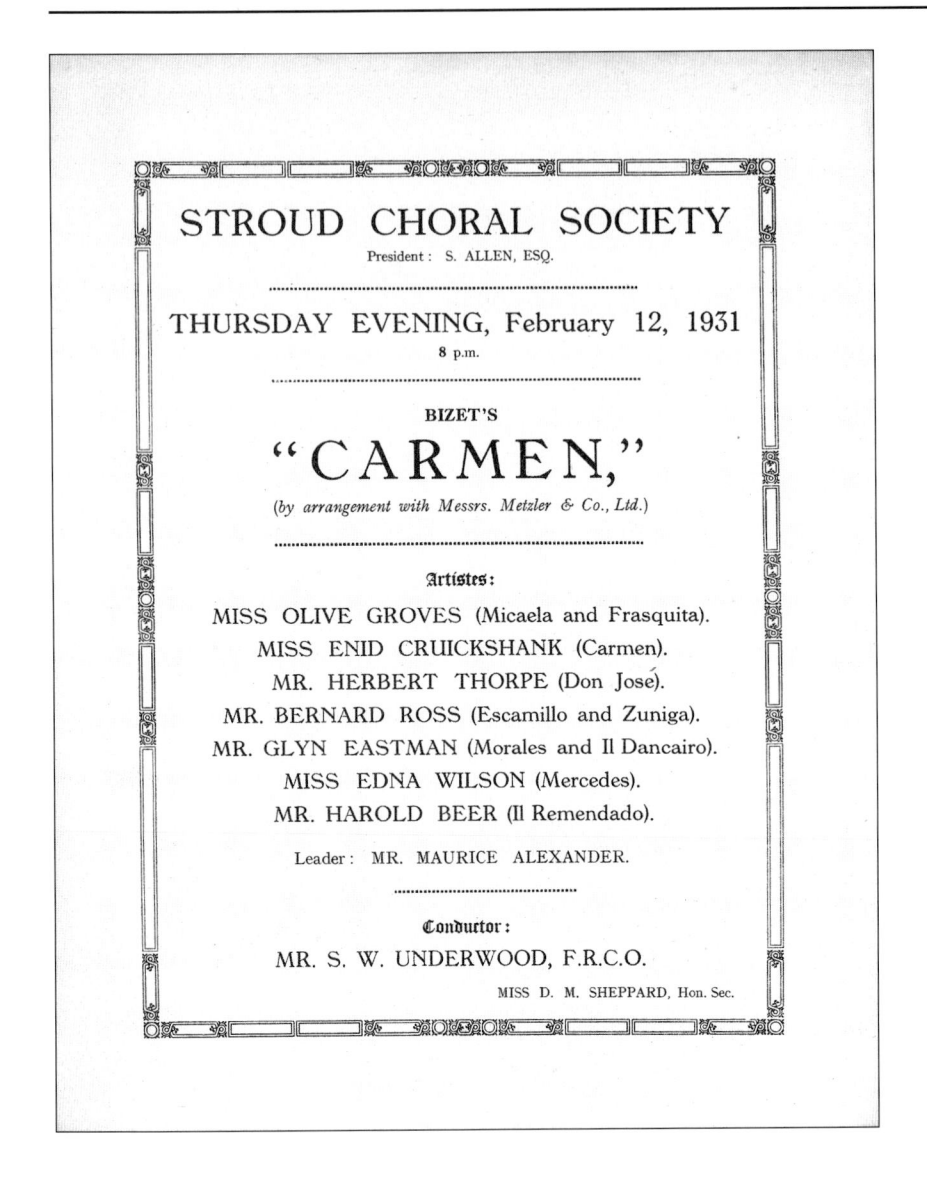

> **STROUD CHORAL SOCIETY**
>
> President: S. ALLEN, ESQ.
>
> THURSDAY EVENING, February 12, 1931
> 8 p.m.
>
> BIZET'S
> **"CARMEN,"**
> (by arrangement with Messrs. Metzler & Co., Ltd.)
>
> Artistes:
> MISS OLIVE GROVES (Micaela and Frasquita).
> MISS ENID CRUICKSHANK (Carmen).
> MR. HERBERT THORPE (Don José).
> MR. BERNARD ROSS (Escamillo and Zuniga).
> MR. GLYN EASTMAN (Morales and Il Dancairo).
> MISS EDNA WILSON (Mercedes).
> MR. HAROLD BEER (Il Remendado).
>
> Leader: MR. MAURICE ALEXANDER.
>
> Conductor:
> MR. S. W. UNDERWOOD, F.R.C.O.
>
> MISS D. M. SHEPPARD, Hon. Sec.

On the whole, Mr Underwood was against the popular approach, feeling that 'the Society should perform work which was worthwhile from an educational point of view and which people ought to know'. Concerts that could be staged in the Parish Church were less expensive to produce. Unfortunately these concerts were prevented because honorary members had paid for their seats and therefore the venue would in most instances have to be in the Subscription Rooms.

Another fund-raising attempt had been to build a new stage for the chorus and orchestra in the Subscription Rooms. This was to be hired out at £3 a time. In 1931 Mr Underwood reported that the Minchinhampton Players would be pleased to stage a play for the purpose of raising funds for the Choral Society. This offer was promptly declined and it was decided that Whist Drives were a better way of making money under the circumstances! The Whist Drives may have paid off as by October 1932 the Society was declaring its biggest balance ever brought forward, £17 10s 10d. It was agreed that the conductor should be paid £12 10s 6d and that in future years he should be guaranteed 15 guineas a year.

February 1931 saw the Society's first ever production of Bizet's *Carmen*. This was a bold, even slightly risky, departure from the usual concert repertoire. Bristol choristers, who had recently given the concert at the Colston Hall, also under Mr Underwood's baton, came to swell the ranks. The reviewer felt that the atmosphere, even though it was a concert version, had been successfully captured and that Bizet's bright tuneful music had delighted everyone. Writing many years later in 1972 Netlam Bigg was to say that this particular concert stood out for him as a 'first': 'When *Carmen* (sung by Enid Cruickshank) sang her famous solo and played her castanets, the audience was not slow to show their appreciation.' A year later while reviewing the February 1932 concert, Goetz's *By the Waters of Babylon* and Purcell's *The Fairy Queen*, the reviewer returns to the previous year's concert with the following remarks: 'We cannot look for a succession of concerts equal to last year's outstanding presentation of *Carmen*. That was recognised as a tour de force, something out of the ordinary, and only obtainable by a supreme effort on the part of the Society, both as regards artistic effort and heavy outlay of money.' The soprano soloist for the 1932 concert was Miss Dora Labbette whose voice, we are told, had been made familiar by wireless and gramophone records, and that 'whilst listening to her faultless singing at this concert it was easy to understand why she has reached the first rank of soprano soloists'. Dora Labbette was also Sir Thomas Beecham's mistress. The French-sounding surname had been deliberately chosen to further her singing career.

By the next year 1933, the Society again seemed dogged by problems with finances. Although the October AGM showed a balance of accounts of £3 2s 8½d, we learn that there was an insufficient amount of money to allow the

Society to purchase material at the cost of £1 10s. This was needed to cover the staging for concerts. This seemed to have been a necessary purchase that was disappointingly beyond the Society's means. It was proposed, as before, that *Messiah* would be a popular choice for the December concert. Again, money was to be saved by using local soloists. The soloists could hardly have been more local than Mrs Sidney Allen who was the wife of the President of the Society. Mrs Allen was to be the soprano soloist in several of the Society's concerts. She was joined in *Messiah* by Miss Mona Hill, contralto, Mr George Taylor, tenor, and Mr Percy Underwood, bass. *Messiah* was deemed to have been a successful concert, 'a good seasonal choice' noted the Journal's reviewer. Even the lack of the trumpeter, Mr E S Smith who was unable to be present, was seen not to have spoilt the performance as Mr P Wheatley had deputised for him on the piano. Determined to avoid a disappointing rendering of the quartet *Since by man came death* Mr Underwood gave that and the ensuing quartet *For as in Adam all die* to the whole choir. The Bristol Choral Society, singing *Messiah* during the previous week had greatly disappointed Mr Underwood by their 'failure to fulfil his expectations' in these quartets so he was taking no chances in Stroud.

Wood's *Master Mariners* and Lang's *The Jackdaw of Rheims* were chosen for the next concert in the spring of 1934. This concert however was cancelled. No reason is given but there may have been some problem attached to the use of the Subscription Rooms. The December concert, *The Jackdaw of Rheims*, part-songs, carols and other Christmas music was billed for the Church Institute in the Shambles. The Journal reviewer states that the Society distinguished itself with some fine singing: 'It is possible that the change to a miscellaneous programme from the usual policy of presenting one big work was not generally approved. But some present must have recalled similar programmes when Mr Hackwood was conductor, so there was a measure of justification for reverting to the past.' This seems to have been the only Society concert ever performed in the Church Institute. Not a totally happy choice, as people deliberately making loud noises outside in the Shambles, and the church clock chiming, spoilt the atmosphere in the quieter more reflective passages of the music.

Whatever had caused the hiccup in 1934, by the following year the Society was back on firmer footing. Netlam Bigg had become secretary on the resignation of Miss Sheppard the previous autumn. The Society had discovered that they could avoid paying Entertainment Tax by the simple expedient of drawing up a set of rules for the Society. There were nine rules headed by the title 'The Stroud Choral Society, founded in 1865.' We learn that the Society was to be called The Stroud Choral Society with the object of encouraging and furthering the art of choral singing. The Society should be managed by the President, Conductor, Hon. Secretary and Hon. Treasurer together with twelve members, all of these to be elected at the AGM of the Society. The fee per season for singing members would be 7s 6d and for Hon Members 10s 6d, the latter would be entitled to two reserved tickets for one of the Society's concerts. At the AGM on February 25th 1935 the President, Mr Sidney Allen, was congratulated on his appointment as High Sheriff of Gloucestershire.

After the successful spring concert of Bach's *Sleepers Wake* and Wood's *Master Mariners* where the eminent soloists Miss Hilda Blake, soprano, and Mr Roy Henderson, baritone, made their mark, the Society produced another 'first' for the December concert by organising a carol service. The Society prepared carefully for this event. The ladies of the choir were asked to wear black veils and black or white dresses. The Marling, High and Central Schools were notified of the concert, though it was made clear to them that no reduction in the price of the programme (6d) could be made. Before the service, the Vicar (the Rev R P Steer) drew the congregation's attention to a beautifully lighted Christmas tree in the north transept of the church. He explained that the children would be bringing books and toys to be placed on its branches. Afterwards, these gifts would be sent to poor homes in distressed areas. It is likely that bringing gifts to the Christmas tree was to happen at the Sunday service and not at the Society's concert. Was this the first time that a Christmas gift service of this type had happened in Stroud? The Journal reviewer comments that this was the first time that the Choral Society had taken part in a carol service of this kind at the church, and that the standard of the singing fully justified the innovation: 'The carols and the instrumental items were very much enjoyed, though possibly many members of the congregation would have appreciated the inclusion of more carols in which they themselves could have joined.' (The congregation had been allowed to start the service with *The First Nowell* and end it with *God Rest You Merry*. Learning from this request, the following year the congregation was allowed to sing *O Come, All Ye Faithful* as well as *The First Nowell* and *God Rest You Merry!*)

At the AGM on February 17th 1936 the Society was back in the red to the tune of £5 5s 5d. Mr Underwood thought 'that the time had come when a change was desirable in the music rendered,' and suggested that the Society should perform Bach's *St Matthew Passion*. He knew that it was a difficult work but as the Bristol Choral Society were rehearsing the same work it was possible that they would be able to give some help. A questioner asked if Mr Underwood thought that the work would appeal to the Stroud people, to which he responded 'nothing we have done for many years has appealed to Stroud, even *Messiah* didn't appeal to Stroud. I am inclined to think that Stroud is not a musical place – perhaps it is the cinema. It is a scattered district but considering the size of the place there is never any interest in serious music.' On a point of interest, *St Matthew Passion* was not the only choice of music that was shared with the Bristol Choral Society. One wonders how much free choice the committee had in the selection of works to perform, as it was obviously much easier for Mr Underwood to work on the same music with both choirs. In the event, it was not the Bristol Choral Society that assisted with *St Matthew Passion* on March 18th 1937, but the Stinchcombe Hill Festival Choir which was 'entirely responsible for the second chorus and the whole performance was a triumph for the conductor Mr S W Underwood, the soloists, the orchestra and the choir'. At the AGM four days later Mr Underwood was presented with a small gift by some members who had appreciated singing *The Passion* under his able baton. This was the first time that the Society had sung Bach's *St Matthew Passion*.

Hoping to give the choir a larger audience, Mr Underwood announced at the Committee meeting in May 1937 that he had approached the BBC with a view to them broadcasting part of the next concert programme. This was to be Handel's *Israel in Egypt* in March 1938. The BBC subsequently declined the offer but sugared the pill by suggesting that a representative would like to be present at the concert. *Israel in Egypt*, again supported by the Bristol Choral Society, was pronounced a 'conspicuous success' though unfortunately a financial loss. John Jacob, the Society's oldest member, thanking Mr Underwood for his hard work went on to say, 'We do not expect to make profits on our concerts. We are really an Educational Body and are trying to increase the appreciation of good music. It is a pity that we cannot do away with a lot of the rubbish, which passes as music today. Much of that we hear on the wireless can be regarded as not worthy even of heathendom. I think it is our duty to preserve the place that real music has in civilisation.' At the end of the 1937–38 season the Society was £13 13s 3d in debt. Mr Underwood felt that in view of this they would not be able to offer Elgar's *Dream of Gerontius* the following year 1939 and suggested Dyson's *Canterbury Pilgrims* instead. In spite of the 1937 Carol concert making a profit of £2 2s, there was not to be a carol concert this year as it was felt that the singing in the last one had not come up to the conductor's high standards. During 1938 the President Sidney Allen, who was to die the following year, reluctantly tendered his resignation due to pressure of work, and Mr John Stuart Daniels took his place.

Sammy Underwood outside his wooden bungalow, Cheltenham Road, Painswick in the 1950s. Note the motorbike and sidecar in the background.

Dark days, post-war blues and an MBE

We lost heavily on our concerts, we have liquidated our reserves, we have a deficit of over £50 and in consequence we have not got a brass farthing with which to start next season.

Treasurer's report, March 1952

For everybody, not just the Choral Society, 1939 was to prove to be a momentous year. On the same page of the Stroud News and Gloucester County Advertiser for Friday, January 27th, in the adjacent column to the review of Dyson's *Canterbury Pilgrims* is announced in bold type **WAR IS COMING**. Major K B Godsell, President of the Stroud Branch of the British Legion was addressing the annual dinner: 'Personally, I see no alternative when you get four Dictators trotting around the continent. We are bound to get involved and the only way to prevent war in my opinion, is to be prepared for war.' How many people reading the report of the Society's concert would also be reading Major Godsell and be wondering what 1939 was going to hold in store for them? The highlight of Dr George Dyson's *The Canterbury Pilgrims* was the soprano soloist Isobel Baillie, making her first appearance with the Society, who completely 'stole the stage' with a superb interpretation of 'The Wife of Bath'. 'Discarding her score and backed by a brilliant orchestra she made the part the most memorable solo of the evening. She was not allowed to resume her seat until she had repeated it.' The previous week the Stroud public may have heard Isobel Baillie on the wireless as the soprano soloist in Beethoven's *Choral Symphony* with the BBC Symphony Orchestra and Choral Society. *The Canterbury Pilgrims* was to be the last concert that the Society would sing in the Subscription Rooms for 37 years.

At the AGM on April 3rd 1939 it was decided that the Society should become affiliated to the National Federation of Music Societies. (The National Federation of Music Societies had been founded in 1935, to aid and assist amateur choirs. By the end of the twentieth century it had a membership of 1,146 choirs.) The President Mr John Daniels paid tribute to the work of Mr Underwood: 'We cannot say too much by way of tribute to our conductor's taste, judgement and musical ability. The singing of the Society has improved so immeasurably in the last eight or ten years so that it is today hardly comparable with years gone by. There can be no question about it that the work of Mr Underwood, and the knowledge he possesses, not only of the way music should be taken, but of voice production and all that goes with good choral singing and proper interpretation of noble music, is what has helped us to reach, what I consider to be a very good standard.' This statement was met with full agreement and applause. The final act of the AGM was to make Mr John Jacob a Life Member of the Society in recognition of the long and valuable service rendered by him to the Society. This was hardly before time. Mr Jacob had been singing with the Society since May 1869 when, aged 19, he sang in Mendelssohn's *St Paul* as a member of the bass section. He was now approaching his 89th birthday. It would have been interesting to know if Mr Jacob agreed with Mr Daniels' interpretation of the ability of the choir in those 'years gone by'!

The second concert of the year on March 30th 1939 (unusually for the Society there was to be three concerts that year) was a much-requested second performance of Bach's *St Matthew Passion*. 'We have not come for a musical treat but to learn, think and wonder,' said the Vicar of Stroud, Canon R P Steer. As the work requires a double choir, the Stinchcombe Hill Music Festival Choir again sang with the Society. 'The high quality of the singing scarcely wavered from the first bar to the last.' It was not until the September Committee meeting, presumably because war had now been declared (September 3rd), that any mention of these 'difficult circumstances' was made. The Committee met to discuss the possibility of continuing the activities of the Society. Mr Daniels, from the chair, proposed that the Society should continue and this was carried unanimously. It was felt that the singing member's subscription should remain at 7s 6d for the time being. At the October Committee meeting it was proposed that the Society should give a performance of Christmas music in the Stroud Parish Church and that this would be an afternoon concert. So began the wartime tradition of the Sunday afternoon concerts.

At the carol service on December 17th, the Journal reviewer was not at all sure what he felt about Alexander Brent-Smith's *A Hymn on the Nativity*. This was its first performance in Gloucestershire having been originally written for and performed at the Three Choirs Festival at Hereford. It was felt that the carols were more enjoyable than the Brent-Smith composition. 'We feel it premature to give any sort of final opinion of the merit of the music. More hearings are necessary, before a matured judgement on it is possible.' *A Hymn on the Nativity* was conducted by the composer. As on the previous occasion the congregation was allowed to sing *The First Nowell*, *O Come, All Ye Faithful* and *God Rest You Merry*. At the retiring collection £14 was taken and this was to be divided between the Polish Relief Fund and the Waifs and Strays Society.

Not unduly perturbed by the ambivalent review of his *Hymn on the Nativity* Mr Alexander Brent-Smith returned to Stroud in March 1940 to conduct the first performance of his *Elegy*, a piece written in memory of Sir Edward Elgar. Originally written five years after Elgar's death in 1934, it was to have been performed at the 1939 Hereford Three Choirs. The threatened outbreak of war cancelled that Festival and it was left to Stroud to have the honour of its first performance.

The *Elegy* portrays the mutual agonies of a man facing death and his final realisation that 'blessed are they who die in the Lord for they rest from their Labours'. 'The words were selected by the composer and the spirit of the music is very closely linked with the meaning of the words' wrote the reviewer. The soprano soloist, Miss Mary Worth, whose top notes flowed in 'effortless, joyous liquidity' distinguished herself in the *Elegy*. However the Society seemed 'a great deal more at home with Dvorak's *Stabat Mater*', the second work of the concert. After the concert Mr Underwood received two letters from Mr Brent-Smith which were read at the AGM to the Society and which paid tribute to the choir: 'Your singers are beautiful to work with. Their keenness, watchfulness and general musicianship make direction a simple task – nay a real pleasure.'

The officers of the Society must have wondered how much longer the choir would be able to keep going. Although by the end of the 1939–40 season there was a credit balance of £14 2s 11d the number of singing members was down from 91 to 73 and Honorary members from 62 to 51. There was uncertainty due to the fluctuating population as to whether the Society would be functioning at the beginning of the autumn season or not. The officers decided to adopt a wait and see policy. Fortunately all worked out well and a most successful concert, Bach's *Christmas Oratorio* was given on December 15th 1940. These wartime Sunday afternoon concerts were to prove most popular. At this concert two long queues, from both the north and south sides of the West door, had formed half an hour before the start of the performance. Even after extra seating had been provided many people remained standing throughout. The soloists Margaret Godley, Joyce Sutton, Emlyn Bebb and Victor Harding all appeared by permission of the British Broadcasting Corporation. The congregation was encouraged to join in 'a number of Epiphany carols'.

In 1941 the Society increased their war effort by producing four Sunday afternoon concerts. As it was impossible to 'black out' the church for an evening performance, the three o'clock start for the afternoon performances had proved an excellent alternative. The vicar of Stroud, Canon R P Steer, told the Society that it gave him great pleasure to let the church be used for the purpose of sacred concerts: 'It provided recreation in the true sense of the word, and many people had told him how they had been helped and uplifted by such opportunities as these occasions afforded.' We are not told what Canon Steer thought about the other uplifting Sunday recreation in Stroud, namely the Sunday evening concerts at the Ritz Cinema, but we do know that other local church leaders in the area were far from happy. For many weeks the local papers had been filled with discussion on the vexed question of Sunday entertainment and it is perhaps partly in answer to this debate that Canon Steer made his announcement.

The Ritz concerts were organised by the Stroud Wartime Entertainment Committee, and were good old fashioned variety concerts featuring musical items such as talent competitions, humorous sketches and jokes, dancing and crooning (the Carroll Sisters), magic and illusions (Chan Dor the Chinese illusionist). The Ritz cinema, situated where we now have the Merrywalks Precinct, was an ideal wartime venue, which would have posed no blackout problems. Members of the Choral Society were also involved with these concerts and during 1941 discussions were held to consider the Society staging a concert at the Ritz. As far as our records show this did not happen, but members were actively involved in promoting the concerts and selling tickets. One popular Choral Society soloist, the baritone Salusbury Baker and his very distinguished violinist wife, Mercia Stotesbury – a local couple who had lived at Stonehouse and later at Pitchcombe – were on the first concert billing at the Ritz on Sunday November 4th 1939.

In March 1942, it was written in the Society minutes that the committee had all taken tickets to sell for the Ritz concert on May 3rd and that all Society members had been encouraged to support this concert. It is not certain why. The star billing seems to have been Gracie Fields' pianist. The last concert at the Ritz was held on December 30th 1945. Whatever the merits and demerits of Sunday entertainment there can be no doubt that these concerts were great morale boosters during very dark times.

There were notable soloists for the 1941 Society concerts. Owen Bryngwyn, a baritone who was also with the BBC, sang in the January recital. 'The lovely voice of Isobel Baillie filled the church' in *Elijah* in February. The reviewer writes: 'Perhaps one of the most striking things about the performance was the "silent applause" which was even more impressive than the clamour that greets a singer in the concert hall. One could feel the air tense with emotional strain and it often seemed that the hushed congregation must burst into audible demonstration of its appreciation.' It is easy to forget how recent is the custom of applause in church. At the recital in April, May Busby was the professional soloist while other solos were taken by members of the Society (Mr Pashley and Miss Lewis). As a note of interest the retiring collection at this concert was for the Council for the Encouragement of Music and the Arts.

In the December concert of Christmas Music and Carols it was a young Stroud soloist, Peter Wood from Uplands, who stole the show. He sang Parry's *Shepherd Boy's Song* to an organ and oboe accompaniment. Again the congregation joined in with *The First Noel, God Rest You Merry* and *O Come All Ye Faithful* and 'really gave of their best'. The Stroud Orchestral Society making their first official appearance accompanied many of the carols. The reviewer rejoiced in a 'typical Christmas custom, the singing of carols in the delightfully appropriate setting provided by Stroud Parish Church. This at least was one feature of the season of peace and goodwill which the war has left untouched.'

Stroud Choral Society.

President: J. S. DANIELS, Esq.

STROUD PARISH CHURCH

Sunday March 15th, 1942,

at 3 p.m.

THE MUSIC MAKERS

EDWARD ELGAR.

BENEDICITE

R. VAUGHAN WILLIAMS.

ISOBEL BAILLIE   GRACE BODEY

ORCHESTRA.

Leader - MAURICE ALEXANDER

Conductor - SAMUEL UNDERWOOD

Accompanist - CONSTANCE BURR.

A COLLECTION will be taken in aid of the Stroud Nursing Association.

Programmes obtainable from Members of the Society, or at Messrs. Grainger's Russell Street, Stroud, or on the afternoon of the performance, at the Church Institute, between 2 and 3 p.m.

The West Door will be open for holders of Books of Words only (Price 1/-) at 2.30 p.m. All seats free after 2.50 p.m.

Cars 4.45 p.m.   *Hon. Sec.*, NETLAM BIGG.

Collins, Printer, Stroud.

For the rest of the war years, in spite of the committee sometimes thinking the Society would have to close for the duration or alternatively thinking that they would extend the singing season through the summer months, it was on the whole business as usual. There were three concerts in 1942 and two concerts each in 1943, 1944 and 1945. A date provisionally fixed for a concert at Painswick on April 20th 1945 did not take place. In December 1945 the Christmas concert reverted to its peacetime place and time and was given on Thursday 13th at 7pm.

During the war years there was a succession of notable soloists that sang in Stroud. Isobel Baillie sang with the choir in February 1941, March 1942 and March 1943. Her concerts were looked forward to and were tremendously popular. When she sang in Brahms' *Requiem* in 1943 the queue outside the church reached down into the High Street as far as 'Messrs Coley's premises' (the chemist) and the programmes for the concert were sold out. For Roy Henderson's concert, Christmas 1942 (Vaughan Williams' *Five Mystical Songs* and *Fantasia on Christmas Carols*) 'a long queue had been formed an hour before the start and the church was filled to capacity'. Roy Henderson was a very distinguished baritone soloist and singing teacher. One of his pupils had been Kathleen Ferrier. He died recently aged 100. Eric Greene (September 1944, *St John Passion,* December 1945, *Christmas Oratorio*) was a notable tenor soloist who sang often in Gloucester and Stroud and was renowned for his evangelist solos. Eric Greene and the bass soloist William Parsons were often on the same concert billing together.

After Bach's *Christmas Oratorio* in December 1945 the reviewer said of the following soloists Kathleen Kay, alto, Eric Greene, tenor and William Parsons, bass, 'their work throughout had been faultless'. Mary (Molly) Lake was a local soloist who had lived at Coaley and Wotton, 'a delightful soprano' (December 1943, *Song of Destiny*), who was also very popular in Gloucester where she often worked with Dr Herbert Sumsion. (Mary Lake went on to found the Stinchcombe Choral Society.)

The Annual General Meetings held in the war years tell us that in spite of considerable population movement in the Stroud area the number of singing members remained relatively stable at between 84 and 90. The Honorary members numbers fluctuated between 40 and 50. All the wartime concerts ran at a deficit and this was in spite of record concert audience numbers. Part of the problem was that the Society could not charge an entrance fee at the Parish Church and there was a reluctance or inability to charge too much for a programme. The early wartime programmes cost 6d rising through 1s 6d to 2s in 1945. The committee seemed to be able to retrieve 90% of this loss from the Carnegie Trust. A £20 legacy from the estate of Mrs Prout was also put towards the deficits. During 1942 the Society suffered the loss of two more members, the Honorary member Beatrice Lady Marling and, on September 7th 1942, John Jacob aged 92. John Jacob had completed 73 years with the Society!

In March 1943 the members at the AGM joined with the President John Daniels, and Sammy Underwood in sending Canon Steer 'good wishes, God-speed and a complete recovery to health'. 'They could not,' said Mr Daniels, 'be too grateful to Canon Steer not only for allowing them to hold their performances in the Church, but also for his kindly interest in their work.' In 1945 John Daniels was re-elected as the Society President, he was also entering his 53rd year as a singing member. In just about all the AGMs there were references to the choir not being able to face the audience and requests for a change. Everyone was in agreement, but no one could think of a solution.

Whether it was the end of World War II and better hopes for the future that lifted the spirits of the Choral members we shall never know but the two concerts given in December 1945 (*Christmas Oratorio*) and April 1946 (*Judas Maccabaeus*) were outstanding. 'To say that this performance was outstanding even in the annals of the Society is a statement of fact,' said the reviewer of the *Oratorio*. 'There was a harmony, a completeness about the whole performance which, was vitally apparent to every member of the congregation, and every word, every note had its charm and effect.' The reviews for *Judas Maccabaeus* were just as flattering. 'Their performance was an outstanding one in every respect, and the church was crowded. A high standard of singing and remarkable discipline of the chorus were apparent, and throughout the whole work there was a complete confidence between the Conductor and the singers.' All the soloists for both concerts received fulsome praise, Elsie Suddaby (*Judas Maccabaeus*) a well-known singer nationally and frequent visitor to Stroud, was 'superb,' revealing her to be the 'truly talented soprano she has always been acknowledged to be'. At the last moment the alto Ann Wood was unable to sing and Muriel Rolf from Gloucester, a mistress at the Stroud Girls' High School, took the contralto solos at short notice and 'proved herself the possessor of a rich voice which gave added appeal to the work'. At the AGM in April

1946, Sammy Underwood stated that the Society could look back on the past season with justifiable pride: 'In our small way we have kept the musical flag of the district flying.'

These successful concerts in the 1945–6 season were undertaken when the Society's numbers, 55 singing members, was at its lowest ever. During the war Stroud had been a reception area for many thousands of evacuees and accompanying adults, and army personnel. Canadians and Americans were also billeted in the Stroud area. The Society minutes for the war years record a continuous changing membership as its members of both sexes were called up or moved away to undertake war work of all kinds. That the numbers of singing members stayed in the 85 to 90 range during the war shows that the Society's ranks were swelled with help from incomers to the area.

The Vaughan Williams concert on December 12th 1946 was the Society's thanksgiving concert to celebrate the end of the war. The first work was Vaughan Williams' *Thanksgiving for Victory*, which had first been sung earlier that year at the Royal Albert Hall. The other two works performed were *Five Mystical Songs* and *Fantasia of Christmas Carols*. Pupils from Stroud Girls' High School, who sang the parts of the children's voices, assisted the choir in its singing of the *Thanksgiving*. Robert Bashford gave the Narration. (Robert Bashford became well-known for his dramatic parts in the Stroud Festival religious plays that were later set up by Netlam Bigg. He was also one of the founder members of the Cotswold Players.) Sammy Underwood's brother Percy took the baritone solo in the *Fantasia of Christmas Carols* (Percy Underwood continued to sing solo parts for the Society until 1955). The leader of the orchestra was Cecil Laubach (who had become the new leader in December 1944). The Vicar of Stroud, the Rev Kenneth Williams, who had replaced Canon Steer, had welcomed the Society and congregation to the church. The reviewer felt that the *Thanksgiving* was a striking work of originality and the Society's interpretation did much to make it the most impressive work of the evening. 'Already acclaimed the finest chorus in the west of England, the choir of over a hundred voices – the largest yet – sang with a precision and finish which have long been the marked characteristic of Samuel Underwood's leadership. To him more than any other man the choir owes its steady progress and high standard of performance at the present time.'

The Society was only too aware of how much they owed, in more ways than one, to their longtime conductor Sammy Underwood. On Monday May 5th 1947 the choir and officers of the Society sprang a little surprise. At an extra rehearsal, called because the choir was to sing at Gloucester Cathedral on May 10th as the sole choir in the Gloucester Music Festival, Sammy was stopped mid-baton and presented

---

HONORARY MEMBER.

Stroud Choral Society.

President: - J. S. DANIELS, Esq.

STROUD PARISH CHURCH

Thursday, December 12th, 1946

at 7 p.m.

THANKSGIVING FOR VICTORY
R. Vaughan Williams.

FIVE MYSTICAL SONGS
R. Vaughan Williams.

Fantasia on Christmas Carols
R. Vaughan Williams.

and other Christmas Music.

MARY LAKE.   PERCY UNDERWOOD.
ROBERT BASHFORD.   High School Choir.

Orchestra - Leader, Cecil Laubach.

Piano   Herbert Sumsion.

Conductor - SAMUEL UNDERWOOD.

A COLLECTION will be taken in aid of the Children's Society and Dr. Barnado's Homes. The South Door will be open at 6.30 p.m. to Holders of Honorary Members' Programmes *only*.

Cars 8.30 p.m.   Hon. Sec., NETLAM BIGG.
Collins, Printer, Stroud.

with a wallet containing £101. The presentation (a collection by members, honorary members and friends from near and far) was to celebrate 40 years of his unbroken conductorship of the choir. Although the presentation was a well-kept secret, Sammy, in his reply said, 'I thought there was a conspiracy of some sort being hatched when I was warned last night to put on my best suit.' He went on to say that his association with the Society over the forty years had been a very pleasant and happy one – perhaps the happiest of all his life 'It will be my desire during my remaining years with the Society to do all I can for you. I love my work and I'm very fond of you.'

The Society crowned the end of the decade with further fine performances. 'The Society had another triumph when an audience of more than 800 listened for 90 minutes in the Stroud Parish Church to Cherubini's *Second Mass in D Minor*' (*Citizen* March 22nd 1948). This was followed by a 'Magnificent' production of Bach's *St Matthew Passion* (March 29th 1949) in which the Choral Society were joined by the Dursley Bach Choir and Stroud High School Choir. Of the soloists, René Soames (a singer of international reputation) sang with a 'flawless earnestness', May Bartlett sang the soprano arias and recitatives 'delightfully', while Grace Bodey sang the contralto parts with 'a perfection Stroud has come to know so well'. Laurence Holmes was splendid as the principal bass soloist and Percy Underwood sang with an 'admirable contrasting vigour'. And not by any means misplaced amongst the principal soloists were Glenys Nelmes, soprano and Jack Poole, tenor in the solo parts they contributed. Sammy's comment given a week later at the AGM, was to say that 'Perhaps they had reached a high water mark as the performance was the most satisfying he had experienced, and for once in his life he felt everyone enjoyed the work, was sympathetic and interested, so that he was able to concentrate from beginning to end. It made his work easy and he was deeply grateful for their attention.'

Photograph taken to commemorate Mr Underwood's 40 years of unbroken conductorship, May 5th 1947. The SCS Committee. William Scott, John Brooke, Mr Fitzwater, Maude Halliday, Jim Wilson, Margaret Bigg, Mrs Fitzwater, Stanley Sullings, Dora Sansom, John Daniels, Sammy Underwood, Netlam Bigg.

The Society accounts for the 1947 – 48 season, as detailed in the AGM of March 22nd 1948, are typical of the Society's financial situation in the late 1940s and early 1950s.

	£	s	d
Income from March Concert 1948			
Sale of programmes	£34	10	6
Half honorary members subs	£23	2	6
Collection (The Society had been given permission to retain part of the retiring collection)	£7	16	6
Expenditure on March Concert 1948			
Soloists	£64	4	0
Orchestra	£134	5	6
Loss on the December (1947) concert	£13	18	7
There was a total deficit on the year of	£93	3	8

Miss Dora Sansom (treasurer) reported that the Arts Council had promised a grant of £50 and they should also receive £35 from the Carnegie Trust, leaving about £6 to be met.

To add to the Society's financial problems, Britain, as it went into the decade of the 1950s, was entering a period of austerity and restraint. Paper, which had been in short supply during the war, had meant that newspapers were reduced in size and fewer books were printed and published. Those books that were made were printed on 'war economy' paper and had to conform to authorised economy standards. Stroud must have had access to a good supply of paper during the war years as the Society programmes were large and mostly printed on good paper. However, during the early 1950s the programmes were produced on poorer quality paper and were reduced in size from around 11½" × 7½" (1948) to 7½" x 5" (1954), only returning to their more usual size in 1956.

For the Society, the first concert of the decade was a fine performance of Elgar's *The Dream of Gerontius* in March 1950. The tenor soloist was the notable singer Heddle Nash who demonstrated his total professionalism by singing the complete part without a score 'this striking technique made it one of the main contributions to a great performance'. 'The orchestra of over thirty players, unconventional in layout and cramped for space in and around the chancel, nevertheless was excellent.' The reviewer talks of the genius of Sammy Underwood in achieving such a distinguished performance for a town the size of Stroud. 'There could have been few Stroud people in the crowded audience ... not conscious of a feeling of pride.' The following week the deputy treasurer Mr Stanley Sullings was able to state that the receipts of £160 for the *Dream of Gerontius* were a record amount and that there was a profit on the whole season of £44. It was unfortunately to be the last profit the Society made for some time.

In September 1950 the Society had been approached by the National Federation of Music Societies, asking for the number of Choral members who would be interested in singing in the Festival of Britain Concert at the Royal Albert Hall on June 2nd 1951. How many members signed up for this is not known but they must have been disappointed when, in November 1950, a letter from the Regional Committee of the Festival of Britain (Bristol), stated that the Society had only been allocated places for one second soprano, one first alto, one second tenor and one second bass. A sub-committee consisting of Mr Underwood, Mr Bigg and Mr Sullings, decided that Mrs Halliday, soprano, Mrs Wright, contralto, Mr Taylor, tenor, and Mr Hodgson, bass, would represent the Stroud Choral Society at the Royal Albert Hall on June 2nd 1951. The Festival of Britain Society has kindly provided details about this concert, which took place on Saturday 2nd June at 3pm. The concert was presented by the National Federation in association with the Arts Council of Great Britain. A thousand representatives of choral and music societies affiliated to the Federation sang under the baton of Sir Adrian Boult a very typical 1950s. programme The programme consisted of Parry's *Blest Pair of Sirens*, Vaughan Williams' *Benedicite*, Elgar's *Prologue* to *The Apostles*, Sullivan's Evening Hymn *O Gladsome Light*, Stanford's *Songs of the Fleet* and Roger Quilter's *Non Nobis Domine*. The soloists were Joan Alexander, soprano, who sang in *Benedicite* and Denis Noble, baritone, who sang John Ireland's *These things shall be*, as well as the solo parts in *Songs of the Fleet*. As part of the programme, the London Philharmonic performed Holst's Ballet Music from *The Perfect Fool* and the Purcell-Bliss *Suite for Strings*.

In this historic event 166 choirs took part. Stroud Choral Society is listed under Bristol and West of England, together with Bath Choral and Orchestral Society, Bridgewater and District Choral Society, Bristol Choral Society, Bristol Philharmonic Society, Bristol Royal Orpheus Society, Cheltenham Male Voice Choir, Cirencester Choral Society, Gloucester Choral Society, Tewkesbury and District Choral Society and Westonbirt and District Choral Society. The Council Members of the Federation, in the Bristol and West of England region, are named as A Barter (Bristol Philharmonic) and A E Craven (Gloucester Choral Society). Out of the 36 council members for the British Isles only one member, Mrs V L Black (Rochester Choral Society, Kent) is a woman!

In December 1951 the high standard of choral singing was continued with the 'deeply moving rendering' of Bach's *Christmas Oratorio parts 1, 2 & 3*. 'The soloists were happily chosen', René Soames and Grace Bodey were 'particularly pleasing', and James Walker 'enhanced his reputation as a bass singer'. 'But it would have pleased the congregation if Miss Nelmes had had more to do, for her pure soprano voice has made her a very popular local soloist.' Glenys Nelmes was a young Society member who had started singing roles in concerts in 1948. In March 1952 the critic was writing that 'with striking ease Miss Nelmes sang the difficult soprano arias and her exquisite tone in the higher register was something which, forgetting all else, made the evening worth while'.

Although between December 1951 and December 1955 the Society produced ten successful concerts, finances remained critical and various measures were undertaken to try and place the Society on a firmer footing. In April 1951, Mr Sullings (treasurer) explained the covenant system whereby a tax-paying member of the Society who undertook to subscribe £1 1s per annum for seven years would bring in £2 per annum to the Society. Mr Sullings reported that he already had five such members. By March 1952 Mr Sullings was reporting: 'We lost heavily on our concerts, we have liquidated our reserves, we have a deficit of over £50 and in consequence we have not got a brass farthing with which to start next season.' It was during 1952 that the committee devised the 'sugar bowl' method of increasing finances. Instead of putting up the annual membership subscription, every singing member was asked to 'voluntarily' place 6d in the sugar bowl at each rehearsal. Some years this was a more successful way of raising money than others. The 1954–5 season only raised £31 5s compared to £41 16s 8d in 1952–3. It was an easy system to monitor and to remind members not to 'forget'! Although decimalization took place in 1971, there is no mention of increasing this amount (2½p) until 1973 when this 'voluntary' donation became 5p. In spite of fluctuations in the sugar bowl revenue, the system continued until November 1976.

During November 1952 the Society's President, John Stuart Daniels, died, and Mrs Sidney Allen took his place. John Daniels had been a very benevolent Society President who for many years had often put his hand in his own pocket to help clear the annual deficit. After his death his nephew, Lionel Daniels, wrote to the Society and suggested that the Secretary, Mr Bigg, should circulate John Daniels' friends with a view to them subscribing to the Choral Society as a memorial to his Uncle. This was done and there is a note in the minutes to the effect that by September 1953 the J S Daniels memorial fund stood at £92. Mrs Sidney Allen was also a most generous benefactor to the Society. She raised money (£41 in 1953) by giving summer Garden Parties for the Society. She also presented baskets of fruit to the committee members at AGMs.

Things were not totally happy with the Society during this period and there were various rumblings of unease and dissatisfaction from all quarters. The committee was pressing hard for a new concert hall in the Stroud area but was getting nowhere. Netlam Bigg wrote frequent letters to the Stroud Urban district Council, the Gloucestershire Education Committee and the National Federation of Music Societies, hoping to get support to press for the new Technical College hall to be adapted to suit performances of choral and orchestral music. The committee was looking for a concert hall big enough to hold an audience of 1,000.

The committee also had a bone to pick with the Gloucestershire Education Committee who were sponsoring Stroud school children to attend choral concerts in Gloucester. The committee wanted the same provision to be made for the Stroud concerts and, backed by Miss Senior, headmistress of Stroud High School, several letters voicing their feelings of unfair treatment were sent to the Education Department.

The treasurer, Stanley Sullings, complained about falling numbers at the weekly rehearsals. The total attendance at rehearsal approximated only 50 or 60 in spite of 120 being on the register. There was also a falling off in audience numbers and some Society members felt that the choice of music might be putting off singers and audience alike.

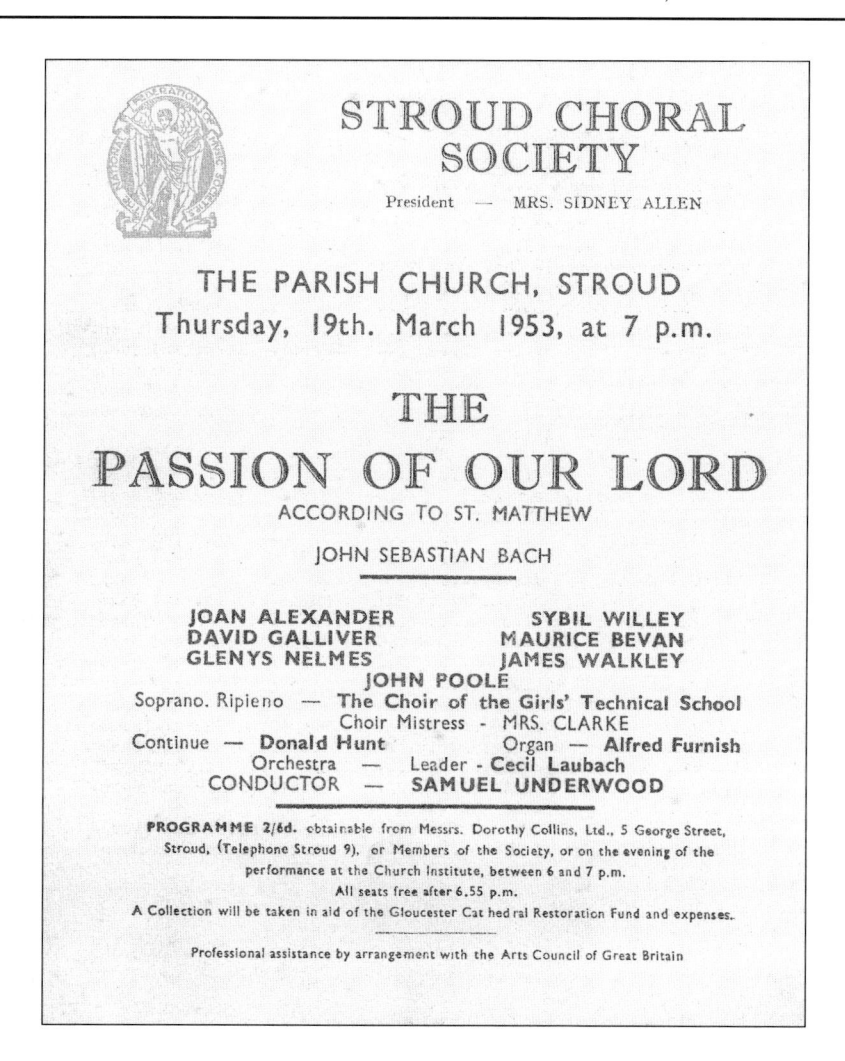

> **STROUD CHORAL SOCIETY**
>
> President — MRS. SIDNEY ALLEN
>
> THE PARISH CHURCH, STROUD
> Thursday, 19th. March 1953, at 7 p.m.
>
> # THE
> # PASSION OF OUR LORD
> ACCORDING TO ST. MATTHEW
>
> JOHN SEBASTIAN BACH
>
> JOAN ALEXANDER   SYBIL WILLEY
> DAVID GALLIVER   MAURICE BEVAN
> GLENYS NELMES   JAMES WALKLEY
> JOHN POOLE
>
> Soprano. Ripieno — The Choir of the Girls' Technical School
> Choir Mistress - MRS. CLARKE
> Continue — Donald Hunt   Organ — Alfred Furnish
> Orchestra — Leader - Cecil Laubach
> CONDUCTOR — SAMUEL UNDERWOOD
>
> PROGRAMME 2/6d. obtainable from Messrs. Dorothy Collins, Ltd., 5 George Street, Stroud, (Telephone Stroud 9), or Members of the Society, or on the evening of the performance at the Church Institute, between 6 and 7 p.m.
> All seats free after 6.55 p.m.
> A Collection will be taken in aid of the Gloucester Cathedral Restoration Fund and expenses.
>
> Professional assistance by arrangement with the Arts Council of Great Britain

Sammy Underwood said that it was a very wrong attitude if members were staying away because the work was too difficult or they did not like it: 'They should sink their own feelings to team spirit, for the sake of the Society.'

The Society members were also unhappy with their committee, voicing some concern as to the way the committee had been formed in the past, and it was suggested that two or three members might retire each year. This was agreed to, but with the proviso that members resigning should be allowed to stand for immediate re-election.

Sammy Underwood continued to ask for a representative of the BBC to attend rehearsals with a view to the choir being broadcast at some point. The BBC on their part seemed very willing, but invariably the only visits they could offer were during the summer months when the choir did not meet. A recording of excerpts of Bach's *St John Passion*, (1955) was made by Mr George Debenham and Mr Philip Daw and sent as a token of friendship from the Society to Stroud in Australia.

The choir had been requested to sing at the Gloucester Music Festivals and at various other occasions during this time, but Sammy Underwood turned most requests down either because of cost or lack of time. A request (October 1952) for the choir to take part in the Coronation Festival at Tewkesbury Abbey was declined for the Society as a whole but individual members were invited to go under their own steam. Choir members did attend the Watkins Shaw lecture on the *St Matthew Passion* arranged by Miss Trent at the Girls Technical School one evening in January 1953.

And threading its way through all these problems, large and small, was the tiresome, seemingly unsolvable, problem of half the members of the choir singing with their backs to the audience!

From time to time references were made to the age of the Society. In 1947 Sammy Underwood said that he was sure that the Society had been founded not later than 1850 and that it must be soon reaching its centenary. At the Annual General Meeting in 1955, Netlam Bigg read a report printed in the Stroud Journal of a performance given on December 30th 1854 and that proved that the Society had been in existence for over 100 years. He went on to say

Stroud Parish Church March 1956. Rehearsal for The Dream of Gerontius. *The choir stand on a specially made platform and is able to face the audience for this special concert.*

that the early minutes had been lost but at that time there was a collection of programmes dating from that time: 'I would like to suggest that we ask the Council to start a Folk Museum at the Mansion House where they could be housed and available for all to see.' It is good at this point to be able to say that Netlam Bigg's hopes for a Folk Museum in the Mansion House in Stratford Park have now been realised.

1956 was a memorable year for the Society as they celebrated Sammy Underwood's 50 years of conductorship. The conductor had chosen Elgar's *Dream of Gerontius* for his Jubilee Concert. Sammy Underwood had taken up his position as organist at Stroud Parish Church in December 1906 and together with that position, the conductorship of the Choral Society.

To begin the celebrations there was to be a lecture on *The Dream* on February 2nd in the Church Institute. This was to be given by Mr Watkins Shaw, honorary librarian of St Michael's College, Tenbury Wells. To encourage children to attend, the cost of a ticket would be 1s, with adults paying 2s 6d. This lecture was to be illustrated by gramophone records.

Harold Watkins Shaw was born in Bradford in 1911. He became a well-known writer, teacher and musicologist. He taught musicology at the Royal College of Music from 1932 to 1933 under R O Morris. He was a lecturer at Worcester College of Education from 1949 to 1971. Watkins Shaw, as he was always known, was a specialist in church music and the *Messiah*. His celebrated edition of *Messiah* was published in 1965. In 1975 he received the OBE.

Following the Elgar lecture there was to be an exhibition of old musical instruments, photographs, scores and concert programmes. The exhibition was to be held in the Stroud Museum at Lansdown and would run from the 1st to 15th March 1956. Amongst the highlights on show was an original Vaughan Williams' manuscript *Benedicite* lent by Mrs Elgar Blake, the composer's daughter. Other items included original scores by Hubert Parry, Alexander Brent-Smith, Rutland Boughton and an original song written by Mr C W Orr of Painswick. Mr Underwood lent three unusual instruments, a sixteenth century Italian virginal, a 200-year-old barrel organ and a bass ophicleide, a forerunner of the bass trombone. 'Beautifully written' labels on the display cases were the work of Mr P Turner of Oakridge and Clarke Bros of Stroud had loaned the radiogram, which had been used to provide background music. There was also a 'striking series' of portraits of the great composers lent by Mrs Sidney Allen. The exhibition proved a great success. The Society in particular thought that much of this was due to the hard work of Mr Lionel Walrond, the curator of the museum. 'It had created much interest in the district and people had even come down from London to see it,' reported Mr Bigg at the AGM in March 1956.

Mr Lionel Walrond arranging old musical instruments as part of the Music Exhibition in the Stroud Museum. March 1st–15th 1956. The Exhibition marked Mr Underwood's 50 years with SCS.

Much thought and careful preparation went into the production of *The Dream* to be performed on March 15th. A new platform costing £60 was made, the cost of which was shared between the Society (using funds from the Daniels Memorial Fund) and the Religious Drama Festival. (The Religious Drama group, founded by Netlam Bigg, were being particularly generous, as apparently they did not require such a large stage for their own use.) For this particular concert, every effort was to be made so that the whole choir would be able to face the congregation and the new platform in the chancel was part of this initiative. Considerable discussion took place as to the concert dress. In the event this came down to the men wearing dark suits and ties, white shirts, and the ladies being able to choose between all black or black skirts with white blouses. A request from the ladies that they should be allowed to wear black lace caps was turned down! Stewards were to be distinguished by having white rosette armbands, and Mrs Maude Halliday made these.

A commemorative programme (which was also the ticket) was to be produced. This was to contain a photo of Mr Underwood and a short history of the choir (thought to be at least a hundred years old), and the complete words of *The Dream*. It would also list the names of the honorary members (76) and the members of the choir (116), the semi-chorus (19), together with the names of the orchestra (47). Two photographs, one of the print of the First Philharmonic 1835, and the second of the choir with Mr Underwood in Stratford Park in 1907, completed the programme. The Stroud Urban District Council had given a grant of £10 towards the cost of producing the programmes. These were to be sold at 7s 6d, 5s, and 2s 6d. The choir were to be allowed to purchase the Commemorative programme at a special rate of 2s. In the event, the sale of the programmes raised an all time record of £116 16s 3d.

The review of *The Dream of Gerontius* was billed in the *Stroud Journal* of Friday March 23rd 1956 as 'A great Act of Worship.' It was felt that this great and moving performance was exactly what Mr Underwood had wished when he chose this work to be performed to mark 50 years of Conductorship of the Stroud Choral Society. Although almost hidden from view in the chancel, the choir was heard clearly above the organ and orchestral accompaniment. The soloists, Nancy Evans, contralto, William Herbert, tenor, Scott Joynt, bass, the organist Claude Allen, and the orchestra were all deservedly praised. All in all it was a stunning success and a 'tremendous tribute to the man on the stand who led it through from start to finish with such consummate skill'. Mr Underwood, speaking later at the AGM, said that he had the feeling that everyone had done their very best to add to this special year. He said that something had happened during *The Dream* to which a member called out, 'Your inspiration Sir.' 'Perhaps it would

Sammy Underwood, March 1956.

be more correct to say my perspiration,' replied Mr Underwood. Through laughter and applause the members then sang a spontaneous rendition of *For He's a Jolly Good Fellow.*

After the performance of *The Dream* a young schoolgirl, Miss J Webster, who was a pupil at Walthamstow Hall, had been moved to write the following poem.

A Conductor's Hands

How still and quiet were his hands
Until his music spoke.
No one would know what fine bright strands
Of sound they could evoke.
But when his poised and tilted head
Lifted towards the light,
How instantly their sleep they shed
And sprang to vivid flight.
No more were they like folded wings
Of doves in noon-day rest,
Now they flashed out to sweep the strings
Up to a mighty crest.
Through hush and shout he led them round
Traversing magic lands,
That perfect miracle of sound
Held on his lifted hands.

To complete the Jubilee celebrations there was a party on May 3rd in the Subscription Rooms. In front of a crowded audience, Sir Steuart Wilson, Head of BBC Music, made a presentation of a cheque for £400, together with a beautifully bound book containing the signatures of his friends and well-wishers.

Later in the year on Sunday November 18th, in celebration of St Cecilia's day, an augmented choir sang evensong in recognition of Sammy Underwood's forthcoming 50 years as organist and choirmaster of the Parish Church.

The year was completed, not just with the December concert of Bach's *Come Redeemer,* Finzi's *In Terra Pax,* and Oldroyd's *Jhesu Christ, Saint Mary's Sone,* but with the knowledge that Mr Underwood was to be named in the New Year's Honours List and would be awarded an MBE for his services to music in the West Country.

The AGM on March 25th 1957 was to be an unusual one insomuch as the conductor was absent for the first time ever. Mr Underwood was at that moment travelling up to London in order to receive his MBE the following day from the Queen at Buckingham Palace. Mr Frank Miller who was now the new President of the Society, following the death of Mrs Sidney Allen the previous autumn, was in the chair. One of the first things Mr Miller did, after explaining Mr Underwood's absence, and paying tribute to Mrs Sidney Allen, was to raise again the question of a purpose-built concert hall for Stroud.

At a later committee meeting in April 1957 there was a discussion, followed by a decision to change the concert day from Thursday to Wednesday. No reasons were given and this seems a puzzling change of policy. Traditionally, going back to the very early days of the Society, Thursday had been the day chosen for the concerts and this was probably because it tied into Stroud's half-closing day. This gave an opportunity in the twentieth century for a rehearsal before the concert, plus time to prepare the venue. (Stroud's early closing in the nineteenth century was very different. Shops closed for lunch, re-opening an hour or so later and then staying open until maybe 8 or 9 o'clock. Early closing, for those shops participating in the scheme seems to have been at 5.30 or 6pm.)

One reason for the change of day from Thursday to Wednesday may have had something to do with Sammy Underwood's punishing, self-appointed, weekly schedule. In addition to giving private music lessons at his home and attending church most days, his weekly timetable during the 1930s and 1940s was generally as follows.

STROUD SINGS

Monday evening	Stroud Church choir practice.	Friday evening	Stroud Church choir practice and extra rehearsal.
	Stroud Choral Society meeting and rehearsal.	Saturday afternoon	Special Service/private rehearsal.
Tuesday evening	Bristol Choral Society meeting and rehearsal.	Saturday evening	Gloucester Orpheus Society meeting and rehearsal.
Wednesday evening	Swindon Choral Society meeting and rehearsal.	Sunday morning	Church service followed by teaching.
		Sunday afternoon	Break at his caravan or on a boat on the canal.
Thursday evening	Gloucester Orchestral Society rehearsal.		
	Gloucester Choral Society rehearsal.	Sunday evening	Church Service.
Friday afternoon	Cheltenham studio, teaching.		

One wonders how any concerts at all could be fitted into this extremely full timetable!

Sammy Underwood had always enjoyed a close working relationship with Gloucester's Dr. Herbert Sumsion. At some time during the late 1940s and at least up to 1958 if not later, whenever possible, Gloucester and Stroud Choral Societies shared soloists. (Peter Hillier, a member of Gloucester Choral Society seems to think that this arrangement continued until Dr. Sumsion's retirement in 1967.) Soloists would perform on Wednesdays in Gloucester and then stay

Percy Underwood, SWU, John Poole, outside Buckingham Palace March 25th 1957. Sammy always referred to his MBE as 'this 'ere honour'.

for the night with Dr and Mrs Sumsion, coming to Stroud to rehearse and perform an entirely different work the next day. Stroud concerts were timed to finish before 10.30pm to allow soloists to catch the late train back to London.

The Wednesday evening concerts continued until December 1959 after which they reverted back to Thursdays. In 1973 the Society's main concerts were moved to Saturday evenings, probably reflecting the demise of Stroud's half-closing day and recognising that many choral members now worked away from Stroud.

At some time in the spring of 1957 Sammy Underwood received a presentation leather-bound copy of *The Dream of Gerontius*, with the title and S W Underwood inscribed in gold on the front. The book was given to him from 'members of his choir in commemoration of his jubilee'. It seems strange that this wasn't included in the presentation and celebrations of the previous year. In a way it would have made more sense to have made this gift a recognition of his MBE – or was it that some members of the choir felt that 1957 more accurately reflected the date of his jubilee?

From the late 1930s through into the 1960s, committee meetings were often held at 'Highmead', the home of Mr and Mrs Netlam Bigg. Netlam Bigg was secretary of the Society from 1934 to 1969. During the 1950s (and probably before) the committee meetings at 'Highmead' were very formal, with members sitting round a huge dining room table, and only expressing an opinion when asked. Netlam ruled with a rod of iron. His wife Margaret, who sang solo contralto parts with the Society, was a gentle, quiet personality. A very rewarding conversationalist lay beneath this reserved manner. Members of the committee in March 1957 were: Mr Frank Miller in the chair; Mr Netlam Bigg – secretary; Mr Stanley Sullings – treasurer; Mr Sammy Underwood – conductor; and Mr E Williames, Rev A F Maltin, Mrs Frank Miller, Mrs Netlam Bigg, Mrs Glenys Jones (née Nelmes), Mrs M Halliday, Mrs Davis, Miss Horle and Miss Senior. At an October committee meeting in 1957 it was agreed to send Dr Vaughan Williams a greetings telegram on the occasion of his 85th birthday on October 12th.

B M W, reporting on both the Society's concerts, Verdi's *Requiem* in March 1957 and Bush's *In Praise of Mary* and Vaughan Williams' *Benedicite* in December 1957, had some thoughtful remarks on the conflict of the old versus the new choral works. She points out that the great choral classics are more likely to be appreciated and pay their way than twentieth century music. Leaving aside modern music in the form of Tommy Steele, Elvis Presley and their like, modern serious music, 'brings more prestige than public support'. She feels that it is easier for the public to understand a familiar classic than 'to struggle with complicated modern rhythms and harmonies'. B M W felt that the Stroud Choral Society did much to dispel feelings of distrust, both in their sure performances of contemporary music, and their reassuring presentation of famous oratorios. Geoffrey Bush's *In Praise of Mary* was a new work first given in public by the Three Choirs in 1955. Given in conjunction with Vaughan Williams' *Benedicite* it was a challenging concert for the audience to appreciate. B M W wondered if it would not be possible, as was done with some BBC concerts, to explain before or during the concert what the new works were about, and what points to watch out for. Failing that, she felt that more programme notes would be helpful.

The Society planned to sing the *St Matthew Passion* on March 26th 1958 and it had chosen a fine group of soloists for this event. Pauline Brockless, soprano, and Grace Bodey, contralto were to be joined by Wilfred Brown who sang the narration, Richard Standen taking the part of Christ with John Carol Case singing the other bass solos. A local singer, John Poole, and the Society's Glenys Nelmes were to take small tenor and soprano parts. However, it was not Pauline Brockless' wonderful voice that delighted the overflowing audience in the church that evening, but that of Glenys Nelmes, whose 'clear voice was admirably suited to the work, which blended well with that of Grace Bodey in the duet *Behold my Saviour now is taken.*' Glenys had been helping to prepare tea for the soloists and orchestra in the Church Institute during the afternoon, when she was called into the church to be told that Pauline Brockless was ill and had lost her voice. Sammy was quite firm and told Glenys that he wanted her to sing the soprano solo. Glenys tells how wonderfully kind and encouraging the professional singers were towards her. One of the arias she had never sung as a solo, and because she had to hurry home to change into a suitable concert dress there had been no time to practise the duet with Grace Bodey. When the time for the duet came, Glenys said that Grace Bodey was 'absolutely marvellous', taking hold of her arm, and whispering encouragingly to her that she could do it and all would be well. Also singing with the choir was the Choir of the Girls' Technical School, and with Claude Allen at the organ and Edwin Brown leading the orchestra, 'worthy of the highest praise', this was to be yet another landmark concert for the Stroud Choral Society. 'Without doubt, all the large audience must have left the church feeling uplifted by such a fine performance.' Although no one knew it at the time, this fine concert was to be Sammy Underwood's last.

On August 10th 1958 Sammy Underwood was taken ill while playing the organ for the Sunday Service. Taken to Stroud General Hospital, he died on Tuesday 26th August. He was aged 77. That same morning, another fine musician with Gloucestershire connections, Ralph Vaughan Williams, also died. In his Obituary, the *Stroud News and Journal* noted that although Mr Underwood had been principally known for nearly 52 years as the conductor of the Stroud Choral Society, he had also conducted the Bristol Choral Society, the Gloucester Orpheus Society and the Swindon Choral Society 'during a long life which he dedicated to music'. 'A man of great ability, Mr Underwood could so easily have become a national figure. But modesty itself, he chose to dedicate his life to the betterment of music in the West Country, and Stroud in particular. He will be remembered by the great men, and the man in the street, by Sir Adrian Boult, whom he helped keep the BBC Choral Society and Symphony Orchestra running during the war, and by the casual visitor to Stroud who attended one of his concerts and marvelled at his ability.'

Sammy's memorial service on Saturday 30th August was attended by hundreds of music lovers. As the congregation assembled, Dr Herbert Sumsion, organist of Gloucester Cathedral, played the *Prelude* and *Angel* song from Elgar's *Dream of Gerontius*. The service was conducted by the Vicar of Stroud, Reverend Arthur F Maltin. Sixty members of the Bristol Choral Society together with members of Stroud Choral Society sang in tribute *O Sacred Head Surrounded* from Bach's *St Matthew Passion*. Mr Frank Miller, President of the Choral Society, and Claude Allen, the Society's accompanist, read the lessons. Sammy's favourite hymn *Through the night of doubt and sorrow* was sung. Many other music societies were represented at this service. As well as the Bristol Choral Society there were the Painswick and Stroud Music Societies, the Stinchcombe Hill Festival choir, the Bristol Royal Orpheus Glee Society, the Gloucester Choral Society and Festival class, the Bristol Philharmonic Society, the Bristol Cathedral Special choir, the Gloucester Orchestral Society, the Gloucestershire Organists Association and the Cheltenham Music Society. Many local church choirs were represented as also were the Stroud Religious Drama Festival, the Music Department of Bristol University, the Westonbirt Society, the Stroud and District Band, the Stroud High School for Girls and the Stroud Technical School. As the church emptied after this memorable service of thanksgiving for the life of an extraordinarily gifted and dedicated man, there can have been no doubt in anyone's mind that they had witnessed the end of a great musical era.

Winds of change

I think most of the performers and congregation enjoyed the Bach and St Nicolas very much. I expect you have had some reactions to the introduction of applause. One assumes the Vicar and P C C did not oppose it, but as some of the members of the Society found it distressing, I hope we shall have the opportunity of a discussion when we meet in the New Year.

Letter to the Secretary, December 1968.

The Society was now faced with the prospect of looking for a new conductor – an activity that none of the committee was at all familiar with! During August the committee had approached Mr Robert Clifford, the recently appointed County Music Advisor for Gloucestershire to ask if he would take rehearsals for the period of Mr Underwood's indisposition and Mr Clifford agreed to this. Now the committee had to look for a permanent appointment. The Parish Church Committee had decided not to continue with a joint appointment, as they preferred to advertise separately for an organist and choirmaster. An advert for a new conductor for the Society was placed in the *Musical Times* and *Musical Opinion*. In the meantime, Mr Robert Clifford would rehearse the Society for the December concert, which was to be Fauré's *Requiem*, Dvorak's *Biblical Songs* and Bach's *Christmas Cantata*. At the November committee meeting it was reported that several applications for the position of conductor had been received and were being considered by the selection committee. By March 1959, the committee minutes announced the appointment of Mr Mark Foster, who in spite of the previous declaration by the vicar, the Rev Clive Cooper, was also appointed organist and choirmaster to the Parish Church.

On Friday March 20th the Stroud Choral Society conducted by Robert Clifford gave a superb performance of Handel's Oratorio *Joshua*. Both the programme notes and the *Citizen* of March 21st 1959, tell us that this was the first time since 1879 that the Society had sung *Joshua*. It was in fact the first time the Society had ever performed *Joshua*. Although a programme had been produced for a concert to be held on December 2nd 1879, it was cancelled with no reason given. Unfortunately another cancellation, due to the illness of the soprano soloist April Cantelo, could have marred this production. Happily, Edna Mitchells, (having learned her part in the plane flying in from Belfast) stepped in at short notice and took her place alongside the other notable soloists, Kathleen Joyce, contralto, Ronald Bristol, tenor, and Richard Standen, bass. The Stroud tenor John Poole sang the part of the Angel. The well-balanced choir gave some fine singing with 'an outstanding chorus in *Glory to God*'. After a rather hesitant start, the orchestra, led by Edwin Brown moved into 'a confident and inspiring performance'. This programme had been chosen to commemorate the bicentenary

New Appointments

Mark Foster has been appointed organist and choirmaster of Stroud Parish Church and conductor of Stroud Choral Society. Mr. Foster was a student at the Royal College of Music after the war and subsequently joined the London Symphony Orchestra. He gave this up six years ago and devoted his attention to the organ. He made rapid strides and eventually obtained the F.R.C.O. diploma. This change from orchestral playing to the organ loft is a reversal of the usual order of things, and Mr. Foster is to be congratulated on his quick attainment of an important post.

Item about Mark Foster from Musical Times *December 1959.*

of the death of Handel in April 1759. B M W reviewing the concert for the *Stroud News and Journal*, commented, 'The performance of this, one of the less well-known of Handel's works, was a fitting commemoration of the death of this great composer.' A critic, R H B, of the *Bristol Post* finished his column with 'the Stroud Choral Society are surely building on the sure foundation laid by their late Conductor Mr Samuel Underwood. With last night's *Joshua* he would not have been disappointed.'

At a busy AGM on March 23rd 1959 Mr Mark Foster was introduced to the Society. Mr Foster told the Society that he was keen to build on the fine foundations laid by the late Mr Underwood and that he would continue to produce both classical and contemporary works. He understood that the Society was anxious to give a concert in memory of Mr Underwood and he thought that Verdi's *Requiem* would be a suitable work if the committee could raise the money. Mr Clifford was thanked for his work for the Society and he replied that he had felt most honoured to carry on, in some small measure, the work of the late Sammy Underwood.

It was at this AGM that Mr Reginald Cox made a presentation to the Society of a set of timpani, which originally had belonged to 'Chew's Band'.

Stanley Sullings, the treasurer reported that Mr Underwood's memorial fund stood at £128 12s 7d. The Society had hoped to complete the organ in the Parish Church as a suitable memorial to Mr Underwood, but a new 16ft reed stop on the swell would cost £450, so it was proposed to see if a second-hand rank of pipes would be available.

Again there was discussion on the need for a new concert hall for Stroud. Yet again it was felt that the new Assembly Hall at Stroud College might be an answer to the problem: 'with a little push, consideration might be given to facilities for concerts and the hall made available to societies.'

After the December concert in 1959, B M W in the *Stroud News and Journal* gave full marks to the new conductor, Mark Foster, and the high standard of singing that augured well for the future. Also giving great pleasure to the audience were the soloists Heather Harper and Grace Bodey, singing beautifully in Vivaldi's *Gloria*, 'a joy to listen to'.

On Thursday March 24th 1960 a performance of Verdi's *Requiem* was given at a memorial concert for Sammy Underwood. It was a moving performance given to a capacity audience. The reviewer felt that 'Many eyes moistened as Mark Foster mounted the rostrum to conduct the *Requiem*. For over 50 years Samuel Underwood had done the same thing and memories of his slightly stooping and grey-haired figure and of the many notable performances he had so skilfully conducted came flooding back.' Much was expected from the well-known soloists, Iris Bourne, soprano, Patricia Kern, mezzo-soprano, David Gulliver, tenor and Marian Nowakowski, bass. The *Citizen* reports: 'Rarely has such a perfect blend of four voices been heard in the centuries-old church than in the wonderfully melodious and moving quartet *Domine Jesu*. Similarly in the touching *Lacrymosa* in which they were supported by the chorus, there was an exquisite expression of emotion.'

In the audience and listening with interest to this concert was Professor Louis H Dierck, one of America's leading conductors. Professor Dierck was on a six-month tour of Europe to study traditional choral techniques. His own choir, founded in 1937, was the Ohio State University Symphonic Choir. In 1955 Professor Dierck had brought this choir to take part in the Welsh Eisteddfod. He had been specially recommended to attend the Stroud concert by the Arts Council. During their stay in Stroud, Professor Dierck and his wife were guests at the home of Mr and Mrs Netlam Bigg.

The Society and friends came together the following Sunday, March 27th 1960 to sing Evensong, at which the Bishop of Gloucester, Dr W M Askwith dedicated a memorial to the late Mr Underwood. After the singing of the *Magnificat* and *Nunc Dimittis*, Glenys Nelmes, soprano, and John Poole, tenor, were the soloists in the first of two Holst *Psalms*. The conductor was Mark Foster and Claude Allen was the organist. The memorial took the form of two new organ stops to replace older ones and the cost, in the region of £250, was met by public subscription. Over £100 of this had been donated instead of flowers at Sammy Underwood's funeral. The engraved brass plate, which the Bishop had dedicated, reads 'To the Glory of God and in memory of Samuel Underwood, MBE, FRCO, organist of this church and Conductor of Stroud Choral Society 1907 to 1958. Two stops of the organ were replaced in recognition of his services to music and the church. Dedicated: March 27th, 1960.' During his address the Bishop described Samuel Underwood as being amongst those who have 'more insight that the average person to reveal the wonders of the universe in which we live.'

From time to time during the twentieth century, questions had been asked as to the age of the Society. During the music exhibition of 1956, when old concert programmes had been on view to the public, curiosity had again been raised about the choir's early beginnings. In 1959 a Stroud solicitor, sorting through old documents had discovered that one bundle had been wrapped up in a poster advertising a concert for November 28th 1848. Also the Society had in its possession the old print showing the Stroud 1st Philharmonic of 1835. John Jacob, a member who had sung with the choir from 1869 to 1942, had given this to them. From Mr Jacob it had been understood that the Choral Society had developed from, or been part of, the Stroud Philharmonic. To this effect, the officers of the Society decided to celebrate in May 1960, what they saw as the 125th anniversary of the founding of the Society.

A celebratory dinner, billed by the Stroud Journal as a 'Unique Event in the Musical World,' was held on May 17th 1960 in the Stroud Subscription Rooms. A special souvenir menu to mark the occasion was printed. From this, we learn that the Society, 160 members and their guests, sat down to the following dinner.

Chilled Grapefruit

Cold Roast Chicken and Wiltshire Ham

New Potatoes

Assorted Salads

Trifle and Dairy Cream

Biscuits

Assorted Cheeses

Coffee

Menu design for SCS 125th year Celebration Dinner, May 1960.

This menu, coming right at the tail end of post-war austerity was typical of the day and reminds us of a time when foreign foods were still mostly enjoyed in their countries of origin.

The toast, 'Stroud Choral Society 1835–1960' was proposed by Mr John Denison, CBE, Music Director of the Arts Council of Great Britain, and the response given by Mr Frank Miller, President of the Society. Mr Netlam Bigg proposed the toast of Stroud UDC and Stroud RDC. In replying, Councillor Thomas John, Chairman of Stroud Urban District Council, told the gathering that 'The local authority has the power to spend up to a 6d rate in promoting art and culture and a 1d rate in this authority produces £1000. While they are conscious of the need for supporting the arts it seems local authorities have not the courage to spend sufficient money in promoting them. I have the honour, or perhaps the misfortune, of being chairman of the Council's finance committee, and I think the amount we give is much too small.' The toast to the guests was given by Mr Stanley Sullings and the reply given by Mr Brian Dunn of the Arts Council and National Federation of Music Societies. Amongst the guests welcomed by Mr Sullings were Dr Herbert Sumsion, Lord Dickinson of Painswick and Captain T A K Maunsell, secretary of the National Federation of Music Societies.

At this celebration, by a curious oversight, the conductor and his wife were omitted from the seating at the top table. Amongst the officers of the Society and special guests at this table were orchestral performers who had been personal friends of the conductor at college. Many people were unhappy about this discourteous act and questions were later asked. In the committee minutes there is a carefully worded letter, dated July 1st 1960, written by Netlam Bigg, which reads as follows: 'At a recent meeting the committee gave careful consideration to the situation arising from the seating arrangements made for the recent Dinner. It was regretted that these arrangements had been the cause of some misunderstandings. Both the committee and Mr Foster unreservedly accepted the explanations which were given at the meeting and it was hoped that everybody would now regard this matter as being closed.' Mr Bigg may well have hoped that this matter was closed, but even today 40 years later, this unkind and unnecessary action is still spoken about with bitterness by members and retired members of this Society.

The celebrations for 1960 concluded in December with *Messiah* in the Parish Church in which 'eight hundred people stood deeply moved as the stirring strains of the triumphant *Hallelujah* Chorus echoed through the building'. The reviewer, R G was obviously impressed with a full congregation, but eight hundred people … ?

During his tenure as conductor Mark Foster encouraged the choir to think of taking performances to other parts of the county. *Messiah* was sung in Malmesbury Abbey on December 16th 1961. This must have been a successful event as the choir made arrangements in February to sing again at the Abbey on March 31st. 'Leave Merrywalks car park at 2.30pm. The committee asks members to bring their own food and the church at Malmesbury will provide tea.' This was to be a repeat performance of the *St John Passion,* which the choir had given earlier in Stroud Church on March 22nd. The notable soloists in the first concert were Iris Bourne, soprano, Wilfred Brown, tenor, and John Carol Case, bass. (In 1997, Mark Foster was presented with a national award, the Sir Charles Groves Prize for music making in the community.)

Just as the Society had got used to their talented new conductor, Mark Foster announced that he was relinquishing the post in order to take up a new position as Head of Music at Cirencester Grammar School (succeeding Peter Maxwell Davies). At the AGM in March 1962, when Mark Foster was presented with a cheque as an expression of thanks for his work during this three-year period, many members voiced their unhappiness at his going. One member was sure that the resignation had been due to the attitude of the Hon. Secretary, Mr Netlam Bigg.

Yet again, the Society had to look for a new conductor and this time the choice fell on Mr Eric Sanders, the Music master at Ross Grammar School. (When Mark Foster left Cirencester Grammar School in 1965 to become principal lecturer in music at St Paul's College, Cheltenham, Eric Sanders became Head of Music at Cirencester.) Once again the Society settled down quickly and happily with their new conductor. At the December 1962 concert of Christmas music, with April Cantelo taking the solos in Fleming's *Five Psalms* and in Mozart's *Exultate Jubilate,* everyone happily felt that the Society was once more back on course. R G reviewing for the *Stroud Journal* so enjoyed the Christmas selection that he felt he would like to hear the Choral Society singing in the Subscription rooms forecourt during the Christmas period – something that the Society has, even now, not got around to doing!

During 1963 and 1964 the choir enjoyed singing traditional oratorios, The Dream of Gerontius, Messiah and Mozart's Requiem Mass. Robert Tear, Barbara Robotham, Ronald Dowd, Roger Stalman, Wilfred Brown and Glenys Nelmes sang at these performances.

The second half of the March concert in 1964 was Benjamin Britten's St Nicolas. A fine performance, which was much enjoyed by the audience, the choir having been augmented by small choirs from Marling School and Stroud High School. After the performance a large bag of sweets was found in a pew and this was passed on to the three Marling boys who had sung the parts of 'The Pickled Boys'. At the AGM in March 1964 a letter from 'The Pickled Boys' was read out. The boys expressed their surprise and delight at receiving the sweets and apologised for a slight musical difficulty, which had occurred during the concert (cleverly overcome by the quick thinking of the conductor). They went on to say how much they had enjoyed singing in the concert and signed themselves, 'Your obedient servants, Marling School Trebles' (Patrick Dickinson, Keith Ricketts and Ivor Ward-Davies). Delighted by this letter, and no doubt with the hope of keeping up the interest of the young choristers, Netlam Bigg dispatched 'two large well filled' bags of sweets to the High School and Marling School choirs.

At this same AGM the Society members were told that, although most choral societies found their finances finely balanced on a 'razor's edge' the finances for the Society gave rise for optimism. Although The Dream of Gerontius had left the Society with a deficit of £59 6s 6d and Messiah a deficit of £9 6s 4d, the Mozart-Britten concert had made the 'formidable' total of £225 19s 5d. This was without the added totals of £100 for the sale of programmes, the honorary members' income of £56 and a grant from the National Federation of Music Societies for £100. However, Mr Sullings warned that as orchestral rates had gone up their next season's soloists rates would have to go up also. (In 1968–69 the following soloist rates were quoted: John Shirley-Quirk £110, Robert Tear £65, April Cantelo £60, Elizabeth Simon £55, John Carol Case £50, Kenneth Bowen £50, Barbara Robotham £45, Wilfred Brown £45, Roger Stalman £45, Honor Sheppard £40 and Elisabeth Holden £40.)

The programme for the Christmas Concert on December 10th 1964 was Ron Nelson's Christmas Story together with Christmas music and carols. 'What a joyful, jubilant prelude to Christmas was Stroud Choral Society's memorable presentation at Stroud Parish Church last Thursday evening' wrote the Stroud News and Journal critic. 'Under the superb direction of their conductor, Mr Eric Sanders, the choir improves all the time and last week they excelled in a brilliant performance.' Ron Nelson's Christmas Story was new to the Society. 'The score is up-to-date but easy on the ear and the use of brass is particularly stirring.' The narration was spoken by John F Evans of Gloucester 'unfaltering and to a soft accompaniment by the organist Claude Allen'. John Carol Case, the baritone soloist for Christmas Story, also sang with the choir during the carols. 'We all cleared our throats and, spurred on by Tony Hewitt-Jones' lively arrangements for the brass ensemble, sang with gusto the five congregational carols in the programme, ending with O Come All Ye Faithful.'

It was John Shirley-Quirk, the well known bass soloist who together with Honor Sheppard, soprano, Elisabeth Holden, alto, and Robert Tear, tenor, gave a 'truly magnificent' performance in Mendelssohn's Elijah on March 25th 1965. The reviewer states that they were 'first-class professional singers'. Again the choir was augmented by a semi chorus made up of singers from Stroud Girls' High School, Marling School and Wycliffe College. The reviewer makes the point that Elijah is second only in popularity to Messiah and having enjoyed a fantastic success when first performed in Birmingham, it has given joy ever since. (Unsurprisingly, Elijah is also the second most frequently performed work in the Society, having been sung 11 times since 1868.)

In December 1965 the Society sang a programme of Christmas music and carols together with Benjamin Britten's Rejoice in the Lamb. The reviewer was disappointed. He felt that Britten's cantata was not a particularly appropriate work. The programme notes tell us that the writer, Christopher Smart, a deeply religious, eighteenth century poet, wrote the text whilst in an asylum, and that 'it is chaotic in form but contains flashes of genius.'

The reviewer was much happier with the following year's St Matthew Passion given on March 31st 1966. It was an 'excellent performance, providing a deeply moving and spiritually refreshing experience.' Helped no doubt by the superb singing of John Carol Case and Kenneth Bowen in their parts of Christus and the Evangelist. The Stroud Girls' High School Choir, trained to perfection by Barbara Thorley, also took part. The review also makes reference to 'the

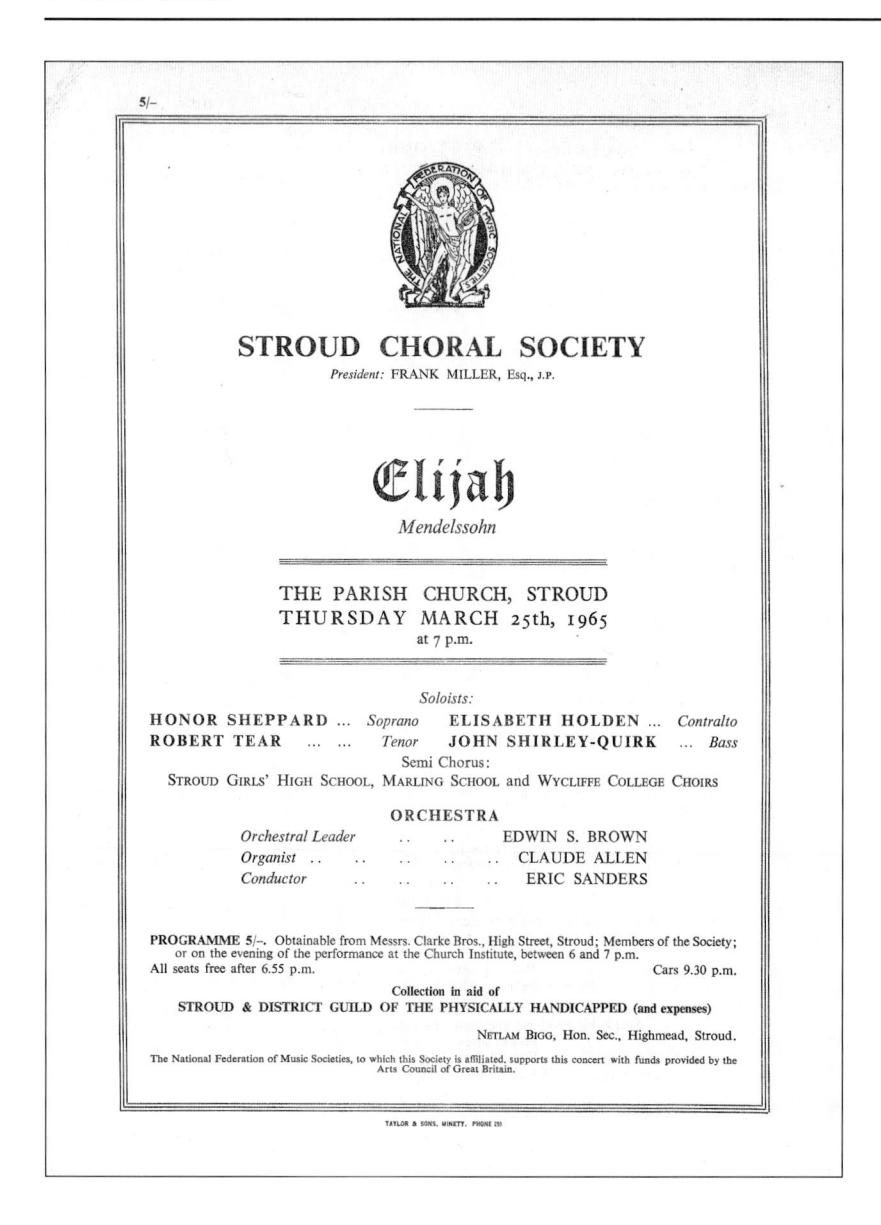

> **STROUD CHORAL SOCIETY**
> President: FRANK MILLER, Esq., J.P.
>
> **Elijah**
> *Mendelssohn*
>
> THE PARISH CHURCH, STROUD
> THURSDAY MARCH 25th, 1965
> at 7 p.m.
>
> Soloists:
> HONOR SHEPPARD ... *Soprano*   ELISABETH HOLDEN ... *Contralto*
> ROBERT TEAR ... *Tenor*   JOHN SHIRLEY-QUIRK ... *Bass*
>
> Semi Chorus:
> STROUD GIRLS' HIGH SCHOOL, MARLING SCHOOL and WYCLIFFE COLLEGE CHOIRS
>
> ORCHESTRA
> Orchestral Leader ... EDWIN S. BROWN
> Organist ... CLAUDE ALLEN
> Conductor ... ERIC SANDERS
>
> PROGRAMME 5/-. Obtainable from Messrs. Clarke Bros., High Street, Stroud; Members of the Society; or on the evening of the performance at the Church Institute, between 6 and 7 p.m.
> All seats free after 6.55 p.m.   Cars 9.30 p.m.
> Collection in aid of
> STROUD & DISTRICT GUILD OF THE PHYSICALLY HANDICAPPED (and expenses)
>
> NETLAM BIGG, Hon. Sec., Highmead, Stroud.
> The National Federation of Music Societies, to which this Society is affiliated, supports this concert with funds provided by the Arts Council of Great Britain.

versatile' County Music Adviser, Tony Hewitt-Jones at the harpsichord and his wife Anita at the cello. At previous concerts mention had been made of Tony Hewitt-Jones' 'lively arrangements' for the brass and timpani.

The concert for Christmas 1966 began with Bush's *Christmas Cantata*. Written in 1947, this cantata for soprano soloist and choir consists of settings of nine carols, five of which are based on traditional tunes. 'The choir sang with obvious enjoyment in this interesting and most acceptable work, while the pure and musical singing of Sheila Armstrong and the sensitive oboe playing of Laura Kane deserve high praise.' Bach's *Cantata no 51* for soprano, trumpet solo, orchestra and organ continuo followed, with soloists Sheila Armstrong and Malcolm Smith (trumpet). 'The audience had the advantage of an excellent translation of the German text in the programme.' Janet Edmunds, contralto, was accompanied by Claude Allen on the piano in a group of four songs. 'The first was a typically tuneful excerpt from Handel's *Solomon*.' The concert concluded with Vivaldi's *Gloria*. 'This fine and melodious work of praise, with solo singers of rare quality, made a most fitting climax to the evening's music making.' The reviewer TSW was far happier with this Christmas concert than the previous year's Christmas performance.

The Society was back on familiar territory with Handel when they sang *Israel in Egypt* on March 23rd 1967. 'This work was given a stirring performance at the Stroud Parish Church on Thursday by the Stroud Choral Society and the choir of the Stroud Girls' High School.' For the performance the soloists were Margaret Duckworth, contralto, Rosemary Thayer, soprano and Robert Tear, tenor. The oratorio is in two parts, the first telling of the plagues of Egypt and the oppression of the Israelites and the second part conveying praise and exultation in typical mighty, Handelian choruses. 'The two choirs, orchestra and organist nobly acquitted themselves in this great work ... This was oratorio in the best tradition and a most exciting musical experience.'

At the AGM four days later, the Society found themselves concerned yet again with money. The treasurer, Mr S Sullings, told the members that there was a total deficit of £112. The members were told that the loss was really to be expected because of the 'freeze' and also because the number of programmes sold had not been enough to cover the expense of the soloists and of engaging the orchestra. 'Thus the Society was not working on an economic basis.' However, Mr Sullings had 'high hopes for a brighter report' at the next AGM and there were sufficient reserve funds to carry them through the next season. Mr Netlam Bigg also pointed out that a drop in the honorary membership from 65 to 50 had not helped the financial situation. He hoped that a 'large scale drive would enable them to recruit more members who were always welcome'. The President, Mr Frank Miller, stressed the need for the arts to act as a balance 'in the practical, material world of today'.

Pleased with the format of their previous Christmas concerts the Society again chose a programme consisting of a cantata, Donald Cashmore's *This Child Behold*, followed by carols for choirs and congregation. Again, the Society was joined by Stroud High School senior choir with their conductor Barbara Thorley. 'The close association of the High School with the Choral Society, a development of recent years, is admirable in every way … They sang with a sweet purity of tone and clarity of enunciation which gave immense pleasure.' The reviewer remarks on the fact that the combined choirs numbered around 150 singers. Getting carried away with his arithmetic he continues: 'with this core of trained singers and congregation of around a thousand it was not surprising that the singing of the congregational carols was lifted high above the usual level.' For this concert the soloists were all local singers, Elizabeth Baker of Edge, Isobel Ridout of Cheltenham, Dennis Weaver of Thrupp and David Purcell of Cheltenham. 'It was a collection of musical talent drawn from the area immediately around Stroud, showing yet again how blessed we are in this way.' 'The Choral Society deserves well of Stroud and the large public response to their Christmas concert must have been encouraging. In spite of all the economic difficulties facing such organisations there is every indication that their future prospects are bright.'

In 1968 the choir prepared for Verdi's *Requiem*. This was to be performed on March 28th and was the third time in the choir's history that the *Requiem* had been sung. In a work that requires dramatic intensity, warm lyrical feeling, fierce climax and lightning changes of dynamics, the discipline and training of the choir by its conductor is paramount. The concert critic EMW praised Eric Sanders saying that he had been perfectly able to achieve all that was required of a good performance: 'I have rarely heard an amateur choir sing with such delicacy and lightness of touch in the pianissimo and staccato passages, nor with such style in the moments of climax.' The soprano soloist Elizabeth Simon was chided for not showing the same 'disciplined delicacy as the choir'. The mezzo-soprano Myra Sanders (wife of the conductor) was praised for her *Liber Scriptus*. The tenor, David Johnston, 'was excellent' and the bass soloist Christopher Keyte's 'quiet, unharrassed and uncluttered voice was a pleasure to hear'. All in all, a performance much enjoyed and appreciated by soloists, choir, orchestra, audience and above all, Eric Sanders, the conductor.

Closely following Verdi's *Requiem* in March, was a performance of Elis Pehkonen's recently written *Requiem* on May 2nd in the Parish Church. Elis Pehkonen was a 25-year-old assistant music master at Cirencester School, working under the direction of Eric Sanders. His requiem had been written in 1967 and first performed in Cirencester in March 1968. The *Requiem* was dedicated to Eric Sanders and this performance had been sponsored by the Stroud Choral Society. Choral members were asked to support the event and those who attended were treated to a unique choral experience. One of the features of the work was the use of three choruses – two semi-choruses and one full chorus – which were sung by 200 children from Cirencester School and Westwood's School, Northleach. There was a large percussion section including xylophones, vibraphones and glockenspiel. Tony Hewitt-Jones at the organ, unable to see the conductor's beat, used a girl pupil standing in the choir stalls to transmit it to him! The reviewer comments that Elis Pehkonen's technique 'comes, perhaps as a shock, but his work has a quality and scope which cannot fail to impress. If, at 25, he can arrange a vast work like this, what will he be doing twenty years hence?'

It was to come as a great shock to the Society, and to Cirencester School, when Eric Sanders at the early age of 43, died on July 28th 1968. He had been ill for only a few weeks. Members of the Society were quite stunned and many received the news with disbelief. It was not just the Stroud Choral Society who had lost a conductor but the Stroud Festival Choir and the Cheltenham Bach Choir. Netlam Bigg speaking on behalf of the Society said, 'Those who had performed under his direction had been thrilled to do so, and the concourse of music lovers in the county would grieve the passing of a man whose wonderful conception of music making had given such joy to so many.' Eric Sanders left a wife, Myra Sanders (a well known professional singer), and a baby daughter.

Once again the Society needed a new conductor. Many members of the committee wished to offer the post to Tony Hewitt-Jones but found themselves in an awkward situation. Tony Hewitt-Jones was County Music Adviser and seemingly not free to apply for the post. The committee did not want to advertise for the position until Mr Hewitt-Jones was free. After much deliberation the committee decided to ask Tony Hewitt-Jones to continue as a temporary conductor for the time being. The proposal, seconded by Mr J Cripps (the Society's new secretary), was carried 9 for, 1 against and 1 abstention.

STROUD SINGS

The December concert for 1968, Bach's *Sleepers Wake* and Britten's *St Nicolas* was performed with Tony Hewitt-Jones as its conductor. For the new conductor it was a wise choice of programme, a blend of old and new which both choir and audience were familiar with. Two of the soloists, Glenys Nelmes (soprano) and Barrie Thompson (bass) were well known and popular singers. The tenor Kenneth Woollam excelled in the Bach: 'a treat that will long linger in the memories of the large audience.' Again the choir was augmented with the semi-chorus from the Stroud High School who were conducted by Barbara Thorley. Again Marling School provided Michael and the three 'Pickled Boys' in the *St Nicolas*. (This time the parts of the 'Pickled Boys' were taken by three brothers Adam, and, twins James and Timothy Greaves.) The orchestra was led by Kenneth Page and the organ played by Claude Allen. The audience were warmly encouraged to join in with *O come, O come Emmanuel*, *All people that on earth do dwell* and *God moves in a mysterious way*. The reviewer found the concert 'a rousing and, quite seriously, thought provoking introduction to the Christmas season' and he found himself hoping that Mr Hewitt-Jones may find it possible to stay and direct the Choral Society for some time to come.

A short letter kept with the 1968 minutes also suggests that at this concert it was probably the first time that applause had been given in the church. The letter asks the secretary if there had been reactions to the introduction of applause: 'One assumes that the vicar and PCC did not oppose it, but some of the members of the Society found it distressing.' The writer hoped that the Society would be able to discuss this point when they met in the new year.

Early in 1969 the committee received a letter from the Herefordshire Community Council to say that in recognition of Eric Sanders' work in the county as conductor of the Police Choir, and as music master at Ross-on-Wye Grammar School, the council would award an Eric Sanders Memorial Prize. This would be in the form of a cash award to be given annually for the next 25 years. Each year at the Herefordshire Music Festival, the adjudicators would nominate a promising entrant from a selected group of classes. This proposal had the support of Mrs Myra Sanders, who had requested that this year the award should go to the most promising performer in the vocal classes.

At the committee meeting on January 31st 1969 a discussion was held about applause at concerts. It was agreed that there should be no applause at Eric Sanders' memorial concert in March and there would be a suitable request to this effect printed in the programme. Mr Hewitt-Jones reported that his six months' sabbatical leave had been brought forward and would now be taken from July to December 1969. This meant that the committee would have to find an acting conductor to begin the 1969–70 season. Richard Latham (director of music at King's School, Gloucester) was to be asked if he would undertake this work.

The chosen work for Eric Sanders' memorial concert was Brahms' *Requiem* and we learn from the programme notes that it was one of his favourite works. The concert took place on March 27th 1969 and was deemed to have been a 'magnificent performance' and a moving tribute to Eric Sanders. 'How deeply moving was the singing of the great passages of comfort from the scripture by the soloists, soprano Helen Greener (a young soloist singing for the first time in Stroud) and Richard Angas (bass) and the fine work of the chorus under the baton of Tony Hewitt-Jones.' 'The soloists gave much pleasure, not only with the technical quality of their work but also because of their obvious sympathy with the mood of Brahms' music. There will undoubtedly always be a warm welcome for them at Stroud.' The impressive orchestra led by Kenneth Page and Claude Allen's expressive organ playing completed this moving requiem.

At the AGM in April 1969 and on the eve of his 70th birthday, Netlam Bigg, secretary of the Choral Society for 35 years, retired. The President, Mr Frank Miller, said that Mr Bigg's name was synonymous with that of the Society. 'It was largely due to Mr Bigg and his association with the late Mr Samuel Underwood and with Mr Stanley Sullings, treasurer, that the Society had attained its present standing.' Netlam's 'incredible performance' over the years had proved a tower of strength to the Society. Mr Miller added that he couldn't speak too highly of the Society's regard for the work that Mr Bigg had done. Netlam and his wife Margaret were presented with a record player by the members of the Society. (Mr John Cripps, who had been assistant secretary for several years, was then elected as secretary.)

In September 1969 the Choral Society unanimously elected Netlam Bigg a Life Member in recognition of his 'sterling work as honorary secretary for 35 years'.

The Christmas concert on December 11th 1969 was a mixture of traditional carols together with Britten's *Ceremony of Carols* and Bach's cantata *Sing Ye the Lord*. This great contrast of styles gave the choir and their conductor Richard Latham plenty of scope for displaying their talents. 'The balance of the singing was generally excellent and the interpretation certainly conveyed the spirit of the music.' The harpist Susan Drake accompanied the choir.

The decade of the 70s was to usher in a new era for the Society. As the links with the old, solid, even Victorian, ethos were broken and the old formalities lessened, a conscious effort was made by the committee to change the feel of the Society from that of a singing class undergoing instruction to one of an association with a corporate character.

Tony Hewitt-Jones had now returned to the Society. He had been studying composition in Paris with the famous teacher Nadia Boulanger. Under his baton a 'convincing and moving performance of Dvorak's *Stabat Mater* was given on March 21st 1970. A stickler for detail, Mr Hewitt-Jones is setting the Choral Society a very high standard which becomes increasingly reminiscent of that other outstanding Choral conductor, the Late Mr Samuel Underwood' quoted the *Journal* reviewer.

In December 1970 the Christmas concert was a pleasing mix of the old and new and comprised of Vaughan Williams' *Fantasia on Christmas Carols*, Britten's *Festival Te Deum* and *Christmas Rounds* composed by the conductor. (We learn from the review that the conductor and his wife had formed the delightful habit of composing musical Christmas rounds and sending them to their friends as Christmas cards.) The baritone Martin Oram pleased the audience with his selection of solo carols and in particular his singing of Cornelius' *The Three Kings* and Coates' *The Calypso Carol,* and 'the clear and sweet soprano voice of Glenys Nelmes' came over well in the Britten's *Festival Te Deum*. Tony Hewitt-Jones enthusiastically and warmly conducted the congregation in *The First Nowell* and *Hark the Herald Angels* in such a way 'as to drive away any lingering power cut blues'.

The following day, December 11th 1970, Frank Miller, the Society's President came into the possession of a black ebony baton, decorated each end with silver and bearing an inscribed plate. This was the baton presented to James Chew in 1850 and found by Howard Beard in a local antique shop. Little by little, the past history of the Society was revealing itself and it was not to be long before a Society member, Mr Leonard Keck, decided to investigate the Society's history further.

The winds of change blew early in 1971 with the arrival of decimalisation. The concert programme for Haydn's *Creation* was priced at 25p and 50p instead of 5s and 10s. The Society was also reminded that in July 1972 the school leaving age would rise from 15 years to 16 years. It was felt that the Society should use 1971 as a campaigning year to encourage those in this extra year at school to think of joining adult societies.

In the autumn of 1971 the Stroud Festival celebrated 25 years of existence. The Choral Society sang Haydn's *Achieved is the Glorious Work* at the closing service of the Festival on October 24th 1971 at the Bedford St Congregational Church.

In November of that year, the Vicar of Stroud, the Rev Peter Minall found himself in disagreement with the new fire regulations demanded for performances held in the Parish Church. The fire regulations stipulated that the south doors had to be open throughout a performance. Failing that, the doors should be changed so that they could be opened outwards in an emergency. Both the Choral committee and the Festival committee wrote to the Vicar saying that they were willing to contribute to the cost of the alteration to the doors. Mr Minall had other ideas. He felt that the cost of work, which had been estimated at £70–£80 was not acceptable. He told the Fire Inspector that he proposed to station stewards at both the south door of the Church and at the Tower door with full instructions on what to do in an emergency! He would, however, comply with the request not to place any extra seats in the aisles either at choral concerts or at Festival plays.

Bach's *Christmas Oratorio* on December 9th 1971 (programme 30p and 60p) completed a successful year for the Society. Young soloists (with Gloucestershire backgrounds) Penelope Birtles, soprano, and Sarah Walker, alto, together with Charles Corp, tenor, delighted the audience. Ysobel Danks led the orchestra which included in its ranks her husband Alexander Kok, the celebrated cellist, and the oboist Celia Nicklin.

1972 dawned with a national fuel crisis affecting most of Great Britain. Many evening classes and other functions were closed. The committee set out to find a way round the problem. Mr and Mrs Miller offered their home as a

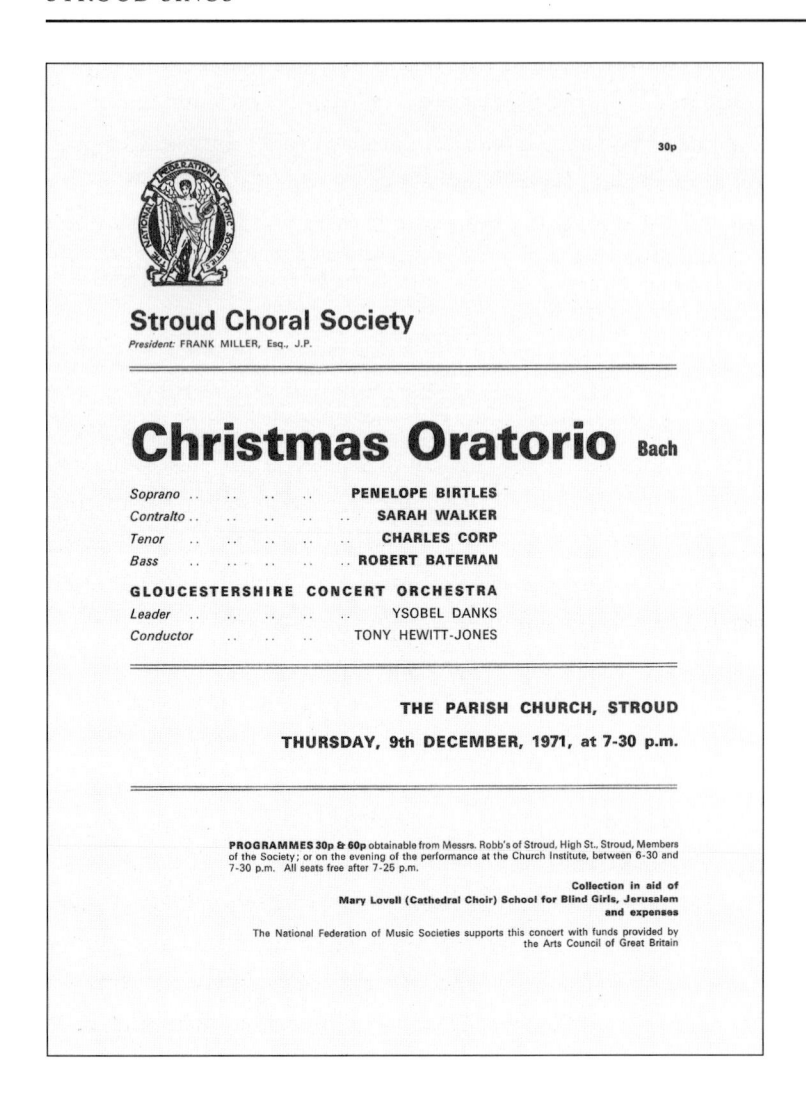

> **Stroud Choral Society**
> President: FRANK MILLER, Esq., J.P.
>
> # Christmas Oratorio Bach
>
> | | |
> |---|---|
> | Soprano | PENELOPE BIRTLES |
> | Contralto | SARAH WALKER |
> | Tenor | CHARLES CORP |
> | Bass | ROBERT BATEMAN |
>
> **GLOUCESTERSHIRE CONCERT ORCHESTRA**
> Leader .. YSOBEL DANKS
> Conductor .. TONY HEWITT-JONES
>
> THE PARISH CHURCH, STROUD
> THURSDAY, 9th DECEMBER, 1971, at 7-30 p.m.
>
> PROGRAMMES 30p & 60p obtainable from Messrs. Robb's of Stroud, High St., Stroud, Members of the Society; or on the evening of the performance at the Church Institute, between 6-30 and 7-30 p.m. All seats free after 7-25 p.m.
> Collection in aid of
> Mary Lovell (Cathedral Choir) School for Blind Girls, Jerusalem and expenses
> The National Federation of Music Societies supports this concert with funds provided by the Arts Council of Great Britain

venue and the sopranos and altos alternated with the tenors and basses on successive Mondays. Fortunately after February 28th restrictions were lifted and rehearsals returned to normal.

The concert on March 23rd 1972 was Handel's *Passion of Christ* and Vaughan Williams' *Mass in G Minor* and was billed as a 'colourful and challenging concert.' Local soloists were chosen, including Glenys Nelmes, soprano, Dennis Weaver, tenor, Frank Miller and John Cripps as bass. In an unusual, but most important departure from the norm, the orchestra led by Farhad Moayedi was a section of the Gloucestershire Youth Orchestra. The Vaughan Williams' *Mass* was to celebrate the centenary of his birth. Later on in June 1972 members of the Society sang at Gloucester Cathedral in a concert to commemorate the Vaughan Williams centenary.

The Choral Society were invited by the BBC to take part in a recording of 'Sunday Half Hour' on July 17th 1972 (to be broadcast on September 3rd). It was hoped that members of the choir would lead the singing and also give an anthem. The music chosen was the *Sanctus* and *Hosanna* from Vaughan Williams' *Mass in G Minor*. The Society was delighted to take part in this event. Unfortunately many people were away and the honour of the Society fell to the small group of choral members who could attend. Leonard Keck was now acting secretary and the minutes for the year 1972 are dotted with copies of the careful letters of enquiry that he wrote to many people and organisations in his research into the history of the Society.

In a 'first' experience for the Society, and probably also the Catholic community, the Choir had received an invitation to take part in the celebration of Mass at the Church of the Immaculate Conception, Beeches Green, Stroud, on Sunday October 15th 1972. The members of the Society sang the Vaughan Williams' *Mass in G Minor* under the baton of Tony Hewitt-Jones in a very beautiful and moving service. Claude Allen was the organist. Afterwards refreshments were provided in the Parish Hall, and members of both the Society and the Catholic community enjoyed and appreciated coming together in this friendly manner. It was not until the decade of the 90s that the Society again sang at Beeches Green.

In November of that year Leonard Keck hosted two evenings for choir members at his home, Tracy House, Houndscroft. On November 6th and November 23rd, members were treated to excellent hospitality, and were able to listen to records and enjoy a delicious buffet. Leonard believed very strongly in the ethos of the Society and was anxious that choral members should get to know each other better. No doubt, some of his feeling of great affection for the choir and its singers stemmed from the research that he was doing into the Choral history.

The calendar year closed with *Messiah* given on December 7th 1972. We learn that the Choral Society had chosen to 'break away from the long established interpretation of this well-known work and was using a recent edition by Watkins Shaw'. The performance was a complete one, with only one of the conventional repeats omitted. The other things that the audience may also have been surprised about according to the reviewer were 'the high speeds that Tony Hewitt-Jones employed in the first three parts which were justifiable and musically satisfying, even if they were unfamiliar'. Also unfamiliar was Mark Deller the counter-tenor (son of the famous counter-tenor, Alfred Deller), who sang the contralto solo part with great success. The reviewer felt that in many instances the use of a counter-tenor instead of the contralto gave a clearer interpretation. The Gloucester Concert Orchestra which included Alexander Kok, cello continuo, was led by Ysobel Danks. After the concert, Leonard Keck wrote to every member of the Society to thank them for their support and hard work and to say how much it was appreciated. After reminding them that the new term would start on January 15th, he wished them all 'a Happy Christmas and Good Health and Blessings for 1973'.

The new year 1973 brought further changes and challenges for the Society. To begin the year the choir started to rehearse the libretto *The Battle of Tewkesbury* (words by Anthony Richards and music by Tony Hewitt-Jones). The libretto gives a vivid account of the Battle and events preceding and following it, dwelling in particular on the desecration of the Abbey by the victorious Yorkist troops and the execution of Lancastrians in spite of Edward's promise of mercy. Finally it tells of the eventual reconsecration of the Abbey. The libretto had been written for the Tewkesbury Festival in 1971 which was the 500th anniversary of the Battle of Tewkesbury. The Society found the work difficult with the weekly rehearsals becoming a battle in themselves. It took a while to create the right evocative feeling before this particular mediaeval battle could be appreciated.

The concert was given on April 5th 1973, and singing with the Society in *The Battle of Tewkesbury* were a semi-chorus of boys from Tewkesbury Abbey and Cheltenham Grammar School. The tenor Neil Jenkins gave another fine performance. The concert also included Sumsion's *Festival Benedicite*. Dr Sumsion, now retired and living in Rodborough since 1967, was present at this performance.

In spite of Mr Keck's best attempts at uniting the choir with social functions the one arranged for April was cancelled through lack of support. At the AGM in April it was revealed that, although the Society had a singing membership of 105, the average weekly attendance was only 65. Mr Keck felt that the Choral Society had 'no identity, no aim, no money and no library and its only assets were the members'. One thing that the Society was united in was the proposed change of concert evening from Thursday to Saturday, a motion that was passed unanimously. Also at this AGM it was decided that the 'sugar bowl' contributions would be raised from 6d to 5p. In future, takings from the 'sugar bowl' were to be announced each week in relation to the numbers present! To brighten the evening the Society was told that the finances were in balance by £87.39. Mr Keck who was now 'active' honorary secretary instead of 'acting' secretary (due to John Cripps' move to London) was happy to announce that his Handbook on the History of the Society would be printed and ready to buy in the autumn. The committee members of April 1973 were President, Mr Frank Miller, conductor Tony Hewitt-Jones, treasurer Stanley Sullings, secretary Leonard Keck, together with Mrs J Wilson, Mrs E Baxter, Mrs K Sandells, Mr N Bigg, Mr R Jones, Miss J Ryland, Mr G Taylor, Mr J Harrold, Mrs M Whiting and Mr P Heymans.

The problem of a concert hall had not gone away, but during this year a feasibility study was undertaken to look into the possibility of building a concert hall on land near to the bus station in Stroud. The choral committee donated £25 toward the cost of this study. The organisation undertaking this work called themselves 'Stroud District Centre Feasibility Study,' President Sir John Marling OBE and Secretary W M F Oliver.

As the Society was run as a Further Educational Evening class it had to submit details of its forthcoming programme of study to the County Education Office in Shire Hall, Gloucester, for approval. Shire Hall had to be notified of any change in the proposed programme. Attendance registers were supposed to be strictly kept and returned to the appropriate office at Shire Hall. The Society always seemed to need chasing for their attendance returns. The Education Office was generating even then a considerable amount of paperwork to do with dates, venues, length of sessions, number of sessions per term (12) and the payment of the conductor (£1.59 a session), the pianist (£1 per session) and the small remuneration paid to the person who kept the register (£8 yearly). Organisations were warned that school children could not attend evening classes unless they were aged 15 on February 1st in any year, and then only with the approval of the Head*master* of the secondary school!

The BBC approached the Society about another 'Sunday Half Hour' for transmission on December 9th 1973. Apparently the BBC felt that the previous one had been 'extremely good'. Tony Hewitt-Jones was happy to comply and signed the choir up for rehearsal on Wednesday October 24th and for recording on Wednesday 31st.

Leonard Keck's 'History of the Stroud Choral Society', 750 copies at a cost of £200, was ready for sale by November 1973. The purchase price was £1 and all proceeds went to the Society. Many members were delighted with this tantalising glimpse into the Society's past, other members were not so sure. One letter on file reads: 'I do not wish to renew my subscription as an honorary member of Stroud Choral Society. I view the dispatch of the Handbook with disquiet as I wonder whether your limited resources could have been put to better effect, and in consequence I do not feel able to support you and I am returning same.' Answering the letter Mr Keck politely pointed out: 'the production of the Handbook is entirely mine, in cost and time and in research. It has taken me nearly two years and the Society will have no costs to face. When I became secretary I felt there was a great need to put the records in order, to preserve those that we had and put them into some permanent form for the benefit of the Society now and in the future. I hope it has not been in vain, and the Handbook will prove a valuable addition to its archive I have no doubt. I mention all this with extreme reluctance. I would have preferred to have kept myself out. But you were not to know. Nevertheless, I respect your decision, and I hope I have been able to correct your feelings. I am returning the cost of the postage which you should not have to face.'

Other letters to the committee about the History were much more complimentary. One from Dr Herbert Sumsion thought that the book would be greatly appreciated and would be particularly valuable for future reference on the history of the Society. A statement with which the present day Society members wholeheartedly concur!

The petrol and heating oil crisis may have been responsible for a smaller than usual audience at the concert on December 8th 1973. The reviewer feared that church heating difficulties may have deterred some listeners. (The Arab oil embargo, as a result of the Arab–Israeli war earlier in the year, had caused a tremendous rise in the cost of both petrol and heating oil. This difficult situation was later also compounded by the miners' strike.) Those who were present at the concert enjoyed the Bach Motet *Jesu, Priceless Treasure,* a selection of carols arranged by David Willcocks and Malcolm Sargent and Byrd's *Mass for Four Voices* which was sung unaccompanied. 'Toward the end of the work the choir were beginning to show signs of tiredness, but they never seemed to have difficulties with the pitch. It was a most acceptable performance, its English conception making an interesting comparison with that of a German choir in the Parish Church some few years ago.'

Early in 1974 Leonard Keck again invited the Society members to an evening of hospitality at his home in Houndscroft, Stroud. More than 75 members of the Society accepted this kind invitation which again took place over two evenings. Members who attended these gatherings recall the friendly welcome and the wonderful food that the Keck family gave them.

On the agenda of the first committee meeting of 1974 was an item agreeing that the experimental change of concert day from Thursday to Saturday had on the whole been a success with the members. In particular the full afternoon rehearsal had been appreciated by all. Another change of image that members were now considering was the possibility of becoming an independent Society as opposed to an evening class.

Tony Hewitt-Jones' choice of Tippett's *A Child of our Time* for the concert on March 30th 1974 was a very personal one. In January 1944, Tony Hewitt-Jones, as a young man of 18 and before going up to Oxford, joined the choir of Morley College, London. He found them rehearsing a strange but fascinating new work which was being conducted by its composer, the Director of Music at that college, Michael Tippett. Tony Hewitt-Jones found himself so overwhelmed by this particular, never to be forgotten experience, that he decided that somehow, he would learn to compose and conduct. In *A Child of our Time* the composer, who was also the librettist, is concerned with the great problem of man's inhumanity to man and it was very much a piece apposite for its time.

Having decided that he would change his course of study from Modern Language to Music when he went up to Christ Church, Oxford, Tony first had to make a small career diversion by being called up to serve in the navy. Here he was trained to interpret signals from German torpedo boats. After the Normandy landings, he was used as an interpreter and was finally stationed at Cuxhaven in Germany where he issued dock passes and translated in a military court. One could well understand the desire that as soon as possible he would want to rehearse Tippett's work with the Choral Society. Although the Society found this a difficult piece to learn, perseverance brought its own reward in understanding and enjoyment. The young soloists, Barbara Yates, soprano, Sylvia Swan, contralto, John Steel, tenor, and David Read, bass, who had so delighted their audience in Dvorak's *Stabat Mater* in 1970, were asked back to sing in this concert. Michael Tippett was also invited to attend. The reviewer comments on the extreme difficulty of the music, 'much of it seemingly having no connection with our accepted keys or harmonies. With so many apparently unrelated sounds going on in choir and orchestra the choir gave the impression of strain in places.' However, the reviewer did feel that 'much credit is due to the choir for their successes.' The Gloucestershire Concert Orchestra was led at short notice by Kathleen Malet, standing in for Ysobel Danks.

On April 8th 1974 the Society held an Extraordinary General Meeting in the Trinity Rooms, Stroud. The committee wished to discuss with the members the possibility of becoming an independent society. The advantages of choosing the length of the evening rehearsals and the length of term were discussed together with finances. The following amendment was carried unanimously:

> Amendment 6b. The meeting should accept, in principle, that the Society become independent with the proviso that the Committee should establish the economic feasibility of such a move.

The proposal to lengthen the evening rehearsal to two hours was passed unanimously, and a proposal to carry on singing through April, May and June received a majority vote. The committee 'came to the conclusion that it would be better' to continue as an evening class for the next season 1974/75 while still working on the proposal of becoming independent the following year.

Meanwhile the Stroud Feasibility Study on a concert hall for Stroud had taken an alarming turn. The President was asked to write to the Stroud District Council to the effect that in the opinion of the committee the Cotswold Players project should not take precedence over the planning of a new hall for Stroud. It was also their opinion that the building of a hall on the site of Bath Street was preferable to the alteration of the Subscription Rooms. The feasibility committee had asked for more money for the study and the Society sent a further £25.

In October 1974 Frank Miller died and the Society unanimously elected Leonard Keck as their new President. Shortly afterwards the committee received a letter from Lord Dickinson kindly offering his services for this post. Frank Miller had discussed his illness with Lord Dickinson earlier in the autumn with a view to Lord Dickinson becoming acting President during Frank's illness. Frank Miller had been President of the Society since 1957. The committee wrote to Lord Dickinson and thanked him for his kind offer, explaining that the Society had already elected Mr Keck.

Mr Keck, as ever, taking the needs of the Society close to his heart, wrote to all the members immediately after the final rehearsal for the Christmas Concert, just five days before the performance. 'There must have been a feeling of keen disappointment, and even despondency at the standard we achieved – it was too bad to be true. The attendance fell below the numbers expected on such an important night, and when this occurs the singing suffers and anxiety increases.' He goes on to gently persuade the members not to lose heart but to pursue the aim of a good choral society with diligence and enthusiasm.

We have been unable to find a review for the concert, Bush's *Christmas Cantata*, Mozart's *Exultate, Jubilate* and Holst's *Christmas Day* which took place on December 14th 1974. However, many good concerts are preceded by disastrous last rehearsals and Tony Hewitt-Jones was later to say how pleased he had been with the choir's unaccompanied singing at the performance.

In January 1975 the Society received a setback in their efforts to have a new concert hall built in or near Stroud, when the acting chairman, John Harrold, read out a letter from the Stroud District Council. This letter stated that the Stroud District Centre Committee felt that 'it was not possible at present to assist in the provision of the type of project envisaged in the report, for a number of reasons not least of which are financial'. They went on to say that when it became possible to reconsider the project, the views of the Choral Society would be made known to the committee.

A wine and cheese social event that Leonard Keck arranged for March displeased the vicar who wrote to say that he was surprised to find that such an event had been organised to take place during Lent.

During the early months of 1975 many extra committee meetings took place to discuss and set out the change of constitution for the Choral Society. The National Federation of Music Societies was helpful with relevant advice and a model constitution. Leonard Keck wrote to all the members in early March 1975 giving a progress report. He told them that the motion that would be put before the members at the AGM would be 'That the present Choral Society shall cease to be an evening class under the auspices of the Gloucestershire County Council and shall become an independent Choral Society, subject to the aims and rules contained in this report.' The letter ended in a typical Keck way: 'This will enable the Society to enter new areas of achievement so that we can together say, "The best is yet to come".'

Handel's *Judas Maccabaeus* was sung in the Parish Church on March 22nd 1975. 'The Choral Society represented the various situations admirably, and they sang with precision. They were ably partnered by the Gloucestershire Concert Orchestra who played well in spite of a few untidy moments. The work had been quite drastically cut, even so, it ran for rather over two hours, and the performance was long enough,' wrote the reviewer.

On March 24th 1975 at the AGM the Society unanimously adopted the proposal to become independent. At this altogether much more upbeat AGM, the members also discovered that the Society finances were in a reasonably healthy state due, some people felt, partly to the sale of the Society Handbook. The Society also received a legacy of £300 from the will of the late Miss Underwood, Sammy Underwood's sister. At the same meeting Mrs Joan Miller presented a cheque for £100 which her husband had bequeathed to the Society. The members themselves, enthusiastic about reclaiming 'their' Society, had also become adept at raising money. Raffles, jumble sales, social events and the President's Evening had raised £100.

At the meeting Mr Keck was unanimously re-elected as President. Other members of the committee were secretary, Sheila Adams, treasurer Jim Wilson, minutes secretary Joan Wilson, together with Mrs Baxter, K Sandells, N Bigg, J Harrold, P Heymans, T Jones, S Sullings, R Wesley, R Wicks and T Jones.

Rejoicing in their new-found freedom, the Society promptly decided upon an extra concert for June. This was to be called a Summer Serenade and was to be a concert of 'lighter' music to include Brahms' *Songs of Love*, Yugoslav Folk Songs and Moeran's *Songs of Springtime*. Ernest Tucker and Claude Allen would play a Beethoven duet. The Cheltenham Chamber Music Group, Ysobel Danks, violin, Alexander Kok, cello, and Douglas Smith, piano would also appear in the programme.

The year was completed with a concert on December 13th to include Buxtehude's *A New-Born Infant*, Charpentier's *Midnight Mass* and Carols for all. This was a 'home grown' concert, using no outside soloists but the conductor had made up for this by choosing Christmas music of very differing styles. The reviewer particularly liked the seventeenth-century composition *A New-Born Infant* finding the interspersion of organ and singing 'extremely attractive'.

The Choral Society began 1976 by rehearsing a newly commissioned work, *Return From a Far Country*. This work, with music by Tony Hewitt-Jones, and libretto by Anthony Richards, had been specially commissioned by Leonard Keck for the Stroud Choral Society. In spite of the work proving difficult to learn, attendance at rehearsals was up and members were obviously making a special effort to produce a successful concert. Not only were the choir carefully preparing for this concert, but it was also arranged that the church bells would be rung for one hour before the concert started and that the clock striker would be disconnected for the duration of the performance. Together with Vaughan Williams' *O Clap Your Hands* and Handel's *Zadok the Priest*, Hewitt-Jones' *Return From A Far Country* received its first performance on April 24th 1976. The reviewer, Farleigh Price (*Citizen*) wrote: '*Return From a Far Country* for soloist, chorus, wind ensemble and percussion was firmly conducted by the composer, Tony Hewitt-Jones and proved an interesting work providing remarkable instrumental and vocal effects. Difficult to perform it was nevertheless rendered with praiseworthy confidence and ability by all concerned and the audience was unstinting in its expression of appreciation.' Much praise was also given to the soloists, Neil Jenkins, tenor and Matthew Clifford, treble.

Later, in June 1976 the Society gave their second Summer Serenade with a programme which included Elgar's *From the Bavarian Highlands*, and Vaughan Williams' *Five English Folk Songs*. Ernest Tucker and Claude Allen again gave a piano duet, but the highlight of the evening was an arrangement for six hands and one piano, played with great verve and enjoyment by Messrs Hewitt-Jones, Tucker and Allen.

As the year ended, with Vivaldi's *Gloria*, Pergolesi's *Magnificat* and excerpts from *Messiah* given to a large audience in the Parish Church on Saturday December 11th, the members felt that they had claimed back their Society with assurance and certainty.

1977 was to be a year of further changes. The members of the Society were soon to learn that Tony Hewitt-Jones wanted to retire at the end of the season. The committee had known this for some while and had been actively researching a new conductor during the previous year. The new conductor was to be David Fysh who was currently

Head of Music at Wycliffe College Junior School. David Fysh had pleased the members of the Society with his pleasant style when he took a trial rehearsal on February 21st.

Tony Hewitt-Jones' swansong was to be Mendelssohn's *Elijah* performed on April 2nd 1977. There was to be an eminent cast of soloists led by a soprano of international repute, April Cantelo. Shirley Minty, contralto, Michael Hartley, tenor, Antony Ransome, bass, who together with Craig Jackson, a young treble, from Tetbury Parish Church took the other solo parts. JT reviewing the concert, also gave high praise to a group of soloists from the chorus, Glenys Nelmes and Jean Lea, sopranos, Valerie Wicks and Mabel Horle, contraltos, whose very pleasing performance in *Holy, holy, holy,* delighted the audience. The reviewer was pleased to find *Elijah* back in production. Having once been a regular item performed by many societies he felt that 'its scores have been collecting dust on the book shelves for many years' (it was previously produced by the Society in 1965). J T felt it was a welcome revival of an old favourite. The chorus thoroughly enjoyed themselves. The Gloucestershire Concert Orchestra, led by Kenneth Moore played to a high standard throughout. The conductor's judgment and interpretation was unquestionable. 'We are truly grateful for the opportunity to hear *Elijah* again.'

At the AGM on April 4th, Tony Hewitt-Jones officially retired. Leonard Keck, reviewing Tony's 'decade of loyal and devoted service' said that he had never spared himself in furthering the Society's interests and that Tony's musicianship had been second to none. 'No doubt, from time to time, he had found his task difficult and frustrating, but he gave his outstanding talents generously with humility and good humour.' Later at a special social evening on April 28th, Leonard Keck presented a cheque and coffee table to Tony on behalf of the Society.

Partly because of activities to celebrate the Queen's Silver Jubilee, partly because Tony had retired, and partly because David Fysh had other ideas, the Summer Serenade did not take place. Instead the choir was invited to attend music workshops, through May and June at Wycliffe Jumior School to get a head start on the music for the 1977–78 season.

No sooner were the Society's annual minutes files reduced to a third of their previous size, than the Performing Rights Society threatened to take over where the Education Office had left off. They would be pleased to have full programme details of the Society's concerts from December 14th 1974. They had been checking their files and found the Society missing! The Secretary, Sheila Adams promptly replied. By return, the Performing Rights Society were back: they needed editors, translators, English text or otherwise, and publishers. Some of this information proved elusive and

Leonard Keck (right), President of SCS, presents a coffee table and cheque to Tony Hewitt-Jones as a mark of the members' appreciation on Tony's retirement in April 1977.

it was an incomplete return that was sent in October 1977, having failed to persuade the publishers of Buxtehude's *A New-Born Infant* to come clean on its editor and translator.

The final change of 1977 was to alter the concert day back to a Thursday! David Fysh felt it was difficult to attract soloists for Saturday evening performances. The year finished with a most successful concert on Thursday December 8th. Joining the choir were the girls of Stroud High School Junior Choir with their conductor Geraldine Brown. Fittingly enough the soprano and contralto soloists, Carolyn Cook and Vivien Price, were both former pupils of the Girls' High School. The concert was a pleasing mixture of traditional and modern carols, together with Vivaldi's *Gloria*. Carolyn Cook, singing a group of songs by Purcell, Fauré and Mozart, was particularly praised in her singing of Purcell's *The Blessed Virgin's Expostulation*.

Stroud Choral Society
Estimates for the Season 1977–78.

Receipts	£	Payments	£
Admissions	192	Professional fees,	680
Christmas	150	including conductor & Accompanist	
Easter	80	Hall, Church, staging &c	270
Hon. Members	15	Programmes, tickets & advertising	100
Programmes	40	Administration	60
Stroud D. Council	563	Miscellaneous	40
Members subs.	145		
N.F.M.S.	30		
Donations	49		
Bank Interest	80		
Social	10		
Miscellaneous			
	1354		**1150**

Reserve at beginning of season	£732
Estimated surplus for season	£204
Estimates reserve at end of season	£936

25th Jan. 1978

There was considerable interest in Stroud when, early in 1978, the BBC announced that it would be filming 'Songs of Praise' from the Parish Church. The service was to be recorded on February 28th and televised on Sunday April 16th. The novelty of appearing 'on the box' was irresistible and tickets were issued both for the rehearsal and the recording. Choirs from local churches together with the Stroud Girls' High School Senior Choir and Stroud Choral Society were invited to attend. The conductor Harry Lyall took all the rehearsals and the recording. In the programme notes choirs were advised to watch the conductor and if he couldn't be seen, then to take the lead from the organist Claude Allen. (So even the BBC had difficulties with positioning the conductor in the Parish Church.) The programme notes sternly advised the participants to 'Ignore the cameras.' The choirs sang separate verses in *Lift high the cross*, *God is working his purpose out*, *Angel Voices ever singing* and *O Thou who camest from above*. Stroud High School Choir gave a solo performance in *Saviour again to thy dear name we raise*. The sound engineers had no problem with the girls' beautiful clear voices, but the cerise and white stripes of the High School blouses caused the camera crew considerable problems! Later, a long-playing record of 'Songs of Praise', taken straight from the broadcast and produced by Cathedral Sounds Ltd, was available for purchase at the Stroud Music Centre at a cost of £2.75. Nowadays, of course, we would just press the button on the video control …

A month after the broadcast of 'Songs of Praise' the choir sang Bach's *St John Passion* in the Parish Church. The Society had assembled an outstanding team of soloists of international repute for the performance with Rogers

Covey-Crump, the Evangelist, Michael George as Christus, Graham Titus, baritone, Susan Campbell, soprano, and Doreen Walker, contralto. J T reviewing in the *Stroud News and Journal* particularly praised the clarity of the fine solo singing in what he acknowledged to be a building with difficult acoustics.

During the year Leonard Keck had been unavoidably absent from some committee meetings and Society activities due to recurring ill health. But whenever possible, he joined in. His cheerful disposition and willingness to work, whether writing letters, speaking on the Society's behalf, or moving furniture for rehearsals and concerts, hid his struggle with leukaemia from many people. He was able to chair a committee meeting in late September but this was his last formal act for the Society. He died on November 22nd on his 74th birthday. It was a great loss. Sheila Adams in her secretarial report in March 1975 in giving thanks to Mr Keck wrote the following: 'his enthusiasm, energy and work for this Society never fails to amaze us and we look to him with respect, affection and admiration in his strivings to make Stroud Choral a happy successful Society.' Although written two years before Mr Keck's death, it exactly summed up the feelings of the Society.

It was a saddened Society that gave the Christmas concert on December 16th 1978. The programme of Christmas music and carols spanned many centuries from the oldest, *Of the Father's heart begotten*, words written in the fourth century, to Rutter's new *Star* and *Donkey* carols. The Rutter carols were part of a group sung by Stroud High School Junior Choir, conducted by Geraldine Brown and 'accompanied beautifully' by Caroline Chew. The main work was Vaughan Williams' *Fantasia on Christmas Carols*. Barrie Thomson, a master at King's School and Cathedral Lay-Clerk, was the baritone soloist.

In February 1979, Mr R A Y Wesley was nominated and elected as the next Society President. Later, his wife Margaret would be the Music Librarian for the Society. These were the first changes in a year that would hold some more surprises for the Society.

On April 7th 1979, Brahms' *German Requiem* was given in the Parish Church in memory of Leonard Alden Keck. Brahms wrote the *Requiem* partly as a commemoration of the dead but also as a comfort for those who mourn. It is a beautiful work with inspired melodies and the soloists Anne Hodges, soprano, and Robert Bateman, baritone, sang 'with attractive voices and very pleasing interpretations'. The orchestral accompaniment was provided by the Gloucester Concert Orchestra, led by Ysobel Danks. For this performance, the organ was not used, apparently owing to difficulties 'caused by distance'. The reviewer missed it!

The programme cover for Brahms' *Requiem* was printed with the new Society logo. This had been designed by Jack Seymour, Head of Art at Archway School. Leonard Keck would have been pleased with this symbol of choral unity. (Prior to this, the Society had sometimes used the crest of the National Federation of Music Societies on their programme covers.)

SCS logo designed by Jack Seymour 1978.

A new era

Nabucco was an excellent concert, the most polished performance that this Society has given since I have been your Conductor.

Eddie Garrard, AGM May 1981.

During several committee meetings in May 1979, anxious discussions took place on the appointment of a new conductor. David Fysh had told the committee that he couldn't continue after June 30th. Many names were put forward as possible conductors but in the end, just three people were asked to take trial rehearsals. For the first time in the history of the Society the choral members were going to be allowed to give their opinions on the appointment of their next conductor! After three lively rehearsals with three good conductors, the Society chose Edward Garrard from Dursley. Just to add to the difficulties of choosing a new conductor, the Church Institute had been out of use due to extensive renovation and the summer workshop rehearsals had taken place in the Church and church vestry. By the time of Eddie Garrard's first official rehearsal the choir was back in a beautifully renovated Church Institute, now to be known as the St Lawrence Hall. (Though still frequently referred to as the Church Institute in the year 2000!)

The last bombshell of the year was the letter written to the President on November 1st 1979 by Claude Allen, tendering his resignation for the end of that year. He wrote that he thought that he had done 'my fair share for the Society, with more than twenty-five years of continuous service, during which time I have worked with or against a typical cross section of conductors'. He goes on to say 'The final decision is not caused by the committee's latest choice. I ought to have left at the same time as David Fysh or even Hewitt-Jones.' Although he had enjoyed the 'leisurely occupation' he knew that the time arrives when all good things come to an end. The Society was stunned, though knowing that Claude was in his mid-70s they should hardly have been surprised. Claude Allen was an outstanding accompanist and his intuitive, sympathetic playing was inspirational.

Claude's organ continuo for *Messiah* on December 8th 1979 was his last official duty for the Society. The soloists, Jillian Whitehead, soprano, Joan Hulbert, contralto, Dennis Weaver, tenor, and James Walkley, bass, together with the choir and its conductor gave a 'high quality' performance of this inspired work.

One of the first things that the Society had to do on meeting after the Christmas break was to change the wording of their new constitution to enable the Society to be registered as a charity. The wording of the constitution as it stood precluded the Society from claiming income tax refunds. The Aims and Objectives of the Society were then amended to the following:

1. To encourage the study and practice of choral singing;

2. To foster the public knowledge and appreciation of such music by means of public performance;

3. To help members to become acquainted with the best choral music of past and present composers.

By order of the Committee.

The committee was assured by the Charity Commission that this wording would enable the Society to be registered. In fact the wording was identical to the Rules of the Society from 1962 to 1975, before the change on becoming independent!

Mrs Mary Smith was welcomed to the Society as the new rehearsal accompanist. Eddie Garrard was thanked for conducting the Christmas concert after so short a time with the Society. The conductor felt that there was an urgent need for more men to sing with the Society and an advert to this effect was placed in the *Stroud News and Journal*. Claude and Mrs Allen were welcomed to the AGM on April 21st 1980. There was to have been an official presentation to them of the radio that Claude had bought with the money donated by the members on his retirement (£100). Unfortunately this radio had developed a slight fault and had been returned to the manufacturers. After the non-presentation Mr and Mrs Allen were unanimously and with great acclaim appointed Honorary Life Members of the Society.

There were two summer concerts by the Society, one on May 10th in the Subscription Rooms, the other on July 5th at the Leonard Stanley Festival. The programme for the May concert was Purcell's *Dido and Aeneas* and Carl Orff's *Carmina Burana*. The reviewer felt that Mr Garrard was to be congratulated on producing such an enterprising programme and was impressed with the precision and clarity of the singing of the choir. Carolyn Cook, returning again to Stroud, delighted everyone with her technical mastery. During the interval, a group of Archway School boys on a Task Force project organised by David Homer, helped with refreshments. Before the performance, the Task Force boys had also sold programmes and translations of *Carmina Burana*. The money from the sale of the *Carmina* translations was given to the Task Force project. This project was the beginnings of the 'Talking Newspaper', a service which provides a taped recording of the local newspapers to the blind. This voluntary service is still running today.

At a concert in May as part of 'Music at the Priory' week Charpentier's *Messe de Minuit* and Pergolesi's *Magnificat* were sung. The soloists were all members of the Society. Marguerite Govier and Heulwen Griffiths, soprano, Elizabeth Griffin, contralto, Ken Plaice, tenor, and Ernest Tucker, bass, were soloists in *Messe de Minuit*. Clare Lavy, soprano, and Christine Pearce, contralto, sang with Ken Plaice and Phillip Young, bass, in the *Magnificat*. Claude Allen made a guest appearance to play Vidor's *Andante Cantabile*.

Ray and Margaret Wesley gave a garden party on July 8th for members of the Society. 'The food, wine and entertainment were excellent and the spirit of friendship in which we all met made the evening one which could not be dampened by the weather.'

When the Society met again in September 1980 they found the Subscription fee was now £10.00 for full paying members and £6.00 for students and senior citizens. The hire of the St Lawrence Hall had risen to £7.50 a week. Kay Sandells was the new Society Treasurer and Heather Cole had taken over from Sheila Adams as Secretary.

In November, the President, Ray Wesley, was invited to attend a meeting given by the Stroud District Council to yet again discuss the need for a new hall in the Stroud area. The members of the Society were keen for Mr Wesley to attend, though most people felt that these discussions were getting nowhere!

On December 13th the Society sang the first three parts of Bach's *Christmas Oratorio*. 'The chorus were well disciplined and accurate. One felt that they had really caught the spirit of the work.' The soloists, Jillian Whitehead, soprano, Clare Griffel, contralto, Dennis Weaver, tenor, and James Walkley, bass, 'combined to make a team with high quality of performance.' The harpsichord part was played in 'fine style' by Mary Smith. So it was a pity that the organ having developed a last minute failure caused the reviewer LB to write that both Claude Allen and the organ were 'certainly missed'.

A familiar face was back at the piano when members began rehearsing after the Christmas break in January 1981. Claude Allen was 'acting' accompanist in Mary Smith's unavoidable absence, due to ill health. The spring concert, *Nabucco*, was to be advertised on 'Severn Sound.' This was the first time that the Society concerts had been advertised on local radio.

There had been mumbling amongst the lady members of the Society who had become tired of wearing all black as their official concert dress. They wondered if this could be changed. The suggestion that they could wear their own pretty blouses with their black skirts for the performance of *Nabucco* in April was countermanded after the concert with strong pleas from members of the audience for uniformity of dress!

At the AGM in May 1981 Mr Garrard said of *Nabucco* that it 'was an excellent concert, the most polished performance that the Society had given since he had been its conductor'. He was particularly pleased by the performance of the amateur orchestra. (The average cost of a professional orchestra was now £750 and professional soloists' fees were from £60 upwards. These factors had to be taken into account when making the choice of the work and the size of the venue was also critical if the Society wanted to keep financially viable.)

Again the Society sang at Leonard Stanley on Saturday June 27th during the third season of 'Music at the Priory'. The concert consisted of Vaughan Williams' *Mass in G Minor* and Handel's *Zadok the Priest* with Claude Allen as organist. The vicar of Leonard Stanley, the Rev G White, wrote to thank the choir and to say that the concert had raised £63.15 for the Belfry Fund.

In September of that year the lady members of the Society were able to go from black to blue, when they chose a pale blue blouse, (at a cost of £6.99) from a selection brought in by the secretary, Mrs Heather Cole. It was reported that the men also approved of the ladies' choice. (Some years later, by the end of the 'blouse saga' the men were reported to be sorry that they had ever shown any interest in the blouses in the first place!)

Claude Allen returned to the Society to resume his accompanist duties on a semi-permanent basis. At a committee meeting on September 24th 1981 it was agreed to increase Mr Allen's fee to £5.00 a night for the 1981–82 season.

Due to the unavailability of the Stroud Subscription Rooms for the autumn concert, Rossini's *Stabat Mater* and Haydn's *Missa Sancti Nicolai* were performed in the Parish Church on Saturday November 28th. Frances Walker, soprano, Diana Walkley, contralto, Noel Drennan, tenor, and Edward Chetcuti, bass, were the soloists. Shirley Gladstone was the leader of the orchestra and Claude Allen the organist. The reviewer thought the chorus to be in good form and praised both the Rossini, 'most impressive and exciting' and the Haydn 'well-controlled, slow chorus work beautifully accompanied by the strings'. What the reviewer didn't like was the austerely printed programme. He would have appreciated a word or two, even in a foreign language, to give a clue as to what was happening in each of the ten movements of the Rossini. L B finished off by saying he 'should surely mention the very fine effect of the pale blue now worn by the ladies of the chorus'.

The committee members' meeting in January 1982 seemed to have many different topics to discuss. There was an urgent need to advertise for a deputy accompanist, as Claude Allen would probably want to 'retire' again soon. The committee wondered if they should look for another rehearsal venue as the fee for the St Lawrence Hall had risen to £8.75 a night. A request to participate in the Leonard Stanley Festival in June was declined due to financial reasons. A discussion about buying folders with the choir's name and logo on (to enclose scores when performing) concluded that at a cost of £7 or £8 each it would be beyond the Society's means.

On March 20th 1982 the Society performed Handel's *Samson* in the Stroud Subscription Rooms. The reviewer states that at first he was surprised to find the oratorio performed in a secular building as opposed to a church: 'But there were some advantages such as better lighting, better visibility without pillars in the way, not to mention coffee during the interval.' The reviewer was also taken aback by the drastic cuts in the oratorio. 'I was somewhat startled to have lost my place in my score. I caught up with the choir some twenty pages later.' However, he conceded that the work would have been impossibly long otherwise. The soloists were Frances Walker, soprano, Diana Walkley, contralto, Basil Matthews, tenor, and Leslie Williams, bass. Although the reviewer was greatly impressed by the standard of the chorus work which 'remained high throughout, showing good diction, expression and full attention', there were criticisms of some aspects of the performance.

During one of the rehearsals just prior to this concert there had been something of an upset between members discussing the lack of support given to attendance by members at the orchestral rehearsal. Heated exchanges were made which resulted in the sudden resignation of the President, Mr R A Y Wesley. The Society was shocked and the committee later wrote to Mr Wesley accepting his resignation with regret and hoping that he would like to reconsider his decision and continue as a singing member. The Society sincerely thanked Mr Wesley for all the hard work he had put in during his years of office, much of which was 'behind the scenes'.

During April 1982, Claude and Kit Allen celebrated their Golden Wedding anniversary. Claude, writing to thank the Society for their card, wrote that he and his wife had enjoyed a marvellous 'Special Day'. He had been told that 'the first 50 years were the worst' – they intended to wait and see!

The Rev Canon E H Tucker had been invited to be the next Society President. In a letter of July 19th 1982 he replied: 'I feel that my qualifications for such a position are lacking in both number and quality, but if the members of the committee wish it, then I am deeply honoured and happy to accept the position.'

A concert version of Edward German's *Merrie England* was sung on June 26th 1982 in the Subscription Rooms. The soloists were all members of the Society. The part of Bess was sung by Glenys Nelmes, Jill-All-Alone, Hilary Penney, Queen Elizabeth, Mary Moore, Sir Walter Raleigh, John Best and the Earl of Essex was Ernest Tucker.

During the autumn of 1982 the Society received with great sadness the news of the death of Claude Allen. Claude died on October 4th. He and his wife Kit had passed away within a few weeks of each other. By chance, on the same day that Claude Allen died, the committee unanimously agreed to write to Mrs Gail Fearnley-Whittingstall to offer her the post of accompanist.

The autumn concert on Thursday November 25th 1982 in the Subscription Rooms was Bruckner's *Mass No 2 in E minor* and Mozart's *Requiem Mass*. The soloists, Mary Jane de Havas, soprano, Sylvia Strange, contralto, Eric Axford, tenor, and David Parsons, bass, were 'fine singers, combining well in the quartet sections'. The reviewer enjoyed the performance, particularly 'those fast fugal movements, which received spirited performances'.

The minutes of the early months of 1983 are mostly devoted to finance. The Society was still practising in the St Lawrence Hall, irrespective of the hiring fee. The treasurer Mrs Sue Davis reported on the financial state of the choir. The summer and November concerts of 1982 had deficits of £1.04 and £17.60 respectively. Fortunately, the Christmas party, organised by Fran Russell and the Social Committee, made a profit of £57.22. The Deposit Account balance stood at a healthy £3,231.51 (including a Legacy of £1,000 and Interest of £99.00). Stroud District Council had cut their grant to the Society from £40 to £20 and the treasurer decided to take this matter up with them. The tickets for the *Creation* in April were to be priced at £2.00 and £1.50 for students and senior citizens.

It was a complete version of Haydn's *Creation* that was performed, much to the reviewer's approval, on April 16th 1983. 'In this performance we had no cuts at all. I am sure Haydn knew best. He wrote *The Creation* in the eighteenth century – the age of perfection. This perfection surely applied to musical form.' 'There was a high standard of singing from the choir with vivid effects from the change of dynamics and tempo, and there was some fine singing in the solo parts.' The reviewer particularly enjoyed *With Verdure Clad* sung by Angela Ayers, *In Native Worth* sung by Eric Axford and *Now Heaven in Fullest Glory Shone* sung by David Parsons. 'Glenys Nelmes and Simon Willink as Adam and Eve sang excellently both individually and in some challenging duets, which required difficult chording and perfect intonation. Shirley Gladstone was the orchestral leader, Gail Fearnley-Whittingstall the repetiteur and all were under the capable baton of the conductor Eddie Garrard.'

Canon Tucker in his new role of President of the Society addressed the AGM in May 1983. In his gentle, courteous manner he first thanked the members for showing so clearly that 'we have a Society to be proud of, numerically, musically and socially.' 'It is evident that everyone here loves music and singing and we are lucky to have a conductor who has many qualities. We expect him to tell us how and what to do and he sets us and himself very high standards. His knowledge and choice of music is very wide and he is a patient and, on occasions, a courageous man with a sense of humour.' The Society was pleased to hear that the year that had started with 67 members had ended with 95. All the members were in agreement on how extremely lucky they were to have found such a talented accompanist in Gail Fearnley-Whittingstall. After the election of officers the new committee for the 1983–84 season stood as follows: secretary, Mrs H Cole, treasurer, Mrs S Davis, minute secretary, Miss C Pearce, NFMS Rep, Mr S Sullings. Committee: Messrs J Best, A Kinsey, S Willink, Mesdames S Adams, B Dunn, S Heymans, K Sandells, H Penney, B Whiting and C Lavy. Librarian, Miss J Cordwell. Social Committee: Mr W Robinson, Mesdames F Russell, G Garrard, and C Lavy.

The summer concert was held in the Subscription Rooms on July 9th 1983. This programme consisted of Vivaldi's *Dixit* and Vaughan Williams' *Five Mystical Songs*. David Parsons was the baritone soloist. The audience were delighted with piano trios and duets by Gail Fearnley-Whittingstall, Eddie Garrard and Ernest Tucker. 'Gail Fearnley-Whittingstall, the accompanist, is to be congratulated on her non-stop performance throughout the concert and Eddie Garrard, the conductor, for his vigorous direction of the choir.'

Two old Choral Society favourites, Brahms' *Requiem* and Fauré's *Requiem* were performed in November 1983. They were also amongst the favourite works of the reviewer, LB, who tells us that the Brahms *Requiem* may have been

SCS, The Church Institute, Monday April 2nd 1984.

written in memory of the composer's mother. Also, that this was the fourth time the reviewer had heard the Choral Society sing this 'beautiful' work since 1961. LB continued, 'I felt that the solo and choral parts of this concert were very well performed. The singing was accurate, in tune, and on time. We heard words well. Expression changes were carefully observed, though some of us felt that the very soft passages in the Brahms could have been softer. But this was not the case in the Fauré, where there was a fine dynamic range.' For this performance the soloists were Jillian Whitehead, soprano, and David Parsons, baritone.

Handel's *Passion of Christ* and Dvorak's *Stabat Mater* were the works chosen for a Passion-tide performance on April 14th 1984. Some members were not too sure about the juxtaposition of these two works, but judging from the reviewer's comments it made for an interesting concert. The reviewer had feared that he would find the Handel 'unduly long.' However, he found himself so interested in the many solo characters, most sung by members of the chorus, that he was ready to revise his opinion of the *Passion*. The chief soloists Glenys Nelmes, soprano, Sylvia Strange, contralto, Eric Axford, tenor and James Walkley, bass, sang with clarity and balance. The reviewer was particularly pleased to hear the Dvorak work as he felt it was not performed as often as it might have been. He appreciated the contrasts in musical style, from serious anthem to dance-like tune, 'sung with fine expression by the chorus'.

Just prior to this concert on April 2nd, the whole choir was professionally photographed at a rehearsal in the St Laurence Rooms. As far as our records show, this was the first time since the 1950s and Sammy Underwood's day that a complete choir photo had been taken.

The Society's AGM in May 1984 was a rather thoughtful meeting. There were many minor difficulties as well as new ideas that the members wished to discuss. Financially the Society had run at a small loss over the season and money had to be withdrawn from the Reserve Fund. In spite of extra funds generated by the activities of the social committee and from other grants, it was felt that the Society had no option but to increase the annual subscription.

The treasurer, Sue Davis, pointed out that 40 rehearsals at £12 for the season represented about 30p a rehearsal. This seemed to be excellent value especially when compared with the cost of other leisure activities. (For instance, the hire of a squash court – £1.90 for 40 minutes, or a swimming session at 52p.) It was decided that in September the new subscription should be £16 for full paying members and £9 for students and senior citizens.

Although the membership stood at 80, again, attendance at rehearsals had fluctuated greatly. This of course put a lot of pressure on the conductor. It was generally agreed to return to a policy of two main concerts a year, which would give a longer rehearsal time. The price of concert tickets was to remain the same.

Everyone agreed that the appointing during the year of a named Publicity Manager, Hilary Penney, and concert manager, Sylvia Heymans, had been a very good idea. Everyone was full of praise for their efforts, in particular Sylvia, who was masterminding all aspects of concert requirements.

In a lighter vein the members had not been able to solve the mystery of the disappearing rehearsal podium! After extensive enquiries it had not been found, but fortunately, and much to Eddie's relief, one of the members, Mr Perkins had kindly provided a new one.

At a busy committee meeting in early June, Canon Tucker raised the issue of the Society's age. The Society was planning a special concert for 1985, to celebrate what was considered to be 150 years of Music Making in Stroud. The committee felt that they couldn't be sure about this date and wondered if they should change the anniversary to 140 years instead to be on the safe side! (The committee were not to know it at the time, but it was actually 151 years of Music Making in Stroud that they were celebrating, and this could be dated from the opening concerts in the Subscription Rooms on Monday, October 27th 1834.)

On June 30th, a lighter-hearted concert featuring Elgar's *The Music Makers* and Coleridge-Taylor's *Hiawatha's Wedding Feast* was performed in the Subscription Rooms. The reviewer reminded us that it was the 50th anniversary of the death of Elgar and also that it used to be said that Elgar could only be properly produced in the three counties of Gloucestershire, Hereford and Worcestershire. The works were accompanied by the piano 'so brilliantly played by Neil Fortin'. The reviewer missed the orchestra, though he felt that 'Elgar with a piano is certainly better than none at all'. The tenor soloist Dennis Weaver was 'greatly admired'.

In September, Society members sang in memory of Claude Allen at a memorial concert at Holy Trinity Church, Stroud. The Choral Society performed Vivaldi's *Gloria* with soloists Glenys Nelmes, soprano, Joan Hulbert, contralto and organist, Christopher Swain. Many individual pieces were performed by Claude's friends and musical colleagues. Among the items, the tenor, Eric Axford, sang Claude's own song *Juniper Hill*. Mary Smith accompanied Shirley Gladstone in Kriesler's *Praeludium* and *Allegro*. Betty Baker sang Mozart's *Agnus Dei*, Jean Lea and Ernest Tucker played the piano duet, Dvorak's *Slavonic Dance in G Minor*. The *Qui Vive* for six hands by W Ganz, was played by Gail Fearnley-Whittingstall, Eddie Garrard and Ernest Tucker. Holy Trinity Church Choir sang Purcell's *Rejoice in the Lord* and there were items by the Wycliffe College Instrumental Group. Before the closing prayer by the vicar, the Reverend Tom Merry, the Society had concluded the concert with the *Hallelujah Chorus* from Handel's *Messiah*.

'The 1984–85 Season promises to be an extremely important one in the illustrious history of the Stroud Choral Society. Something of a jewel in the crown, in fact. At the turn of the year, the Society will begin to mark its 140th birthday and the 150th anniversary of music making in Stroud.' So wrote Carole Taylor in the *Stroud News and Journal*. This was the beginning of a long-sensitive article about the Choral Society, written in August 1984 and detailing much of its early history as told by Leonard Keck in his handbook of the Society which was published in 1973. For many choral members this information about the long history of the Society was quite new.

By the end of the year some arrangements were already in place for the anniversary concert the following year. The members themselves had not been idle on other fronts either. A fund-raising sub-committee had raised £185 from mini-sales during the autumn season. A concert at Painswick organised by Marguerite Govier and Brenda Dunn had raised £30. A tax rebate of £112 was also a welcome addition to the funds. Added to which, the Original Holloway Society had offered to sponsor the anniversary concert. It seemed particularly appropriate that such an old-established Stroud Benefit Society such as the Holloway (1880), should sponsor another old-established Stroud Society.

The calendar year 1984 finished with a performance of Handel's *Ode on St Cecilia's Day* and Britten's *A Ceremony of Carols* on December 8th in the Parish Church. The audience and choir were delighted by the harpist, Liz Fletcher, as she accompanied the *Ceremony of Carols*. Between the choral works Liz Fletcher played a *Sarabande* by Bach and an *Elegy* by Hasselman 'with fine, sensitive interpretation'. Rowena Angell, soprano and Eric Axford, tenor, were the soloists in *St Cecilia's Day* and Rowena Angell and Heather Cole in Britten's *Spring Carol*.

The early committee meetings of 1985 were almost exclusively devoted to the 150th anniversary concert arrangements. The work was to be Verdi's *Requiem* and it was to be held in the Stroud Leisure Centre. The Society was busy looking for local sponsorship and the concert was to be widely advertised in all the local papers, as well as on Severn Sound and HTV. Letters of invitation had already been sent to Princess Anne and Captain Mark Phillips, Prince and Princess Michael of Kent and Colonel M St J V Gibbs, the Lord Lieutenant of the County. Other illustrious people were also invited, including Sir Anthony Kershaw, MP, the Bishops of Gloucester and Tewkesbury and councillor Roy P Nicholas, Stroud District Council. The Rt Rev Robert Deakin, Bishop of Tewkesbury returned a delightful refusal note saying that he and his wife would very much have liked to have come to the concert. He wrote saying that for a short time in the early 1940s he had been a member of Stroud Choral Society. 'Amongst other things I still have a copy of Vaughan Williams' *Benedicite* which we sang at that time under Sammy Underwood.' (March 15th 1942. The Bishop would also have sung Elgar's *The Music Makers!*)

The committee must have breathed a collective sigh of relief when all the arrangements were in place and Verdi's *Requiem* went ahead on April 20th 1985 at the Stroud Leisure Centre in the presence of the Lord Lieutenant of the County. Whether all members could truly envisage 150 years of music making in Stroud or not, there was certainly no doubt that it was an exhilarating concert in which to sing. In spite of the 'somewhat uncertain acoustics' of the Leisure Centre hall the critics were unanimous that both singers and audience enjoyed the occasion. M S writing for the *Citizen* noted that Stroud had turned out in full to support the Society. 'Whether it was cultural loyalty or because

A NEW ERA

"150 YEARS OF MUSIC-MAKING IN STROUD"

Stroud Choral Society and Orchestra present
VERDI'S "REQUIEM"
Saturday 20th April 1985 – 7.30 p.m.

In the presence of Colonel M. St. J. V. Gibbs, C.B., D.S.O., T.D.
The Lord Lieutenant of the County of Gloucestershire

Sponsored by:
THE ORIGINAL HOLLOWAY SOCIETY

Programme 50p

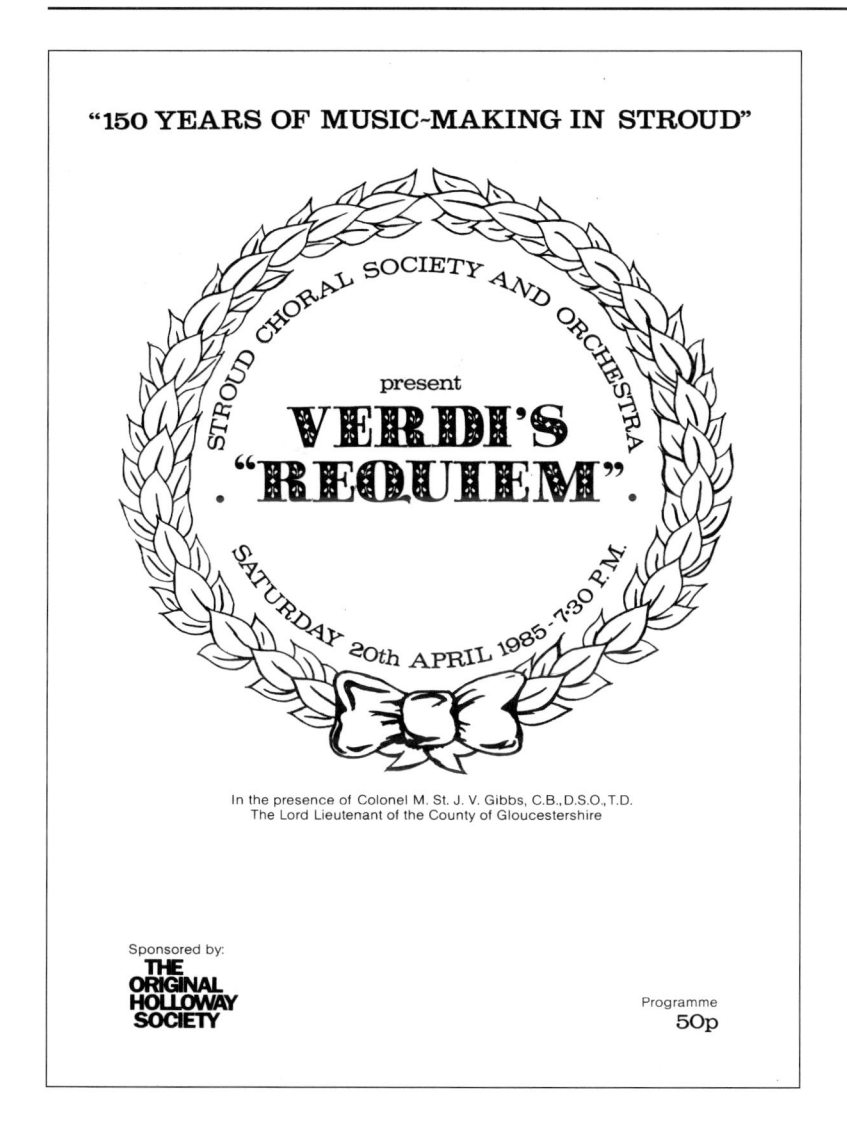

of what this Society had done for music in Stroud over the years, or the infrequent opportunity these days of attending a live performance, there was no mistaking the audience's obvious enjoyment.' M S went on to say 'It is an odd sort of requiem, in its vigorous style, dramatic conception and quasi-operatic approach, devoid of almost any ecclesiastical restraint. But then, Verdi must write like Verdi, and as the Society's conductor, Edward Garrard competently contrasted the excitement of the climaxes with sheer simplicity and beauty, no one bothered about this.'

M R in the *Stroud News and Journal* wrote of the four soloists, 'Francis Walker, soprano, had a beautiful clear, steady voice, and the B flat at the end of the *Requiem* passage (surely the cruellest cadence in the soprano repertoire?) was beautifully executed.' Diana Walkley 'has a fine voice, a true mezzo-soprano. The tenor, William Kendall, was probably the most successful at alternating an operatic quality with lyrical singing as the music demanded. Brian Rayner Cook produced the lovely singing one expects of him.'

Continuing in the tradition of the previous 150 years Eddie Garrard conducted an orchestra of mainly local players, led by Shirley Gladstone. 'Edward Garrard has a clear unfussy beat and was in full control of his large forces. With only one rehearsal of all performers together, it was wonderful that he produced such a unified and successful performance.' M R concluded with good wishes to the conductor and the Choral Society as they start on the next 150 years!

In the Society files there is a charming letter from the Lord Lieutenant of the County, Colonel M St J V Gibbs, thanking the Society for 'a most excellent evening'. He felt that everyone concerned must feel most satisfied at the results of their efforts 'which I know must have been very demanding to have achieved such a high standard'.

The smooth running of this concert must have required considerable management skills and the committee must be congratulated on their efficient arrangements. It was surely a feather in the cap of the concert manager, Sylvia Heymans.

After this concert the Society enjoyed a somewhat quieter year. At a special meeting called for on October 7th the members approved an amended Constitution. One of the new amendments was to automatically give life membership (with exemption from paying subscriptions) to any member who had participated in the Society's activities for 50 years. In common with other choral societies our Society has a record of attracting long-standing members and there is usually at least one recipient of this award singing with the Society.

Poulenc's *Gloria* was the choice of music for the concert on Saturday December 14th 1985 at Stroud Parish Church. The second half of the concert was a progamme of carols for choir and audience. Gail Fearnley-Whittingstall accompanied the choir in the Poulenc, and Glenys Nelmes was the soprano soloist 'producing beautiful tone in the very high notes'. L B noted that 'the final chorus, *You who sit at the right hand,* was pitched very high for both soloist and choir, giving a most brilliant effect. The ending, for solo alone was very dramatic.' Kenneth Cook played the organ for the congregational carols. Unfortunately the organ had ideas of its own, having developed a mechanical fault and threatened to spoil an otherwise harmonious concert.

The spring concert on May 17th 1986 was Beethoven's *Missa Solemnis*. Pleased with the Leisure Centre venue of the previous year and the ability to seat a larger audience, the Society again chose to perform there. The four soloists, Vanessa Young, soprano, Margaret Maguire, mezzo-soprano, Paul Trotter, tenor, and John Davies, bass, had all been students at the Royal Northern College of Music in Manchester. Peter Harney, reviewing for the *Stroud News and Journal* recounted the story of how Beethoven's choir had found parts of the *Solemnis* unsingable. Beethoven was asked to make changes but he had refused to do so. 'To this day it remains one of the most challenging of all choral works which taxes even professional choirs and orchestras. The Stroud Choral Society, under the confident direction of Edward Garrard accepted Beethoven's challenge and gave a memorable performance which will stand as a landmark in its history.'

Members were again involved in self-help activities during the year. A rummage sale one Saturday morning on the Subscription Rooms forecourt raised a surprising £85. A car boot sale in June brought in £192. Sylvia and Philip Heymans opened their gardens again in a kindly fund-raising activity that had become an annual treat as well as a benefit.

An interesting request from Germany gave the committee plenty to think about. Gisela Hanbold of the Göttingen Choir had invited the Choral Society to consider the possibility of a 'twinning' arrangement. The suggestion was that the German Choir should visit Stroud in 1987 with a return visit from Stroud to Germany in 1988. The members, after some discussion, thought that they would like to participate. The committee agreed to work on the physical and financial practicalities of the exercise and reply to the German invitation.

Another intriguing invitation received that year came from the Stroud Rugby Football Club who wondered if the Society could 'put on an entertaining display for twenty to thirty minutes before a suitable home fixture at Fromehall Park'. Sadly the committee declined this novel idea; though some members had rather fancied the idea of choral majorettes!

The new Society secretary, Dr Margery van Zyl, found herself in frustrating correspondence with the Stroud Subscription Rooms management. For some years it had seemed impossible to book the rooms for a Saturday concert in December, even when trying to book over a year in advance. A booking in spring 1985 for December 13th 1986 had been later cancelled and moved forward, due to a double booking, to November 15th. Dr van Zyl, although expressing the Society's wholehearted support of charities, wondered why the Choral Society always had to give way to charity bazaars and antique dealers.

At the earlier than planned date of November 15th the choir sang Purcell's *Ode to St Cecilia's Day* and Schubert's *Mass in A Flat Major* in the Stroud Subscription Rooms. Although the rehearsal time had been shortened due to the earlier performance date the concert was a great success. People leaving at the end of the concert were enthusiastic about the pleasant variety of the music and the polished and responsive performance of the musicians. Both choir members and audience were united in their enjoyment. 'The balance of the choir and the orchestra was good and the young soloists from the Northern College of Music were a joy to look at as well as to listen to.' Of the soloists, Amanda Roocroft, soprano, Alison Hudson, contralto, Colin McKerracher, tenor, John Davies, bass, and Christopher Price, baritone, only Alison Hudson's 'truly beautiful and warm contralto voice' and Christopher Price's 'added confidence and clarity' were mentioned by the reviewer. It was the first time that Amanda Roocroft had sung with the Society and members have since been able to follow her blossoming career with much pleasure and delight.

On December 8th, guests of the Society were welcomed to an informal evening of carol singing, mince pies and wine at the St Laurence Hall. It was a very merry Society that finished the autumn season 1986.

The New Year 1987 found the members rehearsing at a new venue, Marling School. But right from the beginning there was an element of dissatisfaction with the new venue on the grounds that it was changed without enough consultation. The main reason for the change was that the rent of the room was half the cost of the St Laurence Hall, and Marling had a better piano. However it was decided to remain with Marling until Easter and then hold a referendum.

After two letters were sent to the German Choir in Göttingen a friendly return letter was finally received. Items such as accommodation, singing venues and availability of piano and organ were discussed. It had been thought that it would be a good idea for the Göttingen Choir to sing at the Stroud Festival in October. Members were getting used to the idea of entertaining the German Choir and on the whole were feeling enthusiastic about the project. Unfortunately this was as far as it went! From that point on, the Society was unable to raise any further contact with the Göttingen Choir and in view of this, the exchange idea was dropped.

Handel's *Let The Bright Seraphim* and *Let Their Celestial Concerts*, Brahms' *Song of Destiny* and Mozart's *Mass in C Minor K427* was the programme sung on May 9th in the Stroud Subscription Rooms. 'The evening began with a spirited performance of Handel's *Let The Bright Seraphim* by the young soprano, Amanda Roocroft. Her clear phrasing was well supported by the orchestra, particularly the trumpet', wrote J R in a review in the *Stroud News and Journal*. '*Let Their Celestial Concerts* was sung by the choir with enthusiasm and very pleasing phrasing.' The Brahms' *Song of Destiny* 'opened with beautiful lyrical phrases from orchestra and choir in turn, who gave a warm and satisfying performance of this very different work'. Not even the extreme heat of the evening, or the battle with the air-conditioning could mar the second half of the concert. 'The choir, orchestra and soloists are to be congratulated on maintaining their high standard of performance through to the calm of the *Agnus Dei*. Much of this is due to Edward Garrard who was responsible for the quality and musicianship of the evening.'

At the AGM in May, members found themselves voting by 42 to 30 to return to the Church Institute as a practice venue. Somehow this traditional venue, seemed right to many choir members, who felt almost that it was a 'coming home'. Historically the Society's long and strong links with both the Church Institute rooms and the Subscription Rooms are not so easily broken.

Members learnt that their President, Canon Ernest Tucker, was absent due to continued ill health. Typically, Ernest had sent the members one of his sane, cheerful, upbeat letters in which amongst other things he counted his and the Society's blessings. In particular he felt that 'musically, we are blessed with a richly endowed Conductor and a superlative Accompanist'. Sentiments with which the Society most wholeheartedly agreed.

The Treasurer's report showed a good financial situation. Together with the reclaimed tax of £422 from the previous year's covenants and donations from the Original Holloway Society, Unilever, Batricar and Paterson Zachonis, the members themselves were still actively fund raising. Eleanor Boldero's husband Peter kindly ran the Stroud Half Marathon and raised £72.50 for the funds. There was a spate of Subscription Rooms forecourt sales and another car boot sale. The Society had decided to use Leonard Keck's legacy of £1000 to purchase a 'new' practice piano furnished with a lock, cover and wheels. The remainder of this legacy was used to purchase concert folders.

The May AGM 1987 also marked the retirement of Stanley Sullings from his hardworking and conscientious role as the National Federation of Music Societies' representative, a position that he had held for many years. Stanley Sullings had now been with the choir for over 50 years and in recognition of his work was presented with a gift from the Society members. Andrew Maden was to be the new NFMS representative.

On October 4th 1987 'the 41st Stroud Festival was launched on a joyous note with the Grand Opening Concert by Stroud Choral Society'. The Society sang Vivaldi's *Gloria* and Handel's *Let The Bright Seraphim* and concluded the concert with the *Hallelujah* chorus. 'It was a concert which was obviously thoroughly enjoyed by the audience, setting a cheerful and enthusiastic tone for the next fortnight.'

The Stroud Subscription Rooms was packed for the performance of *Elijah* on December 10th 1987. 'It was an impressively dramatic performance with the interpretation of Elijah by Robert Carpenter Turner, setting the scene for an evening of great variety', wrote A H in a review for the *Stroud News and Journal*. *Elijah* was Mendelssohn's second oratorio and was first performed in the Birmingham Town Hall in 1846, where it was received with great acclaim. 'Mendelssohn's work is still a very popular one and the audience were able to hear some beautiful solo singing and chorus work. The large orchestra ably led by Shirley Gladstone, gave strong support. The soprano, Lesley Cox, sang with a beautiful clear tone and all the voices blended well in the quartets. Both the contralto, Kate McCarney and tenor, Paul Trotter, delighted the audience with their obvious enjoyment of the work. The contralto's dramatic singing contrasted later with her beautiful legato singing of *woe unto them who forsake Him*. The chorus produced a balanced and fresh sound and their conductor Edward Garrard managed to combine soloists, chorus and orchestra to produce a most dramatic and satisfying performance.'

The New Year, 1988 brought a new challenge. As part of the ongoing fund raising activities Jenifer Ricketts had thrown down the gauntlet and challenged members to design a Christmas card for the Society. The members, particularly those who couldn't run marathons or conduct mini-auctions, rose to the challenge with enthusiasm and by the deadline of March 28th Jenifer had a full complement of singing robins, reindeers and Christmas trees.

Jenifer's other task for that year was to be wardrobe mistress and consult the lady members on new ideas for concert dress. There had been a general feeling that by now the blue blouses were getting a little tired and new choral members were finding them difficult to obtain. After extensive consultation resulting in the ladies choosing pink and then doing a complete volte-face when they thought pink wouldn't do at all, the project was shelved. However, the topic of the blouses was set to run and run ...

In April 1988 the members were saddened to hear of the death of Netlam Bigg. He had died peacefully in his sleep on April 12th. He was 89. Netlam had been a tireless worker for the promotion of the Arts in Stroud. When you look at the Stroud Festival today and the international reputation that it now commands, you cannot help but be impressed by this man's vision, sparked as it was in the dark days following the end of the Second World War.

The spring concert held on May 14th 1988 was a collection of shorter choral works, Stanford's *Songs of the Fleet*, Parry's *Blest Pair of Sirens* and Elgar's *Songs from the Bavarian Highlands*. The orchestra, again led by the admirable Shirley Gladstone, gave two orchestral interludes. Dvorak's *Carnival Overture* and Glinka's *Ruslan and Ludmilla Overture* were greatly enjoyed. This in spite of the reviewer L B feeling that at times 'the brass were over-enthusiastic'. Christopher Price, the baritone soloist, sang in *Songs of the Fleet*, 'his attractive resonant voice adding greatly to the performance'.

The President, Ernest Tucker, was warmly welcomed, restored to health, at the AGM in May. He in turn said that it was a great privilege to be welcoming members to another Annual General Meeting of one of the oldest societies in the United Kingdom. The President paid tribute on behalf of the members to Netlam Bigg. 'His services to the community were many, including the League of Friends of Stroud Hospital, Scouting, and as founder of Stroud Festival (now in its 42nd year), his association with the Gloucestershire Youth Orchestra, the Three Choirs Festival, County Music Committee and the National Federation of Music Societies, as well as Secretary to this Society for over 35 years.' Canon Tucker went on to say how well Netlam had deserved his MBE in 1968.

As this AGM the Society members were able to persuade Ernest Tucker, by an overwhelming response, to stay on as their President. The members were also delighted to hear that Canon Tucker would be well enough to sing in the next Society concert.

On December 10th 1988 in the Stroud Subscription Rooms the Society presented *Messiah*. This was the 21st time in the history of the Society that *Messiah* had been performed. Eddie Garrard had decided that this should be an uncut version of Handel's most popular work. Another unusual decision was that the soprano, Hilary Greenhill, should sing the aria *But who may abide* instead of the usual contralto or bass. 'It was a packed Subscription Rooms that thoroughly enjoyed the full length production as talented soloists led the way to bring over two and a half hours of quality singing. From the very start the mainly string orchestra supported by oboes, bassoon and harpsichord played with confidence, and the opening recitative and aria from tenor Paul Trotter was sung with great control. When the chorus entered with *And the Glory of the Lord* one was beginning to sit up and take notice.' Richard Greenland's review goes on to say, 'The chorus' performance of *For unto us* confirmed in my mind that we were not in for the usual stodgy, staid *Messiah* most of us have learned to expect, but something more exciting. The contralto, Alison Hudson's voice was extremely rich and beautiful ... and how beautiful was the soprano and alto duet *He shall feed His flock*. From then on, each recitative, aria and chorus were eagerly awaited and three items normally omitted became highlights – particularly the chorus *Let all the Angels* and the contralto aria *Thou art gone up on high* and later the contralto/tenor duet *O death where is thy sting*. The bass, Roger Hewetson and the trumpeter gave a very well balanced performance of *The trumpet shall sound*. However, for me the highest point came seconds from the end. Nearly 2½ hours after the start the chorus came to their concluding effort, and by this stage the sopranos and particularly the tenors must have been vocally exhausted – but each member seemed to have determination to find and use every last resource. To paraphrase King George II at that very early performance, it was here, these last few bars from the end that I felt "heaven opened before me and I felt God's presence." This has got to be one of the most exciting performances of this work ever performed, as also many of the members of the audience were remarking as they left and one must both admire and congratulate their conductor, Edward

Garrard, for producing such a result. As for me, I also went the following evening to their second and equally impressive performance in Gloucester.'

For Christmas 1988 many members of the Society were able to send their nearest and dearest one of a choice of four Society Christmas cards. Madeleine Fowler and our resident artist, Brenda Dunn, had been worthy winners of the 'design a Christmas Card' competition.

Many members of the Choral Society travelled to London on March 12th 1989 to take part in Haydn's *Creation* at the Royal Albert Hall. This was a concert conducted by John Lubbock, together with the Orchestra of St John's Smith Square with soloists Valerie Masterson, soprano, Gwynne Howell, bass, and David Skewes, tenor. Many singers from choral societies all over Great Britain had come together with the BBC Symphony Chorus to sing on behalf of The Royal Marsden Hospital Appeal. Andrew Maden, who had organised the Stroud contingent, was anxious that no one should stray away from the group on account of the probability of not being able to find them again among the 2,500 other singers! It was an exhilarating concert and much enjoyed by the Stroud group.

Verdi's *Pezzi Sacri* and Haydn's *Mass in B Flat* were sung on May 13th 1989 in the Subscription Rooms. The review in the *Stroud News and Journal* is headed 'Ambitious choice pays off.' Certainly it was not easy for the choir to rehearse two such demanding pieces. Rehearsing in eight parts for the Verdi had been hard, ranked around the Church Institute, members complained it was difficult to hear their particular cue. 'Soloists Margaret Langford, Jeanette Massochi, Andrew Telford and Roger Hewetson attained a splendid professional standard which was matched by the superb singing of the choir. From the opening bars of the *Kyrie*, we knew at once that Haydn's music was in safe hands as choir and orchestra rose confidently to the occasion.' The reviewer, C P C, continued by explaining that the Verdi's *Four Sacred Pieces* was formidably difficult for any choir. 'But Stroud Choral Society managed to walk the musical tightrope, conveying the sombre, brooding character of the music. It was a very ambitious choice of music which came off superbly, demonstrating how lucky Stroud is to have so enthusiastic, competent and adventurous a society.'

Two events saddened the members during 1989. In May they learned that their President, Ernest Tucker, was back in hospital. He wrote to the Society later in the year in his friendly manner and asked in view of his 'uncertain mobility' whether the Society would accept his resignation. 'It has been a great privilege to be President for the past seven years and I'm sure you will have no difficulty in finding a more worthy successor.' He finished by hoping the Society was 'keen and raring to go in this delightful pastime of music making'. Michael Gray stepped into the role of Acting President but the missing voice in the bass section was much more difficult to replace!

On October 4th 1989 Tony Hewitt-Jones died from bone cancer, at the early age of 63. He was to be missed in many ways and not only in the musical field. He was noted for his compilation of 'the Anti-Clash Diary' of regional music events which was widely distributed in the county. Tony was a larger than life character as well as a prolific composer and brilliant musician. The Gloucester Three Choirs missed his 'congenial presence and his '32 ft' resonance amongst the second bass line-up'. Tony held an affectionate rapport with young people and had been to the forefront in starting the Gloucester County Youth Orchestra as well as running the County Music Summer Schools. Mrs B Evans, in a written letter to the press recalled, 'I especially remember the Christmas concerts in the Subscription Rooms which somehow started the season in a joyous way.' Tony Hewitt-Jones had written nearly 100 compositions and worked on completing a Choral Mass in the last days of his life. In Mark Foster's opinion, 'His music will outlive many of his contemporaries.' In Tony's memory, the Society sent a donation to the Cobalt Unit Appeal Fund.

The Society members were pleased with their efforts at fund raising during the 1988–89 season, as over £300 had been the result. Mini plant and vegetable sales at rehearsals had produced £11 and a Tupperware order raised £26. Jenifer Ricketts had made a staggering £80 with a sponsored slim. A sale outside the Subscription Rooms produced more than £100. The Christmas cards had made a profit of £65 and later were to add another £77 for funds. Also, £25 had been collected at the AGM.

During the year, Fran Russell had volunteered to become the new choral wardrobe mistress. Initially she had written to the BBC Clothes Show to see if they could offer advice. After that, she and a team of one visited Marks and Spencer and C & A, but were amazed and disappointed to discover that these huge multinational organisations were unable to provide blouses in the numbers required. In the end it was a small clothing shop in Stroud that was able to

STROUD SINGS

Winners of the 'Design a Christmas Card' Competition, Christmas 1988.

meet the request. The new blouses, a tiny flower print on a darker background had their first viewing at the December concert. 'The ladies wore their new blouses and Mrs F Russell, the wardrobe mistress, is to be congratulated on pleasing just about everybody.'

A full audience at the Subscription Rooms on December 9th heard the Society sing Rossini's *Messe Solennelle*. 'For the second time this year, the Society chose a great but rarely performed work and presented it superbly. It was the work of a composer in his seventies and one more famous for sparkling and light-hearted operas. Yet here is a work of strong religious feeling where the words of the Latin Mass are set, nonetheless, in Rossini's exuberant manner.' Superbly accompanying the choir was Gail Fearnley-Whittingstall together with Ian Fox on the harmonium. The soloists, Ida-Maria Turri, Alison Hudson, Gareth Lloyd and Nigel Cliffe 'delighted with their fine singing'. The unaccompanied singing in the *Sanctus* was accomplished 'with confident authority culminating in a triumphant *Hosanna*'. C P C concluded his review with the following encouraging comments: 'The final tribute must, of course, go to the conductor and guiding spirit of the Society, Edward Garrard, who organised the concert and trained the choir, and under whose baton the whole force gave such a worthy account of Rossini's music. It must be stated once more, Stroud is fortunate to have a Choral Society so enthusiastic, so skilled and so adventurous in its choice of material.'

The Choral Society sang in St Mary's Church in Painswick, on March 31st 1990, in aid of Mencap. There was an open invitation to the singing public to join in with this performance and it was an augmented choir of 160 singers that gave a 'memorable rendering of Handel's *Messiah*'. The four soloists, Nicki Jones, Joanne Campion, Andrew Telford and Benjamin Fawdon, 'stood out because of their youth and sensitive interpretation'. Christopher Boodle gave the 'excellent accompaniment' on the organ. 'An evening of music, worship and praise worthy to be repeated', stated the review. At this concert £426 was raised for Mencap.

During the previous year the Society had received a letter from Robert Tucker, the biographer of A Brent-Smith. In the letter he had suggested that as it was the centenary of the birth of the composer Alexander Brent-Smith the Society might like to consider singing his *Elegy in Memory of Edward Elgar*. Alexander Brent-Smith had been born in Brookthorpe and until 1912 was assistant organist at Worcester Cathedral. From 1913 until 1934 he was Director of Music at Lancing College. On returning to Brookthorpe he spent the rest of his life teaching, lecturing and composing. He was the composer of three symphonies, sixteen concertos, ten operas and a multitude of chamber music compositions. It was noted that Edward Elgar had thought very highly of Brent-Smith's music. On March 10th 1940 at Stroud Parish Church, Alexander Brent-Smith had conducted the Choral Society in the first performance of his *Elegy*. In view of the Brent-Smith centenary, the committee and members were happy to include the *Elegy* in their next concert. Although no members of the Brent-Smith family were able to attend this concert, his biographer Mr Robert Tucker was in the audience.

Vaughan Williams' *Sea Symphony* and Alexander Brent-Smith's *Elegy* were performed on May 12th 1990 in the Subscription Rooms. Douglas Drane, music critic for the *Gloucester Citizen,* had more to comment on than the music itself: 'Alas the performance verged on disaster, not because of the choir and orchestra's efforts – though it could be said they had bitten off more than they could chew. No, the main problem was the thunderous noise of the Subscription Rooms' fan inducted air conditioning. One was surprised that conductor Edward Garrard was prepared to continue under such appalling conditions.' Mr Drane's comment on the *Elegy* was that it was difficult to be critical due to the circumstances, but from what he could hear he thought the performance had been worth the effort. Many people thought that the *Sea Symphony* was both exhilarating to sing and to listen to, but there is no doubt that the choir was somewhat thrown by the difficulties. Also singing as best as they were able in the circumstances were Marie-Louise Petit, soprano, and William Armiger, baritone.

News came during the year of three choral members who were not singing due to ill health. Canon Ernest Tucker had recovered enough to attend the concert on May 12th but was not mobile enough after his hip operation to return to choral practices. Jim Wilson and Stanley Sullings had both been suffering from bouts of ill health. The committee was concerned for all three and on behalf of the members sent 'get well' gifts and cards.

There was to be a totally new venue for the Society's Christmas concert on Friday, December 14th 1990. For the very first time in the Society's long history they were to perform at Gloucester Cathedral. The soloists were to be Marie-Louise Petit, Alison Hudson, James Gilchrist and John Rowlands-Pritchard. The concert, J S Bach's *Christmas Oratorio* was to be sung in aid of the Cotswold Care Hospice Day Centre. Both members of the Society and the Costwold Care organisation worked hard on advertising the event and on all the practicalities involved in the concert's staging. The concert was to be sponsored by the Original Royal Holloway Society. For the choir it was a wonderful opportunity to be able to sing such a glorious Christmas work in such an incredibly apt and atmospheric setting. Even the bitter cold and fog of the night, to say nothing of the bitter cold inside the Cathedral could not do anything to mar the warmth of the singing and playing. 'From the first notes of the orchestra leading to the choral outburst of *Christians be joyful* we knew the work was in the hands of players and singers who had firmly mastered it and would give the text a confident and sympathetic rendering', wrote the reviewer C P C. 'The varied moods of the work – lyrical, devout, triumphant – were splendidly conveyed by the singers. They coped successfully with the some-

Rehearsal in Gloucester Cathedral for a performance of Bach's Christmas Oratorio, *December 14th 1990, in aid of Cotswold Care Hospice.*

times formidable demands of Bach's contrapuntal chorus-work, whose intricate fugal windings seemed paralleled in the Cathedral vaulting, picked out in scarlet and gold, high over our heads. One must congratulate singers and players – and the leader of the orchestra, Shirley Gladstone – on a triumphantly successful performance, and the conductor Edward Garrard, on his skill, shown many times before, in co-ordinating so effectively the varied forces under his baton.' Speaking of the concert at a later date, Eddie Garrard said that he thought that the performance of the *Christmas Oratorio* in the Cathedral must rank among the Society's best, and he was sure that the choir and orchestra had enjoyed it as much as the audience obviously had.

The Society sang again in aid of a charity on March 16th 1991 in Stroud Parish Church. The Society, together with visiting singers, performed Haydn's *Creation* for the benefit of the Camphill Village Trust, Newnham-on-Severn.

Monteverdi's *Vespers* and Mozart's *Coronation Mass* had been the music chosen for the May 1991 concert. The Society's singing members were now numbered at 122, and it is possible that after a highly successful December concert members may have felt a little complacent when they started to rehearse the Monteverdi and the Mozart. However, this notion was soon dispelled as the intricacies and difficulties of these works were laboriously struggled and sweated over! From the first rehearsal choir members felt that they would prefer to perform Monteverdi in a church. This time Uplands Church, with its wonderful acoustics (and not so wonderful car parking facilities) was chosen. Sue Edwards, writing in the Society's newsletter, said, 'As is often the case after a highly successful concert, the next one seems impossible to master, but in the end we were able to provide a packed Uplands Church with a rich musical experience – thoroughly exhausting and exhilarating! Alas, although even the standing room was filled and all the tickets were sold, we made a loss on this concert.'

C P C in his review for the *Stroud News and Journal* wrote: 'Monteverdi's *Vespers of the Blessed Virgin Mary* was first performed in the year 1613. The Society, having set itself this challenge, rose to it in fine style. The elaborate settings of the psalms were interspersed with versicles and responses for men's voices in an austere arrangement. These unison passages showed the discipline we have come to expect of the Society, and what a contrast with the rich contrapuntal texture of the psalms. In these, the sub-choir (Glenys Nelmes, Kate Morgan, Olivia Watkins, David Bretherton, James Portbury and Geoffrey Whiley), orchestra and solo singers (Tina Power, Nicki Kennedy, Delyth Mayhew, James Park, David Brown, Niall Hoskin and Philip Webb), alternated, combined and alternated again to create a texture of sound that was always pleasing and sometimes dazzling in its complexity. The choir must have had some anxious moments as they counted the frequently varied beats in a bar – yet none of it showed. We in the audience were only aware of the splendour and excitement of the music.

'The second and shorter part of the programme consisted of Mozart's *Coronation Mass*. Here we were on more familiar ground and the theme was a sense of relaxed enjoyment on the part of the singers, which communicated itself to the audience. It must be said once more that Stroud is fortunate to have a choral and orchestral society, which can give such pleasure so often.'

A formal presentation of a cheque for £825, proceeds of the Cathedral concert in December, was made at the AGM of May 13th 1991. The Rt Rev John Gibbs, chairman of the Cotswold Care Hospice, received the cheque on their behalf. Also present was the Bishop of Gloucester, the Rt Rev John Yates who thanked the Society and spoke of his great enjoyment of the concert and of his delight at its outcome. The Bishop of Gloucester gave a brief outline of the work of the hospice and assured the Society that the money would be put to excellent use. Michael Gray, the Society's President, thanked on behalf of the members, the generosity of the Dean and Chapter of Gloucester Cathedral, the Original Holloway Society, the musicians and soloists, and all who had worked so well to make the evening so memorable and enjoyable.

At the conclusion of this AGM another presentation was made. This time it was to Mrs Freda Bishop: cards, flowers and the Society's good wishes, were to mark her retirement from the choir after 32 years of singing. Members were sad to see her go but Mrs Bishop cheerfully announced her intention of being in the audience at every performance to check that standards were being kept up! Many members of the choir had known Mrs Bishop's friendly face in her other capacity as midwife at Stroud Maternity Hospital.

In September the Society was saddened by the death of their former President, Canon Ernest Tucker, on September 20th 1991. Many members of the Choral Society sang Mozart's *Ave Verum* at his funeral and thanksgiving service at Minchinhampton Church. His daughter, Pat Haine, writing after the funeral said 'the Choral Society was one of the dearest loves of his life and he hated missing anything to do with it. I am sure he was singing lustily the *Ave Verum!*'

On October 5th, Society members joined in a 'scratch' performance of *Creation* in Tewkesbury Abbey in aid of The Hospices of the Marches. Those who attended found themselves deeply moved by the experience. On November 28th the Society led a charity performance of Handel's *Messiah* in St Mary's Church, Frampton-on-Severn, in aid of church funds and the Macmillan Nurses.

The December concert 1991 was to be *The Childhood of Christ* by Hector Berlioz. This work was completed in 1854 and was Berlioz's only oratorio. It was regarded with special affection by its author, but the work was to wait 25 years before it was performed in England.

The members had much enjoyed learning the Berlioz during the autumn session and everyone had enjoyed taking part in the concert on December 7th in the Subscription Rooms. The soloists, Denise Lowis, soprano, sang the part of Mary, Roger Hewetson that of Joseph, and Christopher Price 'conveyed all the brooding terror of Herod'. Michael Power was a notable narrator, 'memorable not only for the quality of his singing, but also for the clarity of his words'. Andrew Maden and James Portbury, members of the choir, confidently sang the parts of Polydorous and the Centurian. 'A beautifully performed trio for harp and flutes, together with the trio and chorus *Now take thy rest* kept the rich, lyrical atmosphere right up to the final chorus *O my soul*.'

To finish the calendar year, the choir gave a Carol Concert at the Church of The Immaculate Conception at Beeches Green, Stroud. The concert was in aid of Cotswold Care Hospice and the Society was delighted at a later date to be able to hand over £550 to Cotswold Care.

On March 15th 1992 members journeyed by coach to the Symphony Hall, Birmingham, and heard the choir of King's College, Cambridge and The Brandenburg Consort in Bach's *St John Passion*. It was a memorable evening.

The choice for the May concert was Vaughan Williams' *Dona Nobis Pacem* and Mussorgsky's *Missa Sancti Nicolai*, arranged by Philip Lane. The Society was very fortunate in having Philip Lane present at the performance. The soloists for the performance on May 9th 1992 were Jillian Whitehead, soprano and William Armiger, baritone. Also singing was a children's choir, mainly drawn from Marling School and Stroud Girls' High School, trained by Kay Sandells and Olivia Watkins. The Society had decided that a recording would be made at the performance. The Mussorgsky is not often sung and the Society felt that such a recording of the *Missa Sancti Nicolai* may be useful for other choirs as well as a record for the members.

In an article titled 'Power and Peace,' C P C writing in the *Stroud News and Journal* describes the *Dona Nobis Pacem*: 'Drama came at once in crashing orchestral chords – made particularly powerful by the brass and timpani over which soared the voice of the soprano soloist Jillian Whitehead. This was an electrifying start. The mood of sad calm in O Man Greatly Beloved was most ably expressed by the baritone soloist William Armiger.' Even more ably expressed was the warmth that the Society felt at the presence of Philip Lane and he was given a standing ovation by the choral members after the Mussorgsky.

There was no doubt that both performers and audience had enjoyed the concert. For many members this was something of a surprise as they had found the works particularly hard to learn. Speaking at the AGM the President Mr Michael Gray echoed the thoughts and feelings of the Society: 'I insisted on giving the chairman Mr Andrew Maden my remarks late after Saturday night's concert. As a consequence I share the general happy mood engendered by the evening, the same sense of euphoria that I felt in Gloucester Cathedral after the *Christmas Oratorio* in December 1990, the only time I have known it in the Subscription Rooms. I even approved the large orchestra, which partnered us so impressively in the Vaughan Williams and the Mussorgsky. I express on your behalf the Society's thanks to Edward Garrard for enlarging and enriching our musical experience through another year with these works by Berlioz, Vaughan Williams and Mussorgsky. Let us congratulate ourselves, those of us who began with such a hearty dislike of the *Dona Nobis* (I include myself) on persevering with it and being rewarded with Saturday's performance. An enthusiastic member of the audience, leaving after the concert, said to me, "150 of you making music – not popular stuff – and what a standard of competence! And a packed hall listening, it says something for Stroud." Yes, and for our Choral Society.'

However the general happy mood and sense of euphoria of the choral members soon evaporated on hearing the recording of this concert. There were angry comments from members. 'It sounded like three singers and a brass band … ' 'The microphones were positioned in front of the orchestra resulting in heavy bass and bassoon sounds and very little from the choir … '. 'Stroud Choral sounded approximately three voices strong instead of eighty to ninety!' 'If other choirs are supposed to be using our tape as a guide then heaven help them because the tape won't!' The members were disappointed not to have had a decent recording of the concert, particularly after the preparation that had been put into the event, and also because they thought that they had sung so well.

On a happier note at the AGM Mrs Freda Bishop was awarded Honorary Membership of the Society and Mr Cuthbert Webb was granted Life Membership. (A member who has participated in the Society's activities for 50 years is entitled to become a Life Member and pay no further subscriptions. An Honorary non-singing member gives a yearly fixed contribution to the Society and is given a ticket to each concert.)

An extra concert was given during November 1992 when the Choral Society and visiting singers gave Handel's *Messiah* on November 28th in the Parish Church. The concert was in aid of the Barnardo's Centenary appeal.

On December 5th 1992 the Society presented Rossini's *Stabat Mater* and Schubert's *Messe As- Dur*. The soloists were Mary Jane de Havas, soprano, Sian Meiner, mezzo-soprano, Philip Harradine, tenor, and Chris Maltman, bass. Together with a full orchestra and a choir of nearly 100, these excellent soloists sang to a capacity audience. 'Rarely can Stroud's Subscription Rooms have been swept by such glorious waves of sound as those heard at the concert given by Stroud Choral Society on December 5th.'

The Society started 1993 with two 'scratch' performances for charity. The first on March 6th was Mozart's *Requiem* in the Parish Church in aid of Cystic Fibrosis. On March 22nd the Society became part of the National Festival to celebrate the 250th British Anniversary of Handel's *Messiah* which was enjoyed, again with visiting singers, in St Matthew's Church, Cainscross. This time the benefit was the Malcolm Sargent Cancer Fund for Children.

Several society members had written to complain about the poor quality of the tapes bought after the May 1992 concert. The secretary Margery van Zyl reported back to the members after she had spoken to the recording engineer and written to the Repertoire Promotion Manager of OUP and the general feeling was that it was difficult to record perfectly outside a recording studio. It had proved difficult to place microphones in the correct position in the Subscription Rooms and in particular it had not been possible to position a microphone close enough to the choir. The orchestra had been large and had included a tuba, four horns, three trombones, three trumpets, two cellos and a double bass. The recording engineer felt that more strings had been needed to give a better balance. The Society members were disappointed, not by this explanation, but because the exercise had not resulted in a representative recorded tape.

The concert on May 15th 1993 in the Stroud Subscription Rooms was Dvorak's *Stabat Mater*. 'Stroud Choral Society's tradition of presenting notable works of great composers was maintained on Saturday', wrote C P C in the *Stroud News and Journal*. 'As always the conductor, Edward Garrard, drew a splendid sound from his singers and players. The soloists (Mary Jane de Havas, Debrah Davison, Philip Harradine, and Stewart Kempster) were a delight to the ear, but their musicianship was fully matched by that of the choir and orchestra. It is hard to pick out individual passages, but the final quartet and chorus will linger long in the memory. The singing was magnificent – especially the crescendo to the *Paradisi Gloria* and the moments of unaccompanied chorales.'

At the AGM in May the Society President, Michael Gray, told the members that the 1992–93 season was 'perhaps one of the most successful in the Society's long history'. 'To date we have produced six concerts and all of them performed with levels of competence of which we may be justly proud.' Grateful thanks to the conductor Eddie and accompanist Gail were warmly echoed by all present. The President reminded everyone that there was yet a seventh concert to come! This concert was planned in order to try and raise funds for the Society itself in particular to be able to fund orchestras. The Rossini, Schubert and Dvorak concerts had required large orchestras, each costing in the region of £700.

The seventh concert of the 1992–93 season took place on June 12th at St Matthew's Church, Cainscross. The programme was Brahms' *Songs of Love* and Elgar's *Songs from the Bavarian Highlands*. Singing with the Choral Society were Stroud Girls' High School Choir with their conductor Gillian Hale. The High School choir presented a series of classical and modern songs. (The latter were much enjoyed by the Choral Society.) A good audience helped to raise over £300 for the Society's orchestra fund.

During that summer, Margery van Zyl had been contacted by the Georgetown Choral Society, Ontario, Canada. The Canadian choir would be visiting England during 1995 and was putting out feelers as to the possibility of a combined concert. The Georgetown Choral Society had also been in communication with Huddersfield Choral Society. The Society members were intrigued by the Canadian proposals. After discussion it was suggested that members would be glad to host the Canadian visitors and they were to be asked about the possibility of joining in with the choir in May 1995 when Stroud would be singing *Elijah* as part of their 150th anniversary celebrations. Late in December 1993, Dr van Zyl received a letter in reply to the effect that *Elijah* on May 3rd would not be possible. 'We were rather excited about it, then came conflicts of dates and a realisation that the amount of music to prepare for concerts plus the *Elijah* might be more than we could muster at the performance level that we wish to have.' Wishing us luck with our celebrational and *Elijah* the Georgetown Choral Society bowed out.

In the autumn of 1993 the ladies of the Society made another blouse suggestion. Some members had not been too happy about the flowered blouses, and again, new members were finding them almost impossible to obtain. This time the choice was white! This had been previously vetoed because many choirs sing (quite sensibly) in white and the Stroud ladies wanted to be different. Apart from 1907 (and the voluminous white blouses), for a great stretch of the twentieth century the choir ladies had mostly sung in all black. To this day the ladies have remained quite happy with their white blouses though perhaps it won't be long before someone suggests 'A coloured scarf on the white blouse … '?

Some members represented the Society at the Hospices of the Marches concert on October 2nd 1993 in Tewkesbury Abbey. The combined choirs, together with the Cheltenham Symphony Orchestra, sang Rossini's *Stabat Mater* and Haydn's *Nelson Mass* under the capable baton of Mark Foster.

The December concert was Puccini's *Messa di Gloria* and Mendelssohn's *Hymn of Praise* which was performed on Saturday 4th at the Subscription Rooms. The critic, C P Campbell, was grateful for the rare opportunity to hear Puccini's *Messa di Gloria*: 'The *Gloria* had a brisk, dancing rhythm while in the *Credo* the words "et resurrexit" were carried on a wave of mounting excitement. That one felt the sensuous power of the music so keenly is a tribute to the musicianship of the performers. The skilful command of a wide range of dynamics is a hallmark of the Society. Occasionally, both here and in the Mendelssohn *Hymn of Praise,* the orchestra threatened to overpower the singers – not least the tenors, who need reinforcements – and tended by sheer volume to obscure some contrapuntal complexities of the vocal scoring of the Hymn. Yet what a splendid sound it all made and how we enjoyed it. Our thanks for another memorable concert go to the choir, the orchestra (leader Michael Parks), the soloists (Tina Power, Glenys Nelmes, Michael Power and Roger Hewetson), and to the conductor, Edward Garrard.'

One interesting addition to the Carol Concert in aid of Cotswold Care at Beeches Green on December 18th 1993 was the carol *Sleep Holy Babe*. This carol had been written by Cuthbert Webb, a long-standing member of the bass section. Cuthbert had been made a Life Member of the Society during the year. It gave the choir great pleasure to be singing one of their members' own compositions.

The year of 1994 started with dissension in the ranks. The reason was the choice of Elgar's *Caractacus* for the May concert. Some members felt that *Caractacus* was more than they could battle with on cold, wet Monday nights after work, and had voted with their feet. Others, who were only too conscious of the fact that a choral work that was disliked at the beginning could end up as a great favourite, decided to stick with it. At the beginning of the 1993–94 season the membership stood at 102, 21 members having left but 14 new members had joined. However only 80 members sang in *Caractacus*.

The committee members were already preparing for the Anniversary concert in May 1995 and had written to Amanda Roocroft asking if she could sing with us on this special occasion. Amanda Roocroft replied that unfortunately she would not be able to sing as she had a previous engagement in Munich at that time. At the same committee meeting in February 1994 it was agreed to award Life Membership to Mr Wilf Robinson.

Elgar's *Caractacus* was sung on Saturday May 7th 1994 at the Stroud Subscription Rooms. Two days before the concert the whole performance had been thrown in jeopardy. The baritone Richard Parry, who was to have sung the demanding title role of Caractacus, was taken ill and could not appear. His dropping out meant a desperate search for a replacement who not only knew the role but who would also be available for the performance. Eddie Garrard was fortunate in finding Niall Hoskin, a baritone who had sung with the Society before. Niall was available to sing on that day but unfortunately had not sung the role of Caractacus before and did not know this particular Elgar work. This did not deter him from taking up the challenge with only 48 hours to go! Niall not only mastered the music but produced a totally confident and superb performance.

The other three soloists for *Caractacus*, Nicola Hollyman, soprano, Mark Milhofer, tenor, and Robert MacDonald, bass, also gave outstanding performances, and together with Niall Hoskin were a great inspiration to all the other singers. Many Society members, who had regarded *Caractacus* with trepidation, were delighted with the outcome of this concert which they felt had succeeded beyond expectation. But over and above Eddie's successful presentation and the audience's full appreciation, was the star of the performance Niall Hoskin. Caractacus, a King of Ancient Britain, was defeated by the Romans, but Niall Hoskin's Caractacus certainly conquered Elgar, and the choir, orchestra and audience warmly applauded him for this.

One unsung hero of the concert was Glenys Nelmes. Glenys had been singing in a concert at Salisbury Cathedral in the afternoon but managed to be back in Stroud in time to sing *Caractacus*.

There were some committee changes during the year. Kay Sandells rejoined as acting minutes secretary. Acting librarians Sue Edwards and Frances Sinden happily handed over the librarianship to Ann Horner and Peggy Quelch. Jackie Martin was welcomed onto the committee as social secretary. A sub-committee for fund raising was set up to include David Coombe, Michael Gray, Pat Robinson and Andrew Maden. Sadly the committee felt it was necessary to raise the annual members' subscriptions to £34, £28 and £22.

Stroud Choral Society took part in the Nationwide *Hallelujah for Hospices* on October 8th 1994 at Gloucester Cathedral. Together with 151 choirs in 151 venues throughout Great Britain Handel's *Messiah* was sung for the benefit of the Hospice Movement. The soloists were Tina Power, soprano, Angela Ayers, contralto, John Rowlands-Pritchard, bass and Michael Power, tenor. Mark Lee was the organist. Radio 2 broadcast the event live. By tuning in and out of many of the performances *Messiah* was more or less broadcast complete!

In November 1994 the Society learned of a generous donation of £600 made by Nuclear Electric towards the 150th anniversary concert. Some years earlier in the 1980s, the offer of a donation from the then CEGB was turned down due to adverse feelings about nuclear power, then held by some members of the Society.

Altogether, 104 singers performed Mozart's *Requiem Mass* and Haydn's *Creation Mass* on December 10th 1994 in the Subscription Rooms. This was a confident, successful performance enjoyed by a capacity audience. 'The Society has, over many years, set itself an uncommonly high standard and it was clear from the opening pages of the *Requiem* that this was to be handsomely maintained.' 'The balance of sound between choir and orchestra was nicely judged … The soloists Nicki Kennedy, Kate Henriques, Andrew Friedhoff and Pam Bordas sang splendidly. In particular the *Benedictus* in the Haydn *Mass* was a memorable piece of quartet singing.' The reviewer finished by congratulating the leader of the orchestra, Michael Parks, the conductor Edward Garrard and the Society 'whose talent, enthusiasm and hard work went to create such keenly enjoyable music'.

Hot on the heels of the Subscription Rooms concert was a carol concert in aid of the Hospice Movement which took place on Monday December 19th at Beeches Green. This concert took place after some very concentrated rehearsals!

Edward Garrard, the conductor of Stroud Choral Society, and the 'architect' of the very successful concert given by the Society in Gloucester Cathedral in December, hands over a cheque for £825, the proceeds of the concert to the Rt Rev John Gibbs, chairman of the Cotswold Care Hospice, May 13th 1991.

Anniversaries and celebrations

On Mount Carmel the prophet Elijah called down flames from heaven. In Stroud, the Choral Society became his fiery glowing vehicle for Mendelssohn's oratorio. The dramatic narrative demands from the performers a wide range of effects, all of which were drawn from them in full measure by Edward Garrard's baton.

Reviewer, 150th Anniversary Concert, May 1995

The new year 1995 found the committee working hard on the preparations for the Anniversary Concert of *Elijah* scheduled for May. Again the committee had written to eminent figures living in Gloucestershire. Prince Charles got in with an early refusal; his equerry had been approached in August 1994, and the reply came in December 1994. 'His Royal Highness has, however, asked me to re-assure you that he much appreciated your kindness in asking him and sends his best wishes for this memorable occasion.' Amongst other august figures who had written to accept the invitation were: Bishop John Gibbs (ex-bishop of Coventry), Bishop Jeremy Walsh (Bishop of Tewkesbury), Roger Knapman (MP for Stroud), David Drew (Labour candidate for Stroud), Alan Caig (director of tourism, SDC), Sybil Bruce (chair of SDC), Peter Woodward Gregg (Redmayne Bentley), Maurice Broadbent (Stroud Festival), John Evans (Stroud Festival), together with the Mayor of Stroud, Pat Cook. For this occasion the Society accompanist Gail Fearnley-Whittingstall and her husband would appear in the category of honoured guests.

The treasurer Adam Smith, reporting to a January committee meeting, stated that although all three concerts produced in the previous nine months had run at a loss, the funds showed an actual increase of £512 in total over expenditure. Committee members were somewhat heartened by this news but still felt that members needed to think about further fund-raising.

Another blow to the committee was the news that because of new fire regulations at the Subscription Rooms the total number of people allowed in the building at any one time, including Subscription Room staff, was reduced to 350! Not over-pleased with the thought of choir and orchestra performing to themselves, the committee wrote urgently asking to be released from their booking for Brahms' *Requiem* in December 1995.

When *Elijah* was first performed in Birmingham Town Hall in August 1846 *The Times* wrote, 'Never was there a more complete triumph', words that the reviewer C P Campbell thought could also be applied to the performance of Mendelssohn's *Elijah* given by Stroud Choral Society on Wednesday May 17th 1995. 'On Mount Carmel the prophet Elijah

ANNIVERSARIES AND CELEBRATIONS

called down flames from heaven. In Stroud, the Choral Society became his fiery glowing vehicle for Mendelssohn's oratorio. The dramatic narrative demands from the performers a wide range of effects, all of which were drawn from them in full measure by Edward Garrard's baton. The choir, orchestra (led by Michael Parks), soloists Nicola Hollyman, Angela Ayers, Iain Sloan, Niall Hoskin, and a group of children from Rose Hill School, of whom Lucinda Dalton and William Bowen sang solo parts, all worked together as one. The scale of this undertaking – some 120 singers and a full scale orchestra, attracting an audience of nearly 600 – reflects handsomely on the cultural life of our town and area. The occasion has been a milestone in the long history of the Society.'

At this concert, the outstanding commitment given to the Society by their accompanist Gail Fearnley-Whittingstall was warmly and deservedly recognised by wholehearted applause from the choir and conductor Eddie Garrard.

Later appreciative letters concerning the *Elijah* concert had been received from Bishop Jeremy (Tewkesbury) and David Drew.

At an upbeat AGM on May 15th 1995, the President, Michael Gray, commented on the improvement in the morale and financial situation of the Society which had culminated in the very successful 150th Anniversary concert performance of *Elijah* on May 13th. The treasurer, Adam Smith, reported that in the twelve months ending on March 31st 1995 there had been surplus income over expenditure of £651. Eddie Garrard, reporting on the season's concerts, thanked everyone for the tremendous success of the Mozart/Haydn concert and for the *Elijah*. After a dreadful afternoon rehearsal and despite difficult acoustics due to positioning of the choir across the width of the hall, the singers and orchestra performed extremely well in an unfamiliar venue. Many people were thanked for their sterling work: Alex Hamilton for the superb *Elijah* programme (the advertising in the programme had netted £505 income), Christine Pearce for the print work she produced through the season, David Coombe, Brenda Dunn and Stephen Hassell for their work on the committee.

Rehearsal in the Church Institute for Elijah, *January 1995. Olivia Watkins, Christine Pearce, Kay Sandells, Joyce Gray.*

Notelets designed as part of fund raising activities in 1995.

Last but not least to be thanked was the fund-raising team led by Pat Robinson. Their ideas for the past season had netted a profit of £495.65. Simple ideas such as choral notelets, book marks and teatowels (now a collector's item) had been sold after weekly rehearsals.

In June 1995 both the *Independent* and *Stroud News and Journal* carried articles about the Society's teatowels! The *Independent*, under the heading 'Andrew throws in the towel' and the *Journal* under the heading 'Russians say "niet" to teatowels':

> A spark of British free enterprise found its way into the heart of the old Communist world in an attempt to raise money for a Stroud choir.
>
> Mr Andrew Maden, the chairman of Stroud Choral Society, tried to sell the group's 150th anniversary teatowels in Moscow's Red Square on a recent trip to Russia.
>
> 'The sale of the teatowels was very disappointing, partly because we forgot to print it in Cyrillic and also because, apart from Lenin, there was only one other person on Red Square when we arrived' he said. 'Perhaps for our 175th anniversary we might consider advertising in the Sverdlovsk News and Journal!'

This article then went on to review the 150th *Elijah* concert.

ANNIVERSARIES AND CELEBRATIONS

In October 1995 Society members were saddened to hear of the death of Cuthbert Webb, a longstanding and recently a Life Member of the Society. A liturgical performance of Mozart's *Requiem* was sung by the Choral Society at the Parish Church on All Souls' Day, November 2nd. This *Requiem* was dedicated 'to the memory of those who have sung with the Stroud Choral Society during the past 150 years and have passed to their rest'. This *Requiem* was conducted by Edward Garrard, the organist was Christopher Boodle and the celebrant, the Reverend Barry Coker.

During 1994–95 there had been some discussion on the whereabouts of 'Mr Chew's timpani'. The Society had wondered about the possibility of repairing and using them. After some difficulty in finding out where they were, Michael Gray went to inspect them at the Chalford Silver Band premises where they had been very kindly stored for some time. He reported back that they were 'enormous, cumbersome, unusable and probably not recuperable!' Several committee members felt that they should be sold for scrap 'as a last resort'. Fortunately at the time of writing, they have been spared this fate, and it is to be hoped that a more fitting home can be found for these antique instruments in their home town of Stroud.

Brahms' wonderful *German Requiem* was the choice of oratorio on December 2nd 1995 at Stroud Parish Church. *The German Requiem* may have been composed in memory of Schumann whose madness and tragic death affected the youthful Brahms deeply. It was written in 1866–67 and Brahms tells us that the aria *Ye now have sorrow* was prompted by the memory of his mother, who died in 1865. The first half of the work was premiered in Vienna in 1867 and had a lukewarm reception! Since then it has become a much loved work which has stood the test of time. This was its 10th performance by the Stroud Choral Society and it ranks in 4th place in the Society's league table of most performed works.

Local singers, Bronwyn Mills and Philip Webb, were the soprano and baritone soloists in this performance. Their clear confident singing was a pleasure to listen to. Members would have liked to have heard more of Bronwyn Mills as she sang only one solo, the aria *Ye now have sorrow*.

To finish 1995, the Society gave a Carols for All concert at All Saints Church, Uplands. Despite the freezing weather outside and the somewhat erratic heating inside, an appreciative audience happily joined with the choir in singing many of the old familiar and much loved carols.

The Society was to perform in four concerts during 1996. In particular, one of the highlights of the year was to be the first performance of a specially commissioned work *The Cotswolds* by John Sanders, this to be sung at the celebration of the Stroud Festival's 50th year in October.

The first concert of the year was to be Dvorak's *Requiem Mass* on May 11th 1996 at Stroud Parish Church. Although the *Requiem* is a beautiful and very rewarding work to sing, many members found the rehearsals hard going. Some of the rehearsals had been double ones with Gail working with lady members in the Church Institute and Eddie rehearsing with the men in the Church. An extra full rehearsal before the performance was also needed. As well as the perceived difficulty of the Dvorak, rehearsals had also been interrupted by power failures and snowfall! The secretary, Margery van Zyl, reporting on the year at the AGM on May 1996, said, 'After many individual doubts about our capabilities and a necessary last minute rehearsal, the work was performed on May 11th with full orchestra and four splendid soloists. The choir enjoyed the challenge of the *Requiem*, in the end, and the audience was full of praise for such a rarely heard but very impressive work.'

The four impressive soloists were Nicola Hollyman, soprano, Helen Greenaway, mezzo-soprano, Stephen Douse, tenor, and Dominic Burns, baritone, 'who sang with professional competence'. 'Against a background of gilded carving and stained glass in the fading light of a spring evening, we listened to the composer's reflections on death, judgement, forgiveness and hope. Dvorak's music spans the range from sombre brooding to the surge of faith, from lyrical calm to dramatic climax. The soft opening theme on the strings, taken up by the choir's almost caressing treatment of the words "requiem aeternam" set the pattern for the fine coordination of voices and instruments. In the past the singers have sometimes been overwhelmed at climactic moments by the weight of orchestral sound. This time the right balance was maintained. Stroud Choral Society under the baton of Edward Garrard, conveyed all these dramatic themes with the confidence and high musicianship we have long come to expect of it.' Eddie Garrard was afterwards to say that this requiem was one of the most moving works in the choral repertoire, sentiments with which his choir agreed.

Although choral members try to be aware of all the extra preparation that committee members are involved with in the production of concerts, it can be easy to overlook the extra work and commitment that friends and family give to the Society: 'The President thanked those who helped at the "front of house" in the Dvorak concert, especially Jean Merrett, Leon Sandells, Philip Heymans and Graham Adams' (AGM 1996). In this book the Society would like to thank all the many friends and family who have helped the Choral Society in whatever capacity, throughout its long and eventful history.

More than 100 members of the Stroud Choral Society were to perform John Sanders' *The Cotswolds* on the final day of the 50th Anniversary of the Stroud Festival. *The Cotswolds* had been commissioned in 1995 by the Choral Society to celebrate the Society's 150th anniversary. John Sanders was the former organist and choirmaster at Gloucester Cathedral who had previously composed several pieces for the Festival in the past.

Of *The Cotswolds* John Sanders said, 'I have tried to capture in music the atmosphere and beauty of the countryside around Stroud.' Apart from the final section, all the words are by Gloucestershire poets. Ivor Gurney's poem *There was Such Beauty in the Dappled Valley* sets the mood and it is followed by Frank Mansell's *Cotswold Choice* in which the author, after considering many local villages, decides finally that he would rather be buried in Sheepscombe. The centrepiece is Maurice Broadbent's *Market Day* in which he reminisces on the importance of Stroud as an industrial town since Roman times. (The words and music vividly evoke the bustle and excitement of days long ago in Stroud's Shambles and High Street.) Leonard Clark's poem *This Night the Stars Shine High Over Birdlip Hill* follows, and the work concludes with a *Canticle of Praise*, a thanksgiving for all God's gifts, using the works of the *Te Deum*, 'We praise Thee, O God.'

Maurice Broadbent was now the Director of the Stroud Festival. He had been involved from the 1950s as both actor and playwright with the Religious Drama Festivals. He and Netlam Bigg had been instrumental in the evolution of the Drama Festival into the Stroud Festival.

As well as *The Cotswolds*, the Society were to sing Lennox Berkeley's *Signs in the Dark*, Vaughan Williams' *Five Mystical Songs* and, to end the concert, Vivaldi's *Gloria*. Singing with the Choral Society were the choir of Rose Hill School (Eddie Garrard is Director of Music at Rose Hill Preparatory School).

The World Premiere of Sanders' *The Cotswolds* was performed on Sunday October 20th 1996 at the Sibley Hall, Wycliffe College, Stonehouse. Both the reviewers, Elizabeth Baker and Cyril Campbell, commented on the double celebration: 'The Festival, begun in 1946, has reached its Golden Jubilee, while the Stroud Choral Society, always closely involved with the Festival, takes pride in the 150 years of its existence.' Both reviewers were in agreement that the whole concert was 'stunning!' As was Margaret Bell, who reported on the concert on behalf of the South West Region of the National Federation of Music Societies: 'A wonderful way to spend a wet Sunday afternoon. I felt particularly privileged to be present at the first performance of the newly commissioned work by Dr John Sanders. *The Cotswolds* was so exciting and tuneful, with the added attraction of a children's choir. I am sure this will remain in the repertoire.' 'Mezzo-soprano Penelope Walker enhanced the work with her heart-warming contribution, as did the heavenly voices of The Angels from Rose Hill School', wrote Elizabeth Baker. Niall Hoskin's beautifully sensitive interpretation of *Cotswold Choice,* with a superb oboe soloist, held both choir and audience spellbound during the afternoon rehearsal and the concert itself.

The reviewers were also full of praise for the other programme items. 'Lennox Berkeley's setting of four poems by Laurie Lee was a decidedly avante-garde composition, technically difficult and not the easiest of music for many of us to enjoy. It is greatly to the credit of the semi-chorus and orchestra that they gave such a competent account of it.' (Laurie Lee was present in the audience.) 'Lennox Berkeley's *Signs in the Dark* had been originally commissioned by the Stroud Festival. It had received its first performance on October 22nd 1967, in the Stroud Festival's 21st anniversary year, and had been recorded on that occasion by the BBC for the 'Music Programme.'

'The Five Mystical Songs by Vaughan Williams are settings of poems by George Herbert, in turn brooding, ecstatic, triumphant ... this work was beautifully handled by the choir and orchestra. The baritone Niall Hoskin sang memorably.' (This was the 6th time since 1923 that the choir had sung *The Five Mystical Songs*.) 'The programme ended with Vivaldi's *Gloria*, crisply sung and complemented by superb trumpet playing and the voices of two well-known local soloists, Tina Power and Sylvia Strange. It was a fitting conclusion to a Cotswold Choral celebration.'

ANNIVERSARIES AND CELEBRATIONS

The final accolade for *The Cotswolds* was the news that the Society had been granted an award by the Performing Rights Society for 'Initiative in Commissioning a Work of Art'. On October 31st 1996, at a presentation in London, Michael Gray, President of the Stroud Choral Society, received the £250 Enterprise Award from Kathryn McDowell, Director of Music at the Arts Council of Great Britain. The award was one of just eight awards to choral societies from all over the country. 'Most of the award winners were societies from the big cities,' said Mr Gray. 'That we were amongst them was extremely gratifying.'

The Society's December concert was Handel's *Judas Maccabaeus* sung on the 7th at Holy Trinity Church, Stroud, to a disappointingly small audience, partly due to clashes of other concerts on the same night. The soloists, Tina Power, Angela Ayers, Bill Bowers-Broadbent and John Rowlands-Pritchard were excellent as was the orchestra, led with great competence by Nicholas Bowers-Broadbent.

Two weeks later, on December 21st 1996, the Choral Society returned to Holy Trinity Church to sing Handel's *Messiah*. Again there were excellent soloists, Tina Power, Angela Ayers, Martin Noel Davies, and Robert Marson. The soloists and choir were accompanied by 'a splendid young organist', Christopher Sparkhall.

Spurred on by the previous year's success in advertising their concert *The Cotswolds* with an eye-catching display (in one of Stroud's vacant shop windows), the Society set out to recreate the Hanging Gardens of Babylon in a shop on the corner of the High Street and Kendrick Street. 'It is a spectacular scene from Verdi's opera *Nabucco*. Cascading foliage and exotic flowers over white arches, trees, river and the shattered golden statue of Baal, portray the final moments of this dramatic work. The poisoned chalice drunk by Abigail, her discarded cloak and head-dress, the ropes and chains of the freed Hebrew slaves and the soldiers' weapons must surely excite the imagination and encourage many to attend this concert. Want to know more of the story? Visit the corner of Kendrick Street and

Michael Gray, John Sanders, Edward Garrard, Maurice Broadbent. 'The Cotswolds' written by John Sanders had its first performance at the Stroud Festival's Golden Jubilee Celebration on Sunday 20th October 1996.

Michael Gray receiving an Enterprise Award on behalf of SCS, presented by Kathryn McDowell, Director of Music at the Arts Council of Great Britain, October 31st 1996.

High Street, look into the window, and then come to the performance of *Nabucco* – listen to the stirring music and let your mind's eye visualise the drama unfolding.' This write up in The *Citizen* was part of the advertising material for the Society's production of Verdi's *Nabucco* to be performed in the Subscription Rooms on May 10th 1997. Just what the inhabitants of Stroud thought about the advertising window is not known, but it was certainly a fine window display and brought the Society literally into the public gaze.

For Verdi's *Nabucco*, the Society returned once more to the Subscription Rooms despite the very restrictive fire regulations. This concert was given before a packed audience whose appreciation led them to applaud the choir after each chorus! The 'excellent, well disciplined orchestra' added to the pleasure of choir and audience, as did 'a superb team of well chosen soloists'. 'The part of Abigail was taken by Frances Walker, whose quality of voice and power was most impressive.' Robert Bateman sang 'with great feeling' in the title role of Nabucco and Garrick Forbes, 'whose splendid wide ranging voice' was used to good effect in the 'taxing part of Zachariah.' Other parts were taken by Neil Fortin who sang the parts of Ismael and Abdulla, and Helen Wright, taking the part of Fenena. A member of the Society, Ann Spargo, sang the part of Anna. 'The choir sang throughout with dedication and a sweet sound with impeccable timing … Perhaps the choir's greatest contribution was the chorus of the Hebrew slaves. There was an audible sigh of pleasure from the audience as this great chorus ended.'

At the May 1997 AGM three long-standing members of the committee, Margaret van Zyl, secretary, Adam Smith, treasurer and Michael Gray, President, stood down. The new Choral Society President was to be our hard-working, brilliant and most patient accompanist, Gail Fearnley-Whittingstall. Hilary Penney became the new secretary, and Olivia Watkins, with assistance from Christine Pearce, the new treasurer. Sue Edwards remained as publicity officer, likewise Eric Martin in his role of concert manager. Other members of the committee were Kay Sandells, Chairman, Pat Robinson, Ruth Fraser, Sally Lamerton, Caroline Bridgens and Susie Salter.

Sue Edwards had added considerably to her role as publicity officer. As well as the usual publicity sent to the press and other organisations she now added 'window dresser' to her job description. She was also producing small, eye-catching folding leaflets, with details of the Society's history, reviews of recent concerts plus rehearsal details, forthcoming events and contact numbers. There could be no excuse for not knowing of the Choral Society's existence! It was Sue Edwards who at the AGM broached the subject of doing something special to celebrate the Millennium ...

The Society also decided to hold Open Evenings at the beginning of each new season. Visitors would be made welcome and the evening would take the form of rehearsing for the first half and socialising with a buffet and drinks in the second half.

The new 1997–98 season started with 116 members on role and five concerts to prepare for. Some members of the Society put forward a request for a sixth concert, a Princess of Wales Memorial Concert in aid of the Memorial Fund to be held in the Cathedral. The only dates that the Cathedral could offer (for October) were too close to other concerts already assigned to the Society, so reluctantly this idea was dropped.

The Society sang at the 51st Opening Service of the Stroud Festival on Sunday October 5th 1997. The service began with Haydn's *The Heavens are Telling* and ended with *Hallelujah Chorus* from Handel's *Messiah*.

On October 18th the Society together with members of the Beacon Singers sang a concert of well known oratorio choruses ending with the *Hallelujah Chorus* at Minchinhampton Church. This was in aid of the Cotswold Care Hospice and was part of the BT Voices for Hospices event.

The Society's main concert for the autumn season took place on December 6th 1997 at the Subscription Rooms. The programme consisted of Schubert's *Mass in G*, Bach's *Magnificat* and Haydn's *St Nicholas Mass*. 'A capacity audience at the Subscription Rooms was treated to three wonderful choral pieces which showed the range and dynamism of Stroud Choral Society at its eloquent best.' The reviewer SP went on to explain that it was unusual to hear these three pieces together on one programme – 'but what clever programming it turned out to be.' Bach's *Magnificat* is known to be a challenging work. 'On the whole, however, it was a commendable performance of this notoriously difficult work ... The *St Nicholas Mass* retained a quality of freshness that communicated itself throughout.' The soloists were Helen Wright, soprano, Angela Ayers, contralto, Neil Fortin, tenor, and Richard Weston, bass. Both the audience and the reviewer were delighted with the New Zealand bass. 'Richard Weston has a quality of technique and accomplishment which should ensure no lack of engagement in future ... The stylish orchestra was superbly led by Nicholas Bowers-Broadbent and really did prove to be the icing on the Christmas cake of a Winter Concert.'

Before the Society members could go home and start icing their own Christmas cakes they had two more concerts to play a part in. The next of these was a 'first' for the Choral Society, who had been invited to sing a group of Christmas carols as part of a concert for Severn Sound's Christmas Celebration. The performance was recorded at the Cathedral on December 18th. There was a short technical rehearsal at the Cathedral at 6.30pm and the concert began at 7.30pm. The Society sang the spirituals *Mary Had a Baby*, and *The Virgin Mary Had a Baby Boy*. In the second half of the programme the choir sang *Jesus Child*. Other people taking part in the concert were the Heron Primary School Mini Choir, the Gloucestershire Youth Jazz Orchestra and Christopher Boodle the organist. The presenter, the Reverend Peter Jackson, ensured that the evening was full of Christmas cheer and it was a happy band of singers that returned to Stroud later that night. All proceedings from Christmas Celebration went to the Severn Sound Money Mountain Appeal for Gloucestershire Charities.

On December 20th 1997, the Society gave a carol concert at Beeches Green where audience and choir joined together in singing with enjoyment the old familiar carols.

But the final icing on the cake for that particular Christmas, was to switch on to Severn Sound on Christmas Morning, and enjoy all over again the Severn Sound Christmas Celebration while preparing the Christmas dinner!

During December 1997, the Society was saddened to hear of the death of Maurice Broadbent, on December 18th, aged 70. He was a well-known figure in the arts world and Director of the Stroud Festival. His commitment to the arts and the Festival was much respected. The Society was pleased and privileged to be invited to participate in the memorial service on January 31st 1998. The choir sang the *Lacrymosa* from Mozart's *Requiem* and *The Heavens are telling* from Haydn's *Creation*. Father Barry Coker, who was President of the Stroud Festival, said, 'He will be greatly missed by the town. He had a great love for this part of the world and great wit.' The Society made a donation to the Festival funds in memory of Maurice Broadbent. The following poem by Michael Holland is a fitting tribute to this larger than life figure.

Maurice Broadbent: A Tribute

No more to walk on Frocester Hill,
The cheery smile, the nod, the wave;
With little Tina faithfully at heel,
Severn wind competing with his breezy air.

We met, we laughed, we chatted (as you do),
His undulating voice in rich brown tone
Listed his boys and girls of Gloucestershire;
Jenny Joseph, Laurie Lee,
Frank Mansell, Leonard Clarke,
And many more, a veritable Who's Who,
of those caught by his twinkling eyes
who melted to coercion for his love, the arts.
And in those same rich tones
Amongst those august names he mentioned me.

Maurice, I'm sure I saw you only yesterday.
It was on Frocester Hill.
I waved and mouthed my silent words,
Hoping the wind would carry them,
You disappeared. Farewell my friend, sleep well.

Tina, the little dog referred to in the poem, was Netlam Bigg's much loved black and white mongrel terrier who Maurice Broadbent had cared for since Netlam's death in 1988. On Maurice's death, Tina went to live with Maurice's nephew. Having had the benefit of three very good owners, Tina died just a few weeks short of being entered into the *Guinness Book of Records* for longevity!

The first rehearsal of 1998, January 5th, was a combined rehearsal and social evening, which was much appreciated by the members. Visitors had been encouraged, in the hope that they might enjoy the 'taster' evening and come back the following week!

In April one of the Society's long-standing members, Joyce Cordwell, was given Life Membership and feted with cards and flowers from the members. When it was discovered that Joyce had actually been with the Society 62 years and not 50, having first attended rehearsals with her mother at the age of 17, it was felt that the press should honour this fact!

During the spring of 1998 the members of the Society worked hard on preparing for their next concert *Carmina Burana*. Sue Edwards and a team of one created three scenes from *Carmina* in an empty shop in the Merrywalks precinct. The scenes in the three windows represented Springtime, the Tavern and the Court of Love. These certainly took the public's eye and the window dressers were frequently interrupted by questions from curious passers by.

Carl Orff's *Carmina Burana* together with Famous Opera choruses were the programme choices for a concert on March 28th 1998 given at the Subscription Rooms. *Carmina Burana* is a collection of thirteenth-century secular songs discovered in a monastery in the Bavarian Alps and first published in 1847. It was not until 1936 that Orff composed his now world-famous oratorio. The members had enjoyed rehearsing *Carmina* and found singing the oratorio, accompanied by a percussion ensemble and two pianos, an exhilarating experience. (The two, top of the range pianos, had been loaned for the occasion by Woodchester Pianos and freely transported and installed by Abacus Removals.) 'The Choral Society, with soloists Maria Lancaster, Bill Bowers-Broadbent and Tony Yates, and accompanied superbly by pianists Gail Fearnley-Whittingstall and Mary Cope, and the Regency Percussion Ensemble, directed by Diggory Seacome, rose to the challenge magnificently and did full justice to the compelling rhythms and rich sonorities. Each of the soloists delighted the audience with their technical competence – Miss Lancaster's perfectly placed top D in the *Dulcissime,* Mr Bowers-Broadbent singing falsetto as the Roasted Swan and Mr Yates' atmospheric tenderness in *Dies, Nox.* The Choral Society hardly put a foot wrong throughout ... and conductor Edward Garrard is to be congratulated on drawing the best from the singers and instrumentalists alike.' Of the popular opera choruses the reviewer chose to highlight the particularly moving chorus *Dido's Lament* sung by the choir and soprano soloists. Also riding high in H P's report for the *Stroud News and Journal* was the playing of the *Scherzo* from Salzedo's *Concerto for Percussion* which received 'well-deserved acclaim for a bravura display of percussive pyrotechnics'.

Shortly after this concert the Subscription Rooms was closed to allow extensive renovations to take place. It was not until December 2000 that the Rooms were re-opened.

The Society had been asked to perform as part of the Wotton festival in early May. On May 2nd 1998, in conjunction with the choir from Rose Hill School, a concert of popular operatic choruses was given. 'Rose Hill's well-trained choir gave renderings of numbers from *Les Miserables* and Lloyd Webber favourites in the first half while the Stroud Choral Society gave spirited performances of choruses by Wagner, Verdi, Orff and Purcell in the second half. Both groups came together to sing the *Easter Hymn* from Mascagni's *Cavallera Rusticana* as a grand finale. All credit must go to Edward Garrard for his work with both groups which produced an excellent concert' (GP). Also adding to the enjoyment of this concert was Georgina Hildick-Smith's flute solo, Colin Davis' *Theme from Pride and Prejudice.*

On June 9th, members attended the Thanksgiving service for the life of James Rennard Wilson (1912–1998) at Rodborough Tabernacle. Jim Wilson had been a long-time member of the Choral Society and had served for many years on the committee.

Stroud Choral Society was well represented by a large group of members at the Royal Albert Hall on Saturday July 11th to take part in the Really Big Chorus event in aid of the Leukaemia Research Fund. They joined with 70 choirs and many individual singers, numbering over 2,000, to sing Verdi's *Requiem,* accompanied by the English Festival Orchestra and conducted by Sir David Willcocks. During the rehearsal, Sir David made the comment, 'How happy I am to see such a large section of tenors' ...! The concert was billed as 'The most awesome Verdi *Requiem* in the Universe'. 'From the first sombre chords of the *Requiem,* through the mighty *Dies Irae,* the glorious *Sanctus,* to the final tumultuous *Libera Me* this enormous choir sang their hearts out! All those taking part were exhausted but exhilarated by such an amazing experience.'

The new season 1998–99 began on September 7th. The subscription rate for this season was £44 for full membership and £36 for retired/non-wages members. The membership for school and college students was free. The committee members for the new season were Gail Fearnley-Whittingstall, President and accompanist, Eddie Garrard, conductor, Kay Sandells, chairman, Hilary Penny, secretary, Olivia Watkins, treasurer, Eric Martin, concert manager, Sue Edwards, publicity. Other members were Caroline Bridgens, Ruth Fraser, Sally Lamerton, Christine Pearce, Pat Robinson and Susie Salter. Jean Bruce-Gardyne joined Ann Horner as Society librarians.

On October 17th members took part in a Choral Workshop at Marling School. The workshop had been promoted by the Society with assistance from the National Federation of Music Societies, and was under the direction of Jeremy Jackman, a well-known choral director. Although a tremendous amount of work and in particular singing exercises took place, the overwhelming recollection of the day is one of laughter and yet more laughter. As for the singing, the improvement over the day was remarkable. Jeremy Jackman was an inspirational teacher. Whether working with Stroud Choral Society or behind the scenes at the BBC singing the 'Blackadder' signature tune he could be guaranteed to bring out the best!

Haydn's *Creation* on November 20th at St Matthew's Church, Cainscross, marked the 200th anniversary of its first performance. It was the Society's 10th performance since 1864. 'Last Saturday in St Matthew's Church,

Window display in Merrywalks Shopping Centre to advertise 'Last Night of the Proms', May 2000.

Cainscross, Stroud Choral Society (conductor Edward Garrard), three first class soloists and an orchestra celebrated the bicentenary of Haydn's oratorio *The Creation*. The soloists Sue Black (soprano), Iain Sloan (tenor) and Richard Weston (bass) all did full justice to their music but often it seemed that they were having to sacrifice finesse to overcome the tidal wave of orchestral sound, good though this was. Richard Weston must be commended for his articulate and sensitive handling of the narrative recitatives, the best of the evening was found in the full-blooded choruses … the evening was one of very enjoyable music making.'

A Carols For All concert was held at Stroud Parish Church on Saturday December 12th 1998. Traditional carols, together with Bach chorales, spirituals, and twentieth-century carols, were accompanied by Gail Fearnley-Whittingstall on the piano and by the organist Andrew Douglas. Mince pies and mulled wine were enjoyed in the Church Institute.

The new year 1999 began with the Millennium in mind. Like every other organisation in the country, Stroud Choral Society also wanted to mark the occasion in some special way. The idea of a Millennium Book had been mooted and this idea was being followed up and evaluated. The suggestion that the Society might like to change their logo to present a fresh image for the new century was also acceptable to the members. A logo competition was suggested and this was coordinated by Susie Salter. The winner of the competition would be announced at the AGM in May. Members were also encouraged to think about the Millennium concert and what form it should take.

The form of the next concert (May 1999) was to be Verdi's *Requiem* and it was the special choice of Conductor Eddie Garrard as it would mark his twentieth year with the Society. The committee circulated other choirs with an invitation to their members to join Stroud for this anniversary concert to be held in the Leisure Centre on May 8th.

As before, the window dressing team set out to publicise the *Requiem* in an eye catching manner. Set against the terrible current history of the war and ethnic cleansing in Kosovo the simple backcloth of pictures of refugees from many twentieth century conflicts, together with white arum lilies, made a most moving statement.

ANNIVERSARIES AND CELEBRATIONS

'Last Night of the Proms', May 6th 2000, Stroud Leisure Centre.

The programme for Verdi's *Requiem* was dedicated to Sylvia Heymans, a much loved member of the Choral Society. Sylvia had died unexpectedly in February 1999 and her committed support of the Society would be much missed.

Apparently when Verdi's *Requiem* was first performed it had given devotees of oratorio a considerable surprise. Nowadays, its dramatic and operatic nature is taken in its stride and we are delighted by its beauty and excitement. The critic H L Vincent wrote that the opening work was 'smoothly sung' but unfortunately from where he was sitting much of the first half was drowned by the timpani and brass, he goes on to say 'that it may have been an acoustic quirk of the hall, but all the same it was a pity'. H L Vincent felt that the soloists were well matched: 'The soprano Shelley Everall and the tenor Bradley Dale, sang as if on stage (well, the music asks for it), whereas the mezzo-soprano, Angela Ayers and the bass, Richard Weston, were restrained but nonetheless musical and telling.' 'Richard Weston has an easy delivery and every word can be heard, Angela Ayers gave a deeply felt account of the *Lux Aeterna* and in the *Agnus Dei,* together with Shelley Everall, gave a beautifully shaped account of this cruelly exposed movement. Bradley Daley has a strong voice which can cut through orchestral tumult – and he needed it at times.' Shelley Everall's entry into the *Domine Jesu* was 'ravishing'. Many members in the audience, if not familiar with this *Requiem*, would certainly have recognised the *Libera Me* from the funeral service of Diana, Princess of Wales and they would have been moved by Shelley Everall's pure, clear singing. The critic felt that the performance had been a 'grand and stirring end to the Society's season'.

At the end of the performance a surprise presentation of an engraved cut-glass decanter was made to Eddie Garrard as a mark of the Society's appreciation of his twenty years as their conductor.

At the AGM in May, Eddie brought in his presentation decanter so that the members could see this splendid gift at close quarters. Some members were curious to know if Eddie had already drunk the contents! Eddie went on to tell the Society how pleased he had been with his anniversary concert, in particular he felt that the discipline in the choir was 'especially pleasing'.

Susie Salter announced that there were 24 entries for the logo competition: there had been a substantial entry from Thomas Keble School and the Society members were pleased and interested to see such a lively collection of designs. The overall winner was Darren Jones of Cashes Green. His mobile, upward-flowing design was felt to best represent the Society reaching out and singing into the future.

Three members of the committee stood down at this AGM. Sally Lamerton was thanked for her work as minutes secretary, Pat Robinson and Christine Pearce (a member for 40 years) were thanked for their support and hard work on the committee over many years. In particular Pat had used her creativity in many fundraising schemes and Christine had produced posters and tickets for many years and recently had been joint treasurer. Special thanks from all members of the Society were given to Glenys Jones (Nelmes) for her excellent singing. Both Christine Pearce and Glenys Jones were made Life Members of the Society. As well as the genuine pleasure that members of the Society felt at the presenting of these long-deserved awards, the laughter that accompanied these announcements was due in part to the comments of the recipients, one of whom was heard to say that she couldn't possibly remember when she first sang with the Society and that she certainly wasn't counting!

There were 111 members that registered in September 1999 for the new choral season 1999–2000. It was to a large majority of this number that the book group reported back in the autumn of 1999 on the Millennium Book feasibility study. Style, quality, quantity and cost had been discussed and the book group were now asking for the Society's mandate in order to proceed. This time the Society would be funding the project and it was felt that the support of at least 65% of the members would be required in order to go ahead. The members responded with an overwhelming 'yes' vote.

At this point, surprisingly enough, the book group had hardly any Choral history to go on other than Leonard Keck's *Handbook of the Society*. It was felt that the best way to proceed was to try to compile an archive consisting of the existing minutes, interesting letters, old programmes and press cuttings. A lively search ensued as to the whereabouts of the old choral programmes which Leonard Keck made reference to in his Handbook. The old programmes were eventually found, safe and sound, having been carefully stored by Stroud Museum since the 1950s.

The old programmes themselves gave useful leads and had researchers looking in many different directions for the next pieces in the jigsaw. The group have been more fortunate than Leonard Keck in his research, as modern science, in the shape of microfilm, had come to their aid. From letters it was noted that Leonard was allowed one morning to search the back copies of the *Stroud Journal* and *Stroud News and Journal*! The Stroud Choral Archives now consist of six, full, lever-arch files and these give absorbing and compelling insights into life and music in Stroud over the last 166 years (1834–2000).

The Society received the sad news of the death of Shirley Gladstone, on October 10th 1999, with sincere regret. Shirley's fine leadership of the orchestra marked the decade of the 1980s and had been much appreciated. Two major Society concerts, Verdi's *Requiem* in 1985 and Bach's *Christmas Oratorio* in Gloucester Cathedral in 1990, had been under Shirley's guiding hand. This was followed by the news of Mabel Hyde's death in November 1999. Mabel had been a long-time member of the Society and was missed by many friends.

The new Society logo made its first appearance on the programme cover for Monteverdi's *Vespers* and Mozart's *Vesperae Solemnes*. The concert took place in Uplands Church on December 11th 1999 and a packed audience listened to 'the beautiful voices of no less than seven soloists and two choirs of eight voices, sing the elaborate psalms and magnificat from the Monteverdi *Vespers*'. 'As the unaccompanied chanted antiphons and responses of the baritones and tenors echoed around the vaulted roof one could imagine being transported back in time to seventeenth-century Venice. An emotional, soul-searching *Nisi Dominus* and the glorious finale of the *Magnificat* were particularly uplifting. Mozart's *Vesperae Solemnes* sung in four parts was lively and confidently performed. The well-known

Laudate Dominum, whose beautiful soprano melody is set against a choral background, was made magical by the clear, soaring, faultless voice of Jane Sherriff and was a favourite of all present.' FS concluded her review by commenting that 'Once again Stroud Choral Society, with an orchestra superbly led by Nick Bowers-Broadbent and under the baton of Mr Edward Garrard, have risen in true style to the challenges set by the ambitious Monteverdi *Vespers* and Mozart's *Vesperae Solemnes*.'

For most people, the Millennium year 2000 dawned with a bright expectation of something new, something different to strive towards or to achieve. In keeping with many other organisations the Stroud Choral Society had thought long and hard about its own celebration of the year 2000. One particularly appealing idea was to produce a concert of Choral Music through the Ages with a famous narrator, childrens' choirs and youth orchestra. Another imaginative idea was to present Haydn's *Creation* with a giant mural of the Creation as a backdrop. This mural would be illuminated during the performance, perhaps by laser beams, to illustrate evolution as it was sung. (It may have been the teachers in the Society that vetoed this suggestion. Already on their knees, the thought of asking schools to design and or produce large sections of 'Creation', as well as to cope with the ever changing curriculum, was one straw too many!)

The one thing the Society was quite certain about was that they wanted young people to be involved with the Millennium concert. The obvious choice for the Society was to ask Eddie Garrard, as Director of Music at Rose Hill Preparatory School, Wotton-under-Edge, if their choir would be able to take part. The Rose Hill Choir contributions had been much appreciated in the past and not just for their ability to sing the difficult parts in works like *The Cotswolds!* Their youth, freshness and enthusiasm for singing is infectious, and with the Society looking ahead, these young singers would embody the hope of a choral future.

With all this in mind the Society decided on a choral 'Last Night of the Proms' to be held at the Stroud Leisure Centre on Saturday May 6th 2000. It was an impressive and impressed audience that came on a gloriously warm May evening to listen to famous oratorio choruses by such masters of oratorio as, Handel, Verdi and Mascagni; to be

Bank Gardens, April 2001, singing into the twenty-first century.

amazed and delighted by the virtuosity of the six hands of Gail Fearnley-Whittingstall, Alison Green and Edward Garrard on the piano; to be enchanted by the flawless performance of Rose Hill choir, particularly moving when they sang Edward Garrard's own composition *We Came into the World;* to appreciate Susan Black's expressively emotive solo in Purcell's *Dido's Lament;* to enjoy a well-balanced orchestra ably led by Nick Bowers-Broadbent and above all, under the baton of Edward Garrard, to join together as one massed choir in the old familiar 'Last Night' tradition and to sing out *Jerusalem, I Vow to Thee My Country* and *Land of Hope and Glory* as our celebration of the millennium.

The last words of this chapter go to the thirteen-year-old senior chorister from Rose Hill School, Frankie Hildick-Smith, whose youthful review leads us towards the next millennium.

> On Saturday 6th May, the Senior Choir sang at a 'Last Night of the Proms' performance with Stroud Choral Society in Stroud Leisure Centre. It was the biggest performance that the choir have sung in and none of us knew what to expect. We had a full rehearsal in the afternoon with the 120 strong Choral Society and the 40 strong orchestra, at first all of the choir were amazed by the standard of singing with which we were accompanying, and hoped we could match their standard. The audience numbered over 400 and was well supported by Rose Hill parents (thank you!) The school choir sang four songs separately, including *Love Changes Everything,* and two songs accompanying the Stroud Choral Society. At the end everyone sang the traditional songs, such as *Land of Hope and Glory,* for these The Rose Hill choir got to go into the audience and wave balloons! As usual *Pomp and Circumstance* finished the evening which was great fun! Many people complimented Mr Garrard on the Senior Choir's performance (although we couldn't praise the audience on their singing!) and the *Gazette* newspaper also wrote a very complimentary report about the evening. Everybody really enjoyed the experience of singing with the Choral Society and the whole concert turned out to be a great success.

Leonard Keck in a letter written to Netlam Bigg in October 1972 made the observation that history was being made all the time and should be worthily kept and not lost forever. We hope Leonard would think that this book is a record worthily kept.

Members of the choir at Rose Hill School, Alderly, with Director of Music Eddie Garrard and the trophy they won in the 1999 Cheltenham Festival.

Let us now praise famous men – and women!

Throughout its long history the Society has been very fortunate in its Officers, and whilst all have contributed greatly to the success achieved, there are some who deserve special mention.

Leonard Keck, Society Handbook, 1973

Samuel William Underwood

If ever a man lived for music, that man was Sammy Underwood.

Dr Herbert Sumsion, August 27th 1958

If the nineteenth-century Choral Society had resounded with the name of Chew, then the twentieth-century belongs to Underwood. Samuel William Underwood was born in Gloucester on May 24th 1881, the eldest son (and one of six children) of Samuel and Elizabeth Underwood. The Underwoods were a well-known local family who kept a general store and off-licence at 58 Castle Street (now Stanley Road), Gloucester. Samuel Underwood attended the King's School where he showed an early interest in music. He became leading chorister at the age of 12 and was known as 'the choirboy with the golden voice'.

Like Chew before him, Sammy Underwood could play many instruments, but was particularly known for his virtuosity on the horn and timpani. He was also a talented organist having gained his associate membership of the Royal College of Organists in 1902 and his fellowship of the Royal College of Organists in July 1905 at the young age of 24.

Before he came to Stroud as conductor of the Choral Society there had been two previous occasions in which he had worked in Stroud. During the final illness of James Chew in the late 1890s Samuel Underwood had played for the services in the Parish Church for several months. In July 1905 he had been

Portrait of S W Underwood as a young man c. 1910.

Ivor Gurney's poem was written before 1911 and this part-song for unaccompanied male voices published in 1932 (perhaps written for the Gloucester Orpheus Choir). Ivor Gurney and Sammy Underwood would have known each other from their time at Gloucester Cathedral in the late 1890s and early 1900s.

appointed organist and choirmaster at Holy Trinity Church, Stroud. Although this position was only held for 4 months until October 1905 it was long enough for the congregation at Holy Trinity to express 'deep regret' at his going.

He returned to Gloucester Cathedral to become deputy organist and lay clerk under the auspices of Dr Herbert Brewer. He had played both organ and piano for the 1904 Three Choirs Festival at Gloucester. The programme for that year included: Bantock's *The Time Spirit*, (conducted by the composer), Beethoven's *Choral Symphony No. 8*, Brahms' *German Requiem*, Elgar's *The Apostles* and Handel's *Judas Maccabaeus*. Herbert Brewer conducted the first performance of his own work *The Holy Innocent*. The programme also included *Elijah*. The trio *Lift Thine Eyes* was sung by Madame Albani together with Muriel Foster and Ivor Gurney! Due to the non-appearance, at the last minute, of the second soprano, Dr Brewer had asked Ivor Gurney (a fouteen-year-old chorister at Gloucester Cathedral) to stand in and take her place.

Many years later, members of the Underwood family still expressed an unhappiness at what they perceived to have been an 'over-looking' of Sammy for a position that the family felt should have been his by right. He had been a 'second choice'. (This is probably a reference to the position of Organist at Gloucester Cathedral on Herbert Brewer's death in 1928.) Fortunately for the Choral Society Sammy was free to serve in Stroud.

The Stroud News of October 12th 1906 carries a long article about the appointment of Mr S W Underwood, FRCO to the position of organist and choir master at Stroud Parish Church. At the end of the article it states that, as a matter of course, Mr Underwood would succeed to the conductorship of the Stroud Choral Society.

During the 52 years that Sammy Underwood, as he was to be universally known, conducted in Stroud, his contribution to the musical life of the West Country was described as 'astonishing' As well as the Stroud Choral

Society he had conducted the Bristol Choral Society for more than 25 years. At some period he had also conducted the Swindon Choral Society, the Gloucester Orpheus, the Gloucester Cooperative Choir, Gloucester Festival Choirs, the Cheltenham Philharmonic as well as other small music groups. In Bristol, on Saturday 8th February 1930, he had shared the conducting at a concert of Richard Wagner's work with the composer's son, Seigfried. During the Second World War, together with Adrian Boult, he was responsible for the continuation of the BBC Choral Society and Symphony Orchestra. Because of his many widespread musical interests and contacts he was able to engage some of the most renowned soloists of the day to perform in Stroud. In 1957 for his contribution to music in the West Country he was awarded the MBE.

For many years Sammy Underwood and Dr Herbert Sumsion, organist at Gloucester Cathedral, enjoyed a close working musical friendship. At the time of Sammy's death in August 1958 Dr Sumsion wrote the following tribute:

> The many friends of 'Sammy' Underwood (as he was affectionately known to everyone) must be so numerous that I count it as a privilege to be allowed to write a few words in memory of him. The eloquent tribute paid to him in your columns of yesterday gives a full

CARTOONS OF LOCAL CELEBRITIES.
(BY "ECHO").

NO. 19—MR. S. W. UNDERWOOD, F.R.C.O.

FAMILIARLY known to our readers as "Sammy," the subject of this week's cartoon owes that familiarity to his mercurial disposition and a popularity engendered by his perennial flow of good humour, wit and genial fellowship.

Cartoon of Sammy Underwood, Stroud Journal, July 8th 1932.

and very vivid picture of him both as a man and musician; and all those that knew him intimately would wish to endorse everything that you have said in your appreciation of him. My own personal friendship dates back to the year 1928 when I took over from him the Festival chorus which he had been training (owing to the sudden death of Sir Herbert Brewer) in preparation for the Three Choirs Festival in Gloucester that year.

I have worked with him on many occasions since then, and always with an increasing admiration and respect for his musicianship and artistic judgement.

If ever a man lived for music that man was 'Sammy' Underwood. In particular he loved any form of singing, and he was, I think, happiest when dealing with choirs and choral societies. He was a unique personality and he had his own individual way of doing most things, both musical and otherwise. The majority of people, having bought a motorcycle and sidecar, would expect to sit on the motorcycle and drive the combination so seated. Not so 'Sammy' Underwood!

I well remember seeing him driving to Stroud, sitting in the sidecar, and driving from this position. Eventually the authorities decided that he should drive in the orthodox manner.

On another occasion, when I was playing the organ for a congregational Broadcast service in Stroud Parish Church and watching his beat in the mirror, he disappeared entirely from my view in the middle of one of the hymns! I found out later that he had climbed to a higher point of vantage because some of the congregation at the back of the church were not watching his beat – a defection that always infuriated him.

Such anecdotes could be multiplied almost indefinitely; and when thinking of 'Sammy' Underwood these and similar occasions inevitably enter one's mind, for they are part of the parcel of the man we knew and loved.

He was himself a singer, and at the annual reunions of the King's School Old Boys' Society he would sing folk songs to his own accompaniment with characteristic humour and artistry.

For many years he was a keen and accomplished timpani player, and he gave this up only when he was capable of miscounting his bars and entering in the wrong place. One such wrong entry would have meant that for him the performance was ruined, though probably no one but himself (and probably the conductor) would have known that a mistake had been made.

In the case of music nothing was for him too much trouble, and no stone was left unturned in his efforts to reach as near to artistic perfection as was humanly possible. He led a full life, and in doing so, he brought endless happiness into the lives of many people. Inevitably, we are saddened by this moment, but at the same time we can be more than thankful for a long life so fully lived.

Personally I shall ever be grateful that for so many years I have been one of the many who have enjoyed his friendship, his musicianship, and his never failing kindness. It is a small wonder that wherever he went he was universally loved and admired.'

Gloucester Citizen, August 27th 1958

Forty-plus years on, there are still many Stroud people who have memories of Sammy, his genial personality, his freedom from conventionality and his fine musicianship. One member of the Society tells, 'He always knew how to get the last ounce of effort out of his choir. He was always striving for the best and didn't mince matters at rehearsals if there was any sign of slackness.'

Another member recalls, 'The final rehearsals according to Sammy were always disasters. We always wondered how the performance would turn out, however as was often the case, everything would go well.'

Glenys Nelmes remembers that those turning up for private singing lessons with Sammy were treated to his special brand of hospitality. The tea, having been brewed in the pot on the hob, where it had been for some time, was readily poured out. The finishing touch, instead of milk, was a spoonful of Horlicks powder. The resulting brew was indescribable! Glenys also remembers accompanying Sammy with fellow members of the Society to sing at Gloucester Prison. During the late 40s and early 50s Sammy trained a small male voice choir at the prison. Groups of singers from both Gloucester Choral and Stroud would attend on different occasions to join the prison choir and give concerts for the other inmates.

Jack Sollars found Sammy a 'remarkable character, though he could be a bit blunt'. As a junior reporter on the *Stroud News* Jack visited Sammy one morning at half-past eleven. Finding him having a meal, tin mug in hand. Jack apologised for disturbing his lunch. 'Lunch be damned this is my breakfast', retorted Sammy. Jack also remembered him being a 'beautiful organist' and in particular he enjoyed Sammy's own setting of the carol *Angels from the Realms of Glory*.

In his latter years, Sammy who hated all forms of self-display, lived quietly in gentle bachelor chaos in a small bungalow on the Painswick Road at Cranham. He was an inveterate collector of old and interesting musical instruments. His small house was shared with this ever-growing collection, particularly of harpsichords and spinets, together with an extensive hoard of music and musical scores.

Sammy Underwood's name is entered in the Musicians Book of Remembrance, held at the Musicians Chapel, St Sepulchre's Church, Holborn.

These last words on Sammy come from an unknown writer in the *Stroud News and Journal* in 1958: 'Sammy Underwood had gifts which might have carried him far among the famed. Instead he preferred to remain in the West getting the unexpected from the ordinary man and woman.'

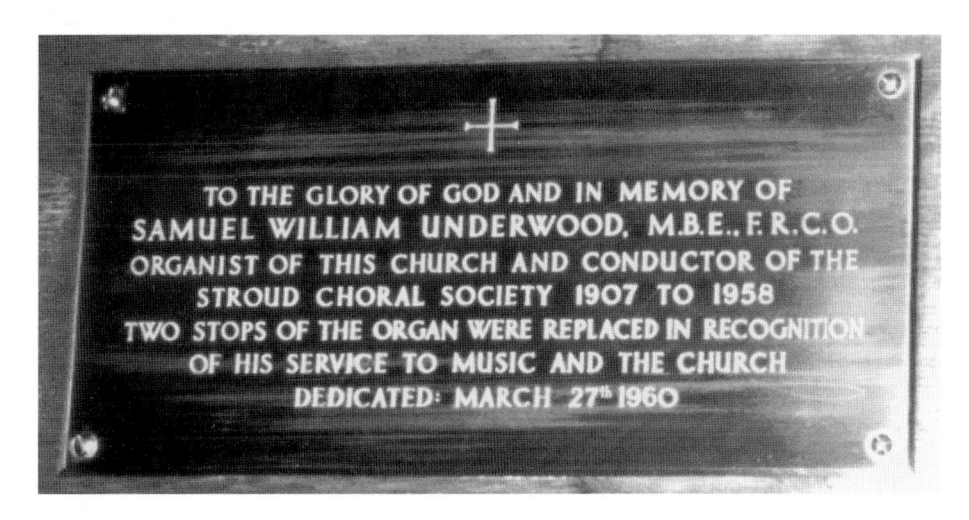

Memorial Plaque to S W Underwood in Stroud Parish Church, March 1960.

John Jacob

He had an impressive association with the Stroud Choral Society in which to the end he maintained a lively interest

Obituary, September 11th 1942

John Jacob is one of the unsung heroes of the Choral Society. It was his thoughtfulness and affection for the Society, one day in March 1935, that has enabled us to study so many of the nineteenth-century programmes that otherwise would probably have been lost.

John Jacob was born in Swansea on July 19th 1850. At some time in the early 1860s he came with his family to live at Ebley. His father, the Rev Elijah Jacob, was Pastor at Ebley Chapel. John was educated at Bussage House School under Mr J Sibree MA. Later, having taken the preliminary examination for the London BA, he served as a master on the staff of the school. For some years he was a private tutor, preparing pupils for outside examinations and the university. It is said that many people thought that John Jacob should have gone on to do greater things with his life. Probably it was because of the indifferent health of his father that he stayed in Ebley, helping with the Chapel activities. He taught at the Sunday school for 60 years. He was the Chapel organist and trained an 'excellent Chapel choir'. During the winter months he trained a choral society 'which gave most successful concerts'. He trained other choirs, including a huge combined choir in 1920, drawn from all the Stroud district's Nonconformist Chapels. The work was to commemorate the tercentenary of the sailing of the 'Mayflower'.

John Jacob was also a committed member of the Stroud Choral Society. In 1923 he boasted that he had not missed a single Society concert for 60 years. This meant that he must have attended his first concert in 1863 aged 13. (*Messiah* in April 1863 or a Miscellaneous concert in December 1863, both under the baton of Mr Helmore.) We cannot be certain when he actually joined the Society though we do know that he sang with the bass section. For many years he served on the committee. Our twentieth-century minutes start from 1926 and these list him as chairman from 1926 to 1937.

STROUD SINGS

In March 1935, when he was 85, he presented the committee with a plain, buff-coloured scrapbook, inscribed to 'The Stroud Choral Society with John Jacob's best wishes March 1935'. The scrapbook held a collection of old Choral Society programmes and included 'Rules for the Stroud Choral Society' dated 1865. Unfortunately this scrapbook was taken apart, perhaps for display in the exhibition in 1956. We are left with the difficulty of piecing bits together and although the programmes are discernible by glued fragments from the scrapbook page we cannot be sure we have the complete collection. It seems that the oldest programme is for *St Paul* May 1869. If this is the first concert that John Jacob sang in, he would have joined the Society at the age of nineteen. When the Society made him a life member in 1939 it would not be surprising if he had been singing for more than 70 years.

John Jacob is credited with giving the Society the 1835 print of the Stroud Philharmonic. It was also John Jacob that expressed the opinion that the Society had its early beginnings in the Stroud Philharmonic Society.

John Jacob died on September 7th 1942 aged 92 after a very active life. Fascinating glimpses of his character, almost 60 years on, came to us in the following passages taken from his obituary. The truth, perhaps, lies somewhere in between!

John Jacob was made a Life Member in April 1939, as he was approaching his 89th birthday. Stroud News, April 14th 1939.

He was a man of stern principle and strong conviction, at times perhaps aggressive, and yet one had never heard anything but regard for him. Those with long memories had vivid recollections of 'old, unhappy far-off things, and battles long ago.' John Jacob had a scent for the fray, was in it to the full, and all the time honoured by friend and foe alike. He maintained his interest to the last, and became one of the most familiar figures in the district.

He was a man of charming disposition, a staunch supporter and firm upholder of organisations and principles that interested him. His kindly personality, gentleness and courtesy had earned for him the regard of all with whom he came into contact, and his familiar figure will be much missed.

Stroud News and Journal, September 1942

FAMOUS MEN — AND WOMEN

Leonard Alden Keck

Where there is more of singing and less of sighing,
Where there's more of giving and less of buying,
A man makes friends without trying.

Chapman (taken from the 'Leonard Keck'
page in the Society Handbook, 1973)

Leonard Keck was born in Cheltenham in 1904 but spent the greater part of his life in Gloucester. His introduction to music was as a boy chorister in Tuffley Church at the start of World War I and in which he continued to serve for some 50 years, several of these as Churchwarden.

As a young man he entered the building industry and trained as an Estimating Surveyor. He later became managing director of Halls & Keck Ltd. He was a Fellow of the Institute of Building and of the Faculty of Building and was twice President of the Builders Federation. He had also served as Chairman of the North Gloucestershire and Herefordshire Training Board for the construction industry.

On his retirement and move to Houndscroft, Stroud, he became a chorister at Amberley Church singing with the tenor section. He donated money for an organ screen and the re-building of the organ at Amberley Parish Church.

Leonard joined the Choral Society in 1970 and in eight years stamped his indelible mark upon it. He was a man of deep musical appreciation, honesty and integrity. Perhaps not since Sammy Underwood himself has anyone carried such a belief in the Society and such a vision for its future. We owe him a tremendous debt of gratitude. He felt that it was important and necessary that the history of the Society should be retrieved and recorded. He felt that it was proper that past members of the Society should be recorded and valued for their contributions. It is from his early research that this book has grown.

It was Leonard Keck who insisted that rehearsal evenings should not just be for singing alone, and that it was important for the development of the Society that members should be able to share fellowship with each other. Never one for talk and no action, he led the way with generous choral 'get-togethers' at his home. It was a great blow to the Society when Leonard died of leukaemia at the early age of 74, on September 22nd 1978. Members of the choir attended his funeral on November 27th at Amberley Parish Church and the following year, in April 1979, Brahms' *Requiem* was sung in his memory.

Claude Victor Allen

Claude Allen provided the continuo and, as is always the case, his presence was a great asset. His masterly, and sympathetic playing of the organ is an added joy to any performance.

B M W, Stroud News and Journal, April 1955

Claude Allen was born near Winchester in 1906 and like Chew and Underwood before him, showed early musical ability. At the age of nine, when organists were few and far between, due to the First World War, he played the organ at Pitt, near Winchester. When someone enquired how he was able to reach the pedals the answer was 'the organ had no pedals!' He attended Peter Symond's School, Winchester from 1916–21 and while he was there he gained his ARCO diploma at the age of 16. This made him the youngest person at that time to have passed this examination.

On leaving school he was awarded the Threlfall Organ Scholarship to the Royal Academy of Music where he studied organ, piano and composition from 1921 to 1923 under the tutelage of Sir Stanley Marchant. (Sir Stanley Marchant was organist of St Paul's Cathedral and later became Principal of the Royal Academy of Music.) Claude Allen gained his FRCO at the Royal Academy.

For a brief time he was the organist and choirmaster of Woburn Parish Church. From there Claude Allen won an organ scholarship to Clare College, Cambridge, where he read Music and Modern Languages, gaining a Batchelor of Music and Batchelor of Arts degrees, and later his MA.

In 1929 Mr Allen joined the music staff at Wycliffe College where he remained for 40 years. During his early years at Wycliffe he wrote six songs which were sung by Jack Toole at a concert in Gloucester. 'Those who sang or heard these songs will not forget their beauty, but they lacked the popular appeal to attract music publishers, and sadly he composed little more' (Obituary, October 14th 1982).

During the Second World War, Wycliffe College was evacuated to Lampeter. On their return Claude and Kitty Allen became houseparents for twelve boys. Mr Allen was always keen to encourage young people especially in the field of music. He would spend many willing hours transposing scores and rehearsing groups. The Wycliffe boys delighted in listening to his organ-playing and soon learned to listen out especially for his variations in the last verses of the hymns!

Mr Allen was as brilliant a pianist as an organist. Many singers were grateful for his excellent and sympathetic accompaniment. A choral member writes: 'Claude was an inspirational organist and could intuitively smooth over mistakes like skipped bars.' He accompanied many of the famous soloists who sang for the Stroud Festival as well as the Choral Society. John Carol Case apparently always asked for Claude to play for him. The baritone Brian Rayner Cooke once brought a piece of Handel which had only the singer's line and asked him to fill in the accompaniment 'which he did with such panache that afterwards it was acclaimed as more Handelian than Handel!' At one concert where Claude had accompanied the singer Angela Beale in songs by Ralph Vaughan Williams, the composer's widow afterwards said, 'Ralph would have been delighted with the sensitive playing of his songs.'

Claude was organist at Holy Trinity Church for 14 years, the post being taken on his retirement from Wycliffe in 1968. It is reported that at the annual Holy Trinity Concert, when the Vicar Ernest Tucker and Claude entertained, the audience was 'considerably larger than average'.

Claude had been the Society accompanist since December 1954. His modest and self-effacing manner hid a strong sense of humour, which often caught people out, and he was an excellent and amusing compere of musical evenings. Finding a replacement for Claude after his 'second retirement' from the Society in 1982 was far from easy.

Canon Ernest Tucker and Claude Allen, Holy Trinity Church, Stroud, July 1982.

Gail Fearnley-Whittingstall

Currently, the choir has the services of an excellent accompanist, Gail Fearnley-Whittingstall who rarely misses a rehearsal and performs amazing feats of part-reading without turning a hair!

Ernest Tucker, March 1985

Gail Fearnley-Whittingstall has been the Society's stunningly successful accompanist since the autumn of 1982. Her lifelong love of music began at boarding school in Bath. Her talent was spotted early and the school encouraged her to develop her potential to the full. It was a while before Gail settled on the piano as her instrument of choice but once having made this decision there was no looking back. In 1958 she successfully gained her LRAM in piano at the early age of 19.

Unfortunately, having achieved this early success, Gail found that her youth worked against her when she tried to find employment. Gail tells how she remembers sitting in endless interviews for accompanists jobs only to be turned down, her talent disregarded, because of her age. For a while she was forced to give up the idea of becoming a professional accompanist. Instead Gail turned to teaching and for four years she taught at St Margaret's School in Shrewsbury.

After the teaching post Gail found the next few years fully occupied in the role of wife and mother. With two children very close in age, the hectic demands of motherhood meant little time for much music outside the home. Unfortunately her first marriage did not last. Some time later she met – over the bridge table – George Fearnley-Whittingstall who became her second husband in 1974. If Gail had found her hands full with two children, with a new baby and three children belonging to George, life was very full indeed!

In spite of such a busy family life George began to encourage Gail to think of her music again. Soon she was playing once more, taking part in competitions and eventually teaching in Chepstow, her childhood home.

The daily journeys undertaken across the Severn Bridge were beginning to take their toll on George and eventually the family moved to Eastington. Once settled into their new home Gail turned her mind to thoughts of work again. She placed a small advertisement offering her services as accompanist in the Stroud Music Centre. At this particular time the Society was anxiously seeking a new accompanist and

Gail Fearnley-Whittingstall, Summer 1998.

this advert was spotted by Eddie Garrard. The members of the Society could hardly believe their good fortune when Gail arrived to play for her first rehearsal one Monday night in the autumn of 1982. Gail has been with us ever since.

Gail still leads a very full life. Not content with helping out with the ever-growing clutch of grandchildren, supporting George with his political commitments or breeding Labradors, she is also on the local committee of the NSPCC. Gail also helps with music at Rose Hill School in her position as accompanist.

Not just an accompanist for the Choral Society, Gail has also performed in concerts as a pianist in her own right. (For the very difficult piano part in *Carmina Burana,* March 1998, Gail and fellow pianist Mary Cope visited Woodchester Pianos for extra practice on the pianos to be used in the concert!)

Over the years Gail has come to mean much more to the Society, not just as accompanist but also as a teacher and a good friend. This Society was delighted when, in 1998, Gail accepted its request to become its President.

Edward Garrard

This has got to be one of the most exciting performances of Messiah *ever. One must both admire and congratulate the Conductor, Edward Garrard, for producing such a result.*

Richard Greenland, December 1988.

Like many good musicians before him, Eddie Garrard showed an early preference for music. Inspired by music on the radio and parents, who enjoyed music making in the home, Eddie began playing the piano at the tender age of three and joined a church choir when he was five! He has been involved in church music ever since. At primary school Eddie made his mark composing music and later learned the violin while he was at Cheltenham Grammar School. At fifteen he became organist and choirmaster at Prestbury Church.

Eddie would have liked to have taken up music professionally when he left school but his parents were keen for him to have a more conventional career. So instead of a musical career Eddie found himself working in accountancy with a Cheltenham firm.

Away from work Eddie continued to be involved in music and he was one of the founder members of the Cotswold Savoyards in the 1960s. At 21 he was invited to be the musical director of the Dursley Operatic Society where he stayed for ten years. After a break he returned to the DODS in the mid-1980s and has been actively involved until recently. He particularly enjoys music in the theatre and the more dramatic side of music.

From time to time Eddie was invited to play and tour professionally, but the demands of his then young family (he and Glennis have six children) would have been incompatible with this lifestyle. During this time Eddie was continuing with private teaching of piano and singing as well as conducting and running church choirs.

By 1978 Eddie came to the momentous decision to 'give up the day job' and devote all his attention to music. 'I was fed up with working for other people and I had just had enough of not being involved more fully in music.' Having taken his LRAM and LGSM externally, Eddie's first job away from accountancy was as a teacher in a private school in Thornbury. Later he was to become Director of Music at Rose Hill School, Alderley near Wotton-under-Edge where he very happily remains to this day.

In the autumn of 1979 the Stroud Choral Society were actively seeking a new conductor. After auditioning several candidates the post was offered to Eddie Garrard. Over twenty years later Eddie is still wielding his baton at the helm of this Society. At an interview given to Victoria Temple for the *Stroud News and Journal* in June 1999 Eddie remarked, 'They said they were looking for somebody to take on the post long term, and that is certainly what they have got.' Adding, 'Conducting is what I wanted to do. I suppose it's because one gets completely involved in the overall picture of the music rather than one particular aspect.' Certainly this Society has been luckily blessed with noted long-term conductors and Eddie is well set to join this illustrious band!

Like Chew and Underwood before him, Eddie is also involved in a multiplicity of musical activities. As well as DODS, Stroud Choral Society, church choirs and private tuition, Eddie is very involved in the musical life of Rose Hill School. He has taken the Rose Hill Choir abroad to perform and included in their repertoire have been Eddie's own compositions. The school has competed successfully at the Cheltenham Festival where they have won the 'Age 12 and under' category for mixed and single sex choirs several times. The Rose Hill Choir was a finalist in the National Festival for Youth in 1998–9 and runners up in the HTV 'Sing Out 2000'. Eddie and the choir particularly enjoyed performing at Euro Disney! Working with young people and introducing music into their lives has give Eddie much pleasure. He doesn't underestimate the importance of music in the lives of young people.

It has been said that Eddie is 'unflappable', the 'anchor of the Society who always gets us out of difficulties, musical or otherwise'. Eddie certainly has to think on his feet at times. He has had to cope sensitively with many situations. For example, musicians who have brought the wrong instruments to rehearsal and need the orchestral parts rewriting, a soloist who cancelled (through illness) two days before a concert leaving very little time to find a substitute, soloists who have learnt the 'wrong' Mozart and need rehearsing in the 'right' work between the rehearsal and the concert, to say nothing of keeping his 100 or so choristers in check. Then ... there was the lady harpist who confided in Eddie the startling information that she wore knickerbockers when playing, to discourage members of the audience from gazing up her skirt!

Happily, together under Eddie's guiding baton, the Choral Society looks set fair to sing on into the twenty-first century.

Conductor Eddie Garrard at his home in Cam, June 1999.

Soloists of note

My experience has satisfied me that in every musical performance – be it oratorio or opera – important as is efficiency in the choral and orchestral departments, success, in a great measure, depends on the judicious selection of principals.

Ex-impresario, Stroud Journal, March 1868.

Stroud Choral Society wishes to put on record its very grateful appreciation to all the soloists who have contributed to its concerts throughout the Society's long existence. We have chosen to highlight a few of these soloists to illustrate the wide musical experience they have demonstrated during their singing careers and draw the attention of our readers to some of the names with which they will be familiar but possibly unaware of their connection with this Society.

We apologise to readers and soloists for any omissions that they would have liked to have seen included.

Sir Charles Santley (bass baritone)
- Born Liverpool 1834
- Died London 1922
- Studied in Milan and London
- Studied under Garcia, noted Spanish bass
- Noted for singing oratorio
- Wrote books on singing
- Sang in English premier of Gounod's *Faust* 1863
- Knighted in 1907
- Ex-impresario's choice for Stroud Choral Society *Elijah* May 1868

Barri Odoardo (tenor)
- Born Edward Slater 1844
- Died London 1920
- Irish composer of English drawing room songs, *The Boys of the Old Brigade* 1874
- Sang for Stroud Choral Society May 1881

Robert Watkin Mills (bass-baritone)
- Born Painswick, Glos 1856. Died 1930
- Educated at Painswick Public Grammar School
- Studied under Dr Samuel Sebastian Wesley, Gloucester Cathedral
- Studied in London under Edward Holland
- Studied in Milan under F Blasio
- Sang for Stroud Choral Society April 1910

Elsie Suddaby (soprano)
- Born Leeds 1898
- Died Radlett 1980
- Trained originally as a pianist
- Famed for her lovely pure soprano voice
- Made her reputation in singing oratorio
- One of original sixteen singers in Vaughan Williams' *Serenade to Music* 1938
- Sang for Stroud Choral Society November 1927, November 1937, November 1938, March 1946, November 1948

Roy Henderson (bass-baritone)
- Born Edinburgh 1899
- Died 1999
- Remembered as Kathleen Ferrier's teacher
- Studied at Royal Academy of Music
- Became Professor of Singing 1940–74
- Conducted many choirs
- Conducted Nottingham Oriana 1936–52
- Sang for Stroud Choral Society February 1935, December 1942

Isobel Baillie (soprano)
- Born in Hawick, Scotland.
- Died Manchester 1983
- Studied in Manchester and Milan
- Debut at Hallé Concert Manchester 1921

Madame Albani, Mrs Patey, Mr Santley and Mr Lloyd were professional soloists on the major choral festival circuit. In this print they are shown at the Leeds Music Festival in 1886. Also in 1886 they were soloists at the Three Choirs Festival at Gloucester. At Gloucester they were engaged for the following fees: Madame Albani 450 guineas, Mrs Patey 200 guineas, Mr Santley 200 guineas and Mr Lloyd 180 guineas. It was Mr Santley that Ex-impresario had wanted SCS to engage for the role of 'Elijah' in May 1868.

Madame Albani, c 1900

Miss Elsie Chambers, 'The well known Stroud Contralto Gold Medalist', c 1909. Miss Elsie Chambers and her sister Zoura were members of an 'old and accomplished Stroud family' who lived in Stratford Road, Stroud. Zoura was a gifted water colour artist who had exhibited at the Royal Academy Summer Exhibition. Elsie was a professional singer of international repute who had performed for Sir Henry Wood and other leading composers. Elsie Chambers sang three times with SCS. Messiah February 1909: 'This was, we believe, practically the first appearance of Miss Chambers in Oratorio, and the impression she created was most favourable.' Elijah, March 1923: 'Miss Elsie Chambers can always be heard at her very best in Oratorio work, and particularly she has made the Contralto role in Elijah her own peculiar study, and, whether interpreting it in London or the provinces, she has always been successful and received unstinted appreciation.' Messiah, April 1924: 'The restrained power always behind the artistic treatment of the Contralto solos was a feature of Miss Elsie Chamber's performance. Richness of tone and tenderness of expression characterised each of her efforts, giving new value to such well-known numbers as "He shall feed his flock" and "He was despised".'

Chosen by Toscanini for performances of Brahms' *Requiem*

One of the original 16 singers in Vaughan Williams' *Serenade to Music* 1938

Made her American debut in 1933

Taught at Royal College of Music 1955–57, Cornell University and Manchester School of Music

Autobiography *Never Sing Louder than Lovely* 1982

Awarded CBE 1951

Awarded DBE 1978

Sang for Stroud Choral Society January 1939, February 1941, March 1942, March 1943

René Soames (tenor)

Born Canterbury 1903

Won a choral scholarship to Canterbury Cathedral

Joined both BBC Chorus and BBC Singers 1937

Excellent interpreter of Peter Warlock and Works of the French School

Known for his opinion that few singers understood the psychological approach to singing and that English singers should know English works first

Sang for Stroud Choral Society March 1947, March 1949, March 1951

Heddle Nash (tenor)

Born in London 1894

Died 1961

A chorister at Westminster Abbey

Studied singing in London and Milan

An outstanding tenor, specialising in works of Mozart and Rossini

Very successful at oratorio

Considered one of the finest interpreters of Elgar's *Gerontius* which he recorded in 1944

Sang for Stroud Choral Society March 1950 (*Gerontius*)

James Walkley (bass)

Has enjoyed many years as a noted Gloucestershire soloist

A Lay Clerk at Gloucester Cathedral

Has sung solo parts in oratorio with many English Choral Societies

SOLOISTS OF NOTE

Sang in first public performance of Honegger's *Cantate de Noël* with the London Symphony Orchestra
Has made many radio and television appearances
Became very well known for teaching voice production and for teaching singing in schools and colleges
Founded the Cheltenham Bach Choir in 1946
Founded Philomusica of Gloucestershire in 1966
Awarded an MBE for Services to Music in Gloucestershire
Sang for Stroud Choral Society December 1951, March 1953, March 1955, December 1961, March 1962, March 1964, December 1979, December 1980, April 1984

Elsie Morrison (soprano)
Born in Australia
Won Melba Scholarship in 1943
Came to England in 1946
Joined Sadlers Wells, making her debut in 1948
Married to the bass Kenneth Stevenson
Sang for Stroud Choral Society December 1950, November 1952, December 1953

Heather Harper (soprano)
Born in Belfast 1930
Created role of Lucie Manette in Britten's *Tale of Two Cities*
Also role of Mrs Coyle in *Owen Wingate*
Awarded CBE 1965
Continued singing career until 1984
Became Professor of Singing at Royal School of Music 1985
Sang for Stroud Choral Society December 1955, December 1959

Jennifer Vyvyan (soprano)
Born Broadstairs 1925. Died 1974
Studied at Royal Academy of Music with Roy Henderson
Joined Glyndebourne in 1948
Created Penelope Rich in Britten's *Gloriana* 1953
Well known for oratorio particularly works by Elgar and Howells
Sang for Stroud Choral Society March 1955, December 1957

Dame Janet Baker (mezzo-soprano)
Born in Hatfield, near Doncaster 1933
Sang in the Leeds Philharmonic Choir
Soloist in Haydn's *Nelson Mass* 1953
Studied in London with Helen Isepp and Meriel St Clair
Joined the Ambrosian Singers in 1955
Awarded second prize in the Kathleen Ferrier Competition 1956
Made her opera debut in 1956 at the Oxford University Opera Club
Equally renowned for Lieder or Oratorio
Retired from Operatic stage in 1982
Awarded CBE 1970
Awarded DBE 1976
Awarded CH 1994
Sang for Stroud Choral Society December 1960

Robert Tear (tenor)
Born Barry, Glamorgan 1939
Choral scholarship to King's, Cambridge
Studied singing under Julian Kimbell
Appointed Lay Vicar St Paul's Cathedral
Worked with Ambrosian Singers
Operatic debut 1963 Britten's *Turn of the Screw*
Covent Garden debut 1970 as Lensky in *Eugene Onegin*
Became a conductor
Awarded CBE 1984
Sang for Stroud Choral Society December 1963, March 1965, March 1967

Sarah Walker (mezzo-soprano)
Born Cheltenham 1943
Studied at Royal College of Music 1961–65
Made her opera debut 1969
First appearance at Glyndebourne 1970
A noted recitalist
Awarded CBE 1991
Noted for her sartorial elegance (the Union Jack dress) when she sang *Rule Britannia* at the Last Night of the Proms in the late 1990s
Sang for Stroud Choral Society December 1971

Felicity Lott (soprano)
Born in Cheltenham 1947
Made her operatic debut in Mozart's *Zauberflöte*
Particularly fond of works by Richard Strauss

Made her debut in America in Chicago 1984 at the Metropolitan Opera, New York 1990
Member of the Songmakers Almanac
Awarded CBE 1990
Awarded DBE 1996
Sang with Stroud Choral Society June 1972, December 1974

April Cantelo (soprano)
Born Purbrook, Hants, 1928
Studied piano at Royal College of Music
Studied singing with Julian Kimbell
Joined New English Singers, Dellar Consort and Glyndebourne Chorus
Married to Colin Davis 1949 (divorced 1964)
First solo *Barbarina and Echo* with Glyndebourne in Edinburgh 1950
Joined English Opera Group 1963
Created Beatrice in Williamson's opera *Our Man in Havana* 1963
Recital programmes ranged from lute songs to Monteverdi, Lieder and modern
Particularly well known for her interpretation of Baroque music, Mozart and songs of Richard Strauss
Known also for her interest in the problems of actor/singers
Lectureship at Canterbury University
Sang for Stroud Choral Society April 1977

Brian Rayner Cook (baritone)
Graduated in music from Bristol University where he developed interests as an organist and conductor
Specialised in singing at the Royal College of Music
During these postgraduate studies, won all the major singing prizes
Awarded a Kathleen Ferrier Memorial Scholarship in 1969
Travelled extensively and has sung in many European countries
Has also sung in South America, Canada, Israel and Egypt
Peter Maxwell-Davies and Roger Smalley have composed for him
Appeared in two First Nights at the Proms as well as a Last Night at the Proms in 1980

Took part in a series of *Face the Music* on television in 1983
Opened the BBC World Service live Invitation Concerts in 1984
Has made many recordings including opera, oratorio and song
Sang for Stroud Choral Society April 1985

Angela Ayers (mezzo-soprano)
Read Music, French and German at Sheffield University
Studied singing under John Dethick, Paul Hamburger, John Carol Case, April Cantelo and Stuart Smith
Participated in master classes at the Britten-Pears School, Aldeburgh
Has broadcast with BBC Singers and Monteverdi Choir
Many recitals covering a wide repertoire
Special interest in English Song, Lieder and French Mélodies
Sang for Stroud Choral Society April 1983, May 1995, December 1996 (twice), December 1997, May 1999

Niall Hoskin (bass-baritone)
Born 1953, Isle of Wight
Choral Scholar of Clare College, Cambridge
Studied with James Atkins in Cambridge
Sang with Wakefield Cathedral Choir. Baritone solo in première recording of Kenneth Leighton's *Sequence for All Saints*
Performed frequently in opera, oratorio and recitals
Recital at St George's, Bristol with the Bridge Quartet
Has performed the major song cycles of Schubert and Schumann with pianist Clare Wilding
Joined the Stan Tracey Orchestra in 1999 to celebrate the centenary of Duke Ellington's birth
Sang for Stroud Choral Society
May 1991, May 1994, May 1995, October 1996, December 2000

SOLOISTS OF NOTE

Christopher Maltman (bass)
    Born in Cleethorpes, Lincs 1970
    Studied at the Royal Academy under Mark Wildman
    Won a number of prizes including the Anna Instone Memorial Award
    Studied in Italy with Silvio Bruscantini
    Sings with Welsh National Opera
    Also noted for his oratorio and recital work
    As part of the Lyndon Ensemble toured and led Music Workshops in schools
    Finalist in the Cardiff Singer of the World 1997 where he won the Lieder Prize
    Sang for Stroud Choral Society December 1992

Amanda Roocroft (soprano)
    Born in Lancashire 1966
    Studied at Royal Northern College of Music
    Won International Young Singer of the Year at Llangollen in 1985
    Made her operatic debut in Cardiff in 1990 with Welsh National Opera as Sophie in *Der Rosenkavalier*
    Made her Covent Garden debut as Pamina in *The Magic Flute* 1991
    Glyndebourne debut 1991 as Fiordiligi in *Cosi Fan Tutti*
    Starred as Mimi, in *La Boheme* Royal Opera House 1996
    Sang role of Cleopatra in *Julius Caesar* Royal Opera House 1997
    Debut in Munich 1998 as Amelia in *Simon Boccanegra*
    Made Fellow of the Royal Northern College of Music 1998
    Appeared at NY Metropolitan 1999 in role of the Countess in *Marriage of Figaro*
    Sang role of *Jenufa* at Glyndebourne 2000
    Sang for Stroud Choral Society November 1986 (first professional engagement), May 1987

Susan Black (soprano)
    Has sung with ensembles from the Royal Philharmonic to the Band of the Grenadier Guards
    Extensive repertoire ranging from Purcell to Bernstein
    Operatic roles include title role in Puccini's *Tosca*, the Countess in Mozart's *Marriage of Figaro*, Eurydice in Offenbach's *Orpheus in the Underworld* and Giulietta in *Tales of Hoffman*
    Oratorios have included Mozart's *Requiem* and *Exultate Jubilate,* Haydn's *Nelson* and *Teresa* Masses and Elgar's *Starlight Express*
    Has toured South Africa as guest soloist with the Lydbrook Silver Band
    Sang for Stroud Choral Society November 1998, May 2000

Glenys Nelmes (soprano)

Throughout Glenys' long, loyal association with the Stroud Choral Society she has been our soloist many times. Now, enjoying a less hectic timetable, Glenys remains invaluable during rehearsals where she often takes the solo sections. Glenys has kindly given us the following profile of her singing years:

'I was born in South Wales and from an early age was encouraged to enter local competitions for solo singing and piano playing. In my teens I was invited to join a local Ladies choir where I had the privilege to sing small solo parts alongside such fine singers as Isobel Baillie and Kathleen Ferrier. After attending teacher training College in Salisbury my first solo debut was in Salisbury Cathedral as the Angel Gabriel in Haydn's *Creation*. Later I was to perform throughout South West England and also in York Minster. On arriving to teach in the Stroud area in 1947 I joined the Choral Society and sang my first solo role from Chandos' *Te Deum* in December 1948. I studied oratorio with Samuel Underwood who gave me many varied opportunities for solo work.

After Sammy's death I trained with Astra Desmond at the Royal Academy of Music in London where I concentrated on the operatic works of Mozart, Puccini and Verdi. (Astra Desmond was a noted contralto who had sung with the Society in 1944). One of the highlights of my solo career was the Countess in *Marriage of Figaro* with the Oxford Opera Group. I have been a member of the Cheltenham Bach Choir, St Cecilia Singers and a founder member of the Capella Singers and Philomusica of Gloucestershire. In later years I studied English Song with Barry Faber of Cheltenham.'

Unanswered questions, unsolved mysteries

Nor can we be absolutely sure that the records we have in each of the earlier years represent the whole story

Leonard Keck, 1973

In Leonard Keck's 1973 *Society Handbook* he expressed the hope 'that any innaccuracy or omission that may in time be revealed, will be understood and corrected'. It is true that, although the present day Society now knows much more about its origins and background, it can still echo Leonard's words about a history that is still incomplete and one that still raises puzzling questions.

Who was Ex-Impresario?

We are told, in his letters to the *Stroud Journal* in the spring of 1868, that he had been a Director of English and Italian Opera Companies and organised musical performances on a large scale in this and other countries. He was now retired from active management and had reassumed his own name. He declined to make himself known to the Stroud public and tried to explain his position. 'I cannot conceive that any good would arise from the publicity. Having friends who hold extreme views and who regard with no great favour "theatrical people", I tremble at the thought of the fearful denunciations which, on discovering what manner of man I formerly was, in a fit of virtuous indignation they would heap on my grey hairs on bald head, whichever it is; - indeed, I dare not anticipate the consequences of such a discovery.' We know Ex-Impresario had been in the Stroud area for a few years as he states himself to be alarmed at the extent of deterioration of musical taste in the country as a whole and in Stroud in particular during 'the last two or three years.' From his letters it is obvious that he is a person of great musical knowledge and experience and of very decided views. His character leaps from the page, educated, articulate and forceful. It doesn't seem possible for him to have remained incognito for long, surely the minute he gave any musical opinion, he would have given himself away!

What brought Ex-Impresario to Stroud? Did he remain in the area? We could find no reference to him after May 1868. Perhaps he spent the rest of his retirement in a more affluent area than Stroud, where the hiring of expensive soloists would have presented fewer problems.

Where is Mr Chew's engraved presentation baton?

This ebony baton, engraved on silver with the dedication to Mr Chew and the date October 12th 1850 was stolen c 1996. The Society has recorded this baton as stolen and placed its description on 'TRACE,' a search database where stolen items are identified and matched against recovered property. In the meanwhile readers are asked to keep an alert eye open at Antique Fairs, car boot sales, auctions and bric-a-brac shops for Mr Chew's baton.

What happened to Mr Chew in the late 1850s?

James Chew's Obituary makes reference to something that happened in the late 1850s. The Obituary charts James Chew's progress as Conductor of the Stroud Choral Society: 'The original class existed for about twenty years under Mr Chew's conductorship and then was abandoned under regrettable circumstances which is unnecessary to relate. It was resuscitated a few years later by Mr Helmore but no classical work was attempted, the programme being confined to glees, songs, etc.' What were these 'regrettable circumstances' that caused the Society to be abandoned and what part did Mr Chew play in this? Why did it receive a mention in his Obituary? These regrettable circumstances cannot have been of a scandalous nature as Chew's position as church organist and choirmaster was never in jeopardy. Does the mention of 'classical work' as opposed to 'glees and songs' give us a clue? Was the Society's production of the new Oratorio *Moses* in October 1856 such a disastrous event that James Chew felt that he could no longer continue with the conductorship of the Society? The concert was given under the auspices of the Stroud Philharmonic and the composer, J M Capes, an amateur musician had seemingly written the work to be performed by the Stroud Philharmonic Society. The critic remarks that the Band 'has reached a very creditable state of efficiency but does not pretend to be a first class musical organisation. Even if members were as skilled as the Royal Italian Opera Band, their number is too small, and they have not among them the variety of instruments necessary to form a complete orchestra.' Whatever the problem, there is no doubt that Chew and or others, were deeply affected by some jostling for musical ascendancy taking place in Stroud at that time.

Where is the original print of the 1st Philharmonic 1835?

We learn from many sources that the Society had an early print by an unknown artist of the Stroud Philharmonic 'shewing a group of musicians playing *Queen of My Soul* and dated 1835'. We no longer have this print in our possession. At some point, either for Sammy Underwood's jubilee programme in 1956 or for Leonard Keck's Handbook in 1973, a photograph of the print was taken and the print itself was removed from the Society's ownership. Where is this print now?

What is the significance of the very early choral programmes in the Society's ownership?

The Society has in its archives eight old programmes for choral concerts dated 1828, 1829, 1831, 1835 and 1836. Two of the programmes, 1828 and 1836 are for Music Festivals taking place over several days. The Music Festival of 1828, that took place perhaps in Derby (the heading of the programme is lost), was for the benefit of the General Infirmary. The Festival in April 1836 took place at Exeter Hall, London and was for the benefit of Charing Cross Hospital. Four programmes are for concerts at the Theatre Royal, Drury Lane, in 1829 and 1831. Of the two remaining programmes, one is for the 1st Annual Meeting of Amateurs of Classical Music, June 15th 1835 at Bedford Square, London. The other programme is for the 7th meeting of the 3rd Season of the Choral Harmonists Society at the London Tavern, Bishopsgate Street on May 22nd 1835. This latter programme has a quaint note to the effect that 'Books of the words may be obtained of the Waiters on every Evening of Performance, price 1s'.

The programmes for all these concerts consist of very similar works. Many of the Handel oratorios such as *Messiah, Solomon, Israel in Egypt* together with Purcell, Beethoven, Mozart, Spohr, Haydn's *Seasons* and *Creation* and Rossini's *William Tell* were performed. Miscellaneous concerts contain opera choruses, arias, airs, glees and ballads. On both September 11th 1828 and on April 22nd 1836 Handel's *Messiah* was sung 'with additional accompaniments by Mozart.'

Some of the soloists listed in the later programmes are of interest to us as they also sang in Stroud. Miss Woodyatt (from the Nobilities concerts, London and Musical Festivals) Mr Sapio and Mr Machin (principal singers at the Royal Festival, Westminster Abbey) and Mr Bishop (first tenor, Theatre Royal) sang at the opening concerts of the Subscription Rooms in 1834. Throughout the 1830s Miss Woodyatt, Mr Sapio and Mr Machin were soloists with the Stroud Philharmonic. Mr Braham and Mr Bishop are also soloists of note, listed in some of the old programmes and also appearing in concerts at Stroud.

One soloist's name of significant importance is that of Balfe. Michael Balfe (1808–70) was principal baritone at the Theatre Royal, Drury Lane. He was also a young popular composer and Rossini was said to have been impressed by his work. His most well known work was *The Bohemian Girl* first staged at Drury Lane in 1843, with its well-known popular song *I Dreamt that I Dwelt in Marble Halls*. (*The Bohemian Girl* was a particular favourite of Sir Thomas Beecham.) Balfe also wrote *Come into the Garden Maud*.

It is said that Balfe bridges the gap in British Opera between Arne and Sullivan. Our programme for Exeter Hall 1836 has 'Balfe' written in pencil on the outside and underlined where it appears inside. Whether this is by his own hand or by that of a follower is not known. Mr Balfe was singing in the quartet *Benedictus qui venit* from Mozart's *Requiem*.

Balfe's overture *The Siege of Rochelle* had its first performance in the Subscription Rooms in April 1836, and he sang at the Assembly Rooms in Cheltenham in September 1839. Balfe also undertook a tour of the West Country in the 1840s. He conducted Jenny Lind's Grand Miscellaneous Concert at the Shire Hall in Gloucester on November 27th 1848 (a Morning Concert, Doors open at Twelve o'clock, and commence at One o'clock). *The Siege of Rochelle* was again performed. Was it possible that he came to Stroud to listen to the Misses Williams and the Stroud Choral Class in the Subscription Rooms on the following evening?

Why do we have these old programmes? Who did they belong to and what was their connection with the Choral Society?

Who was the Stroud Oratorio Society?

In December 1845, in the *Wilts and Gloucestershire Standard,* under a heading *'Mapping v Music'* a curious little story unfolds. Forty members of the Stroud Oratorio Society were due to give a concert of 'the celebrated oratorios of Handel, Haydn, and other eminent performers' in the Assembly Room at the King's Head on November 25th. Unfortunately on the appointed day this spacious room 'was fully occupied by numerous surveyors, mappers, sketchers, and other parties employed in forming the plans and sections of the Thames Valley and Cheltenham and Oxford Railways'. We are told that these gentlemen were reluctant to pack up their maps for the Stroud Oratorio and instead gave them £40 to go away! The choir relocated to the White Hart Inn where the concert took place. Although the audience was large 'little gratification was experienced' and the Oratorio Society was 'condemned'. It was reported: 'There was more noise than music – more voices than harmony.' The item ends with the statement: 'We are sorry for this, as from the name of the Society we were led to expect better things, and that improved musical taste and talent were about to develop themselves amongst the mechanical classes of the country.'

The following week there was a letter from Stroud, dated December 5th 1845, written by 'One of the Society'. (This nineteenth-century custom of using pseudonyms on letters in print has somewhat impeded our early research!) 'One of the Society' did not want the group to fall into disrepute and felt the need to explain that only 'a portion of the whole Society, and who, generally speaking, had not acquired such proficiency in music, as its more experienced members' were able to be present.

'The concert lately given at Stroud (October 6th 1845) by the whole of the Society, was, by competent judges, considered extremely well executed.' In the light of this, the writer felt that the Cirencester concert should not be judged as a true example of the capabilities of the Society.

So who was the Stroud Oratorio Society? Obviously it was a choir of some size, maybe as many as 80 members. Who was their conductor? If it was James Chew this would make more sense of the presentation of the baton five years later in 1850 by the Society now known as Stroud Choral Society.

TOP OF THE STROUD CHORAL POPS

This is only the second time that Handel's masterpiece has ever been performed in Stroud, the other occasion being in the year 1817 when it was given in the parish church. The performance caused a great sensation, but the generation who listened to this sublime composition then is nearly swept away, and it is probable that not more than one or two were present on Tuesday night.

Review of Messiah, April 1863

The *Messiah* (Handel)	1863	1865	1870	1875	1883	1888	1903
	1906	1909	1915	1924	1930	1933	1944
	1952	1960	1961	1963	1972	1979	1988
	1988	1990	1992	1993	1994	1996	
Elijah (Mendelssohn)	1868	1884	1894	1897	1907	1923	1941
	1965	1977	1987	1995			
The Creation (Haydn)	1864	1868	1886	1910	1927	1971	1983
	1991	1994	1998				
The German Requiem (Brahms)	1912	1922	1933	1943	1954	1961	1969
	1979	1983	1995				
Judas Maccabaeus (Handel)	1865	1878	1933	1946	1952	1975	1996
St Matthew Passion (Bach)	1937	1939	1947	1949	1953	1958	1966
Christmas Oratorio (Bach)	1940	1942	1945	1951	1971	1990	
Stabat Mater (Dvorak)	1921	1940	1952	1970	1984	1993	
Gloria (Vivaldi)	1959	1966	1976	1979	1987	1996	
Five Mystical Songs (Vaughan Williams)	1923	1930	1942	1946	1983	1996	
Sleepers Wake (Bach)	1925	1935	1950	1961	1968		
St John Passion (Bach)	1944	1955	1962	1962	1978		
Hymn of Praise (Mendelssohn)	1895	1904	1908	1941	1993		
Requiem (Verdi)	1957	1960	1968	1985	1999		
Hiawatha's Wedding Feast (Coleridge-Taylor)	1906	1914	1928	1984			
Dream of Gerontius (Elgar)	1913	1950	1956	1963			
Two Psalms (Holst)	1943	1953	1959	1974			
Voces Clemantium (Parry)	1903	1910	1929	1950			
Ceremony of Carols (Britten)	1961	1969	1984				
Samson (Handel)	1866	1873	1982				

CONCERTS 1830-39

DATE		PROGRAMME	CONDUCTOR	VENUE
1834	November 26th Concert	Formation of Stroud 1st Philharmonic Society Soloists Miss Powell, Mr Ryall, Mr Bishop	Leader Mr Uglow	Stroud Subscription Rooms
1835	November 17th Concert	Stroud Philharmonic Society *Queen of my Soul* Soloist Mr Sapio		Stroud Subscription Rooms
1835	December 22nd Concert	Stroud Philharmonic Society Soloists Miss Woodyatt, Mr Sapio	Pio Cianchettini Leader Mr Evans	Stroud Subscription Rooms
1836	January 18th Concert	Stroud Philharmonic Society Soloists Miss Wagstaff, Mr Sapio, Messrs Wood and Gabb	Pio Cianchettini Leader Mr Evans	Stroud Subscription Rooms
1836	February 19th Concert	Stroud Philharmonic Society Soloists Miss Woodyatt, Mr Sapio, Messrs Wood and Gabb	Pio Cianchettini Leader Mr Evans	Stroud Subscription Rooms
1836	April 5th Concert	Stroud Philharmonic Society Soloists Miss Clara Novello, Mr Sapio, Messrs Wood and Gabb	Pio Cianchettini Leader Mr Evans	Stroud Subscription Rooms
1836	November 16th Concert	Stroud Philharmonic Society		Stroud Subscription Rooms
1836	December 22nd Concert	Stroud Philharmonic Society Miss Clara Novello, Mr Sapio		Stroud Subscription Rooms
1837	January 19th Concert	Stroud Philharmonic Society Miss Woodyatt, Mr Machin, Mr Sapio	Mr Amott Leader Mr Evans	Stroud Subscription Rooms
1838				
1839				

CONCERTS 1840-49

DATE		PROGRAMME	CONDUCTOR	VENUE
1840	January 20th Concert	Stroud Philharmonic Society Benefit of Casualty Hospital Miss Bruce, Mr J Parry	Leader Mr Evans	Stroud Subscription Rooms
1841	April 14th Concert	Stroud Philharmonic Society Grand Miscellaneous Concert Miss Woodyatt, Mr Sapio, Signor Borrani	Pio Cianchettini Leader Mr Evans	Stroud Subscription Rooms
1845	October 6th Concert	Stroud Oratorio Society Selection of Sacred Music – Handel's *Messiah*, *Samson*, *Judas Maccabaeus* Haydn's *Creation* Benefit of the Casualty Hospital		Stroud Subscription Rooms
1845	October 18th Report	£15 3s 6d received by the Stroud Casualty Hospital, proceeds of the Benefit Concert		
1845	November 25th Concert	Stroud Oratorio Society Selection of Sacred Music – Handel's *Messiah*, *Samson*. *Judas Maccabaeus* Haydn's *Creation*		White Hart Inn, Cirencester
1846	February 10th	A Mr Chew Concert – no details	Mr Chew	Stroud Subscription Rooms
1847	July 21st	A Mr Chew Concert – no details	Mr Chew	Stroud Subscription Rooms
1848	August 3rd Choral meeting	Stroud Atheneum – no details		Stroud Subscription Rooms
1848	November 28th Choral meeting	Stroud Atheneum Chorus *Hail Smiling Morn* Songs, duets, madrigals and ballads The Misses Williams	Mr Higgs	Stroud Subscription Rooms
1849	August 10th	A Mr Chew Concert – no details	Mr Chew	Stroud Subscription Rooms

CONCERTS 1850-59

DATE	PROGRAMME	CONDUCTOR	VENUE
1850 April 4th	A Mr Chew Concert – no details	Mr Chew	Stroud Subscription Rooms
1850 October 17th Concert	Selection of Sacred Music, 1st and 2nd Movement, Mozart's *12th Mass*.	Mr Chew	Stroud Subscription Rooms
1851 March 13th Concert	*The Desert Flower*, *The Gypsy's Life*, *The Bluebells of Scotland*, miscellaneous selection including instrumental solos. Benefit of the Casualty Hospital	Mr Chew	Stroud Subscription Rooms
1852 February 3rd	A Mr Chew Concert – no details	Mr Chew	Stroud Subscription Rooms
1852 April 15th	A Mr Chew Concert – no details	Mr Chew	Stroud Subscription Rooms
1852 December 16th	Mr Evans and Mr Chew Concert – no details	Mr Chew	Stroud Subscription Rooms
1852 December 28th	Mr Evans and Mr Chew Concert – no details	Mr Chew	Stroud Subscription Rooms
1853			
1854 January 16th Concert	Handel's *Haste Thee Nymph* and miscellaneous selection including instrumental solos. Stroud Mutual Improvement Society	Mr Chew	Stroud Subscription Rooms
1854 October 2nd Public Soirée	Miscellaneous selection Stroud Mutual Improvement Society	Mr Chew	Stroud Subscription Rooms
1854 November 9th Concert	In aid of widows and orphans of the Crimean War Programme unknown	Mr Chew	Stroud Subscription Rooms
1854 December	Stroud Choral Society. Programme unknown Stroud Benevolent Society	Mr Chew	Stroud Subscription Rooms
1855 October 10th Annual Soirée	Choruses, duets, songs and glees Stroud Mutual Improvement Society.	Mr Chew	Stroud Subscription Rooms
1856 October 23rd Concert	Oratorio Cape's *Moses* (first performance) Stroud Philharmonic with Stroud Choral Society	Mr Chew	Stroud Subscription Rooms

1857/59

CONCERTS 1860-69

DATE		PROGRAMME	CONDUCTOR	VENUE
1862	September 9th Advert	Choral Classes commence Mondays and Fridays, 5 shillings a quarter	Mr Helmore	Blackboy Schoolroom
1862	October 18th Notification	Choral Classes postponed due to illness of Mr Helmore		
1863	February 10th Concert	Glees, Part Songs, Choruses	Mr Helmore	Stroud Subscription Rooms
1863	April 28th Concert	Handel's *Messiah*, celebrating the marriage of Prince of Wales March 10th 1863.	Mr Helmore Leader Mr Chew	Stroud Subscription Rooms
1863	May 28th Concert	Members of the Choral Society sang at the opening of St Mary's Church, Tetbury.	Mr Helmore	St Mary's Church, Tetbury
1863	December 1st Concert	Mendelssohn's 195 Psalm 'Come let us sing' and miscellaneous selection.	Mr Helmore Pianist Miss Clark	Stroud Subscription Rooms
1864	April 12th Concert	Haydn's *Creation*	Mr Helmore Leader Mr Chew	Stroud Subscription Rooms
1864	December 20th Concert	Haydn's *Seasons* and miscellaneous selection. Cornet solo Mr Chew	Mr Mann	Stroud Subscription Rooms
1865	May 23rd Concert	Handel's *Judas Maccabaeus*	Mr Mann Leader Mr Chew	Stroud Subscription Rooms
1865	September 13th AGM	Rules of Society changed. Object of Society: 'To form a union of best vocal amateur talent of Stroud and Neighbourhood, for the study and practice of the higher class of musical compositions'.	President J E Dorington Esq in Chair	Blackboy Schoolroom
1865	December 12th Concert	Handel's *Messiah*	Mr Mann Leader Mr Chew	Stroud Subscription Rooms
1866	May 8th Concert	Handel's *Samson*	Mr Mann Leader Mr Chew	Stroud Subscription Rooms
1866	December 20th Concert	Mozart's *12th Mass*	Mr Mann Leader Mr Chew	Stroud Subscription Rooms
1867	May 14th Concert	Handel's Festival Selection of 1862 as performed at Crystal Palace	Mr Brind Leader Mr Chew	Stroud Subscription Rooms
1867	September 28th Accounts	Annual accounts. Balance of 19 shillings and 1 pence.		
1867	December 17th Concert	Miscellaneous selection.	Mr Mann Pianist Miss Clark	Stroud Subscription Rooms
1868	May 12th Concert	Mendelssohn's *Elijah*	Mr Mann Leader Mr Deane	Stroud Subscription Rooms
1868	December 17th Concert	Haydn's *Creation*	Mr Mann	Stroud Subscription Rooms
1869	April 29th	Death of Mr Mann, aged 34		
1869	May 13th Concert	Mendelssohn's *St Paul*	Mr Brind	Stroud Subscription Rooms
1869	December 20th Open Night	Musical Entertainment. Selection of Haydn's *Creation* and Spohr's Cantata *God Thou Art Great*.	Mr Brind	Unknown

CONCERTS 1870-79

DATE		PROGRAMME	CONDUCTOR	VENUE
1870	March 24th Concert	Handel's *Messiah*	Mr Brind Leader Mr Chew	Stroud Subscription Rooms
1870	April 28th Private Soirée	Unknown	Mr Brind	Stroud Subscription Rooms
1870	September 9th AGM	Public Meeting to dissolve Stroud Choral Society Mr Brind to continue with Choral Classes		Corn Hall
1870	October 3rd Choral Class	Mendelssohn's *As Pants the Hart* Sterndale Bennett's *May Queen*	Mr Brind	Corn Hall
1873	May 7th Concert	Handel's *Samson*	Mr Brandon Leader Mr Chew	Stroud Subscription Rooms
1874	December 11th	Service	Mr Chew	Stroud Parish Church
1875	April 14th Concert	Stroud Music Festival Handel's *Messiah*	Mr Brandon Leader Mr Chew	Stroud Subscription Rooms
1875	April 15th Secular Concert	Stroud Music Festival Miscellaneous selection	Mr Brandon Leader Mr Chew	Stroud Subscription Rooms
1876				
1877	November 5th Choral Class	Rehearsals commence for Handel's *Judas Maccabaeus*	Mr Brandon	Corn Hall Monday 8pm
1878	May 16th Concert	Handel's *Judas Maccabaeus*	Mr Brandon Leader Mr Chew	Stroud Subscription Rooms
1879	February 3rd Choral Class	Unknown	Mr Brandon	Unknown
1879	August 27th Choral Class	Rehearsals commence for Handel's *Joshua*	Mr Brandon	Corn Hall
1879	November 29th Notification	Notice in *Stroud Journal* to postpone concert of Handel's *Joshua* to have taken place December 2nd (programme produced)	Mr Brandon American Organ Mr Chew	Lansdown Hall, Stroud

CONCERTS 1880-89

DATE		PROGRAMME	CONDUCTOR	VENUE
1880	January 26th	Notice in *Stroud Journal* that classes are to commence practice of Sterndale Bennett's Cantata *May Queen*		Lansdown Hall, Mondays 8pm
1881	May 15th Concert	Sterndale Bennett's *May Queen*	Mr Brandon Leader Mr Chew	Stroud Subscription Rooms
1882	April 14th	Handel's *Acis and Galatea*, Romberg's *The Lay of the Bell*	Mr Brandon Leader Mr Chew	Stroud Subscription Rooms
1882	October 16th	Stroud Choral Class. Notice of start of season To rehearse Handel's *Messiah*		Corn Hall Mondays 8pm Ladies afternoon class 3pm
1883	April 14th	Handel's *Messiah*	Mr Brandon Leader Mr Chew	Stroud Subscription Rooms
1883	October 8th	Stroud Choral Class. Notice of start of season To rehearse Mendelssohn's *Elijah*		Corn Hall Mondays 8pm Ladies afternoon class 3pm
1884	May 1st	Mendelssohn's *Elijah*	Mr J Hunt Leader Mr Chew	Stroud Subscription Rooms
1884	October 13th	Stroud Choral Class. Notice of start of season To rehearse Haydn's *Creation*		Corn Hall Mondays 7.30pm
1885	April 28th	Haydn's *Creation* 'was unavoidably postponed'		
1886	December 9th	Haydn's *Creation*	Mr Brandon Leader Mr Chew	Stroud Subscription Rooms
1887	April 28th	Cowen's *The Rose Maiden*	Mr Brandon Leader Mr Chew	Stroud Subscription Rooms
1887	August 25th	A Promenade Concert. Postponed due to Inclement Weather	Mr Brandon Band of 2nd Volunteer Battalion Glos. Regiment	Stratford Park
1887	September 1st	The Promenade Concert. Postponed		
1887	September 2nd	The Promenade Concert		Stroud Subscription Rooms
1888	February 7th	Handel's *Messiah*	Mr Brandon Leader Mr Chew	Stroud Subscription Rooms
1888	October 8th	Stroud Choral Class. Notice of start of season		Corn Hall Mondays 7.30pm
1889	December 5th	Mendelssohn's *St Paul* Cowen's *Sleeping Beauty*	Mr Brandon Leader Mr Chew	Stroud Subscription Rooms

CONCERTS 1890–99

DATE		PROGRAMME	CONDUCTOR	VENUE
1890	January 13th	Stroud Choral Class. Practices to resume on Monday 13th January at 8pm. Handel's *Messiah* Concert in March. No concert details found		
1892	April 28th	Bennett's *The Ancient Mariner* miscellaneous selection	Mr Hackwood Leader Mr Butland	Stroud Subscription Rooms
1893	April 27th	Smart's *The Bride of Dunkerron* miscellaneous selection	Mr Hackwood Leader Mr F J Mann	Stroud Subscription Rooms
1894	April 12th	Mendelssohn's *Elijah*	Mr Hackwood Leader Mr J W Mann	Stroud Subscription Rooms
1895	April 25th	Rossini's *Stabat Mater* Mendelssohn's *Hymn of Praise*	Mr Hackwood Leader Mr Woodward	Stroud Subscription Rooms
1896	November 24th	Spohr's *Last Judgement*, Stanford's *The Revenge* Postponed from the Spring owing to small-pox epidemic at Gloucester	Mr Hackwood Leader Mr Mann	Stroud Subscription Rooms
1897	November 30th	Mendelssohn's *Elijah*	Mr Hackwood Leader Mr Woodward	Stroud Subscription Rooms
1899	March 6th	Death at the age of 75 of Mr James Chew		

Postcard franked 1901

CONCERTS 1900-09

DATE		PROGRAMME	CONDUCTOR	VENUE
1901	April 18th	Sterndale Bennett's *May Queen*	Mr T Hackwood	Stroud Subscription Rooms
1903	February 19th 3pm	Miscellaneous selection S W U played the horn in the Band	Mr J Edis Tidnam	Stroud Subscription Rooms
1903	February 19th 8pm	Handel's *Messiah* S W U played the horn in the Band	Mr J Edis Tidnam	Stroud Subscription Rooms
1903	December 10th	Parry's *Voces Clemantium* Composed for the 1903 Hereford Festival	Sir Hubert Parry	Stroud Subscription Rooms
1904	April 7th	Hodson's *Golden Legend* The composer, Rev Mr Hodson, present	Mr J Edis Tidnam	Stroud Subscription Rooms
1904	December 8th	Mendelssohn's *Hymn of Praise* miscellaneous selection S W U played the horn in the Band	Mr J Edis Tidnam	Stroud Subscription Rooms
1905	March 2nd	Sir Frank Bridge's *Flag of England* miscellaneous selection	Mr J Edis Tidnam	Stroud Subscription Rooms
1906	February 22nd	Coleridge-Taylor's *Hiawatha* miscellaneous selection	Mr J Edis Tidnam	Stroud Subscription Rooms
1906	April 26th	Handel's *Messiah* S W U played the horn in the Band	Mr J Edis Tidnam	Stroud Subscription Rooms
1907	April 11th	Mendelssohn's *Elijah*	Mr S W Underwood	Stroud Subscription Rooms
1907	July 4th	Open Air Concert. Postponed	Mr S W Underwood	Stratford Park
1907	July 18th 3pm and 7pm	Open Air Concert	Mr S W Underwood	Stratford Park
1908	January 23rd	Miscellaneous selection	Mr S W Underwood	Stroud Subscription Rooms
1908	May 5th	Mendelssohn's *Hymn of Praise* Brewer's *Sir Patrick Spens*	Mr S W Underwood Dr H Brewer	Stroud Subscription Rooms
1909	February 11th	Handel's *Messiah*	Mr S W Underwood	Stroud Subscription Rooms

CONCERTS 1910-19

DATE		PROGRAMME	CONDUCTOR	VENUE
1910	April 7th	Haydn's *Creation* Parry's *Voces Clementium*	Mr S W Underwood	Stroud Subscription Rooms
1911	February 23rd	Handel's *Acis and Galatea* Gounod's *Faust* (selections)	Mr S W Underwood	Stroud Subscription Rooms
1912	February 15th	Brahms' *Requiem* Schubert's *Unfinished Symphony*	Mr S W Underwood	Stroud Subscription Rooms
1913	April 10th	Elgar's *Dream of Gerontius*	Mr S W Underwood	Stroud Subscription Rooms
1914	February 5th	Coleridge-Taylor's *Hiawatha* Brahms' *Song of Destiny*	Mr S W Underwood	Stroud Subscription Rooms
1914	December 16th	Miscellaneous selection	Mr S W Underwood	Stroud Subscription Rooms
1915	April 6th	Mendelssohn's *Elijah*	Mr S W Underwood	Stroud Subscription Rooms
1915	December 7th	Handel's *Messiah*	Mr S W Underwood	Stroud Subscription Rooms
1916 to 1919		No performances		

A typical example of Edwardian humour!

CONCERTS 1920-29

DATE		PROGRAMME	CONDUCTOR	VENUE
1920	February 19th	Elgar's *The Banner of St George* Stanford's *The Last Post* miscellaneous selection	Mr S W Underwood	Stroud Subscription Rooms
1920	December 16th	Miscellaneous selection	Mr S W Underwood	Stroud Subscription Rooms
1921	May 3rd	Dvorak's *Stabat Mater*	Mr S W Underwood	Stroud Parish Church
1922	May 11th	Brahms' *Requiem*	Mr S W Underwood	Stroud Parish Church
1922	November 30th	Stanford's *Revenge* Coleridge-Taylor's *Death of Minnehaha* miscellaneous selection	Mr S W Underwood	Stroud Subscription Rooms
1923	March 15th	Mendelssohn's *Elijah*	Mr S W Underwood	Stroud Subscription Rooms
1923	December 13th	Holst's *Festival Chimes* Vaughan Williams' *Five Mystical Songs*	Mr S W Underwood	Stroud Parish Church
1924	April 3rd	Handel's *Messiah*	Mr S W Underwood	Stroud Subscription Rooms
1925	March 26th	Bach's *Sleepers Wake* Holst's *Hymns from Rig Veda* Purcell's *Dido and Aeneas*	Mr S W Underwood	Stroud Subscription Rooms
1926	May 6th	Vaughan Williams' *Towards the Unknown Region* Parry's *Jerusalem*, miscellaneous selection	Mr S W Underwood	Stroud Parish Church
1927	January 13th	Haydn's *Creation*, Parts I and II Schubert's *Unfinished Symphony* Brahms' *Song of Destiny*	Mr S W Underwood	Stroud Subscription Rooms
1927	March 31st	Elgar's *For The Fallen* Bach's *Come Redeemer* miscellaneous selection	Mr S W Underwood	Stroud Subscription Rooms
1928	January 26th	Coleridge-Taylor's *Song of Hiawatha*	Mr S W Underwood	Stroud Subscription Rooms
1928	November 1st	Purcell's *King Arthur* Parry's *The Glories of Our Blood and State* miscellaneous selection	Mr S W Underwood	Stroud Subscription Rooms
1929	April 30th	Mozart's *Requiem Mass* Parry's *Voces Clementium* miscellaneous selection	Mr S W Underwood	Stroud Subscription Rooms

CONCERTS 1930-39

DATE		PROGRAMME	CONDUCTOR	VENUE
1930	January 23rd	Handel's *Messiah*	Mr S W Underwood	Stroud Subscription Rooms
1930	April 8th	Parry's *Blest Pair of Sirens* Vaughan Williams' *Five Mystical Songs* Bach's *The Peasant Cantata*	Mr S W Underwood	Stroud Subscription Rooms
1931	February 12th	Bizet's *Carmen*	Mr S W Underwood	Stroud Subscription Rooms
1932	February 3rd	Goetz's *By The Waters Of Babylon* Purcell's *The Fairy Queen*	Mr S W Underwood	Stroud Subscription Rooms
1933	March 14th	Brahms' *Requiem* Handel's *Judas Maccabaeus*	Mr S W Underwood	Stroud Subscription Rooms
1933	December 19th	Handel's *Messiah*	Mr S W Underwood	Stroud Subscription Rooms
1934	December 10th	Lang's *The Jackdaw of Rheims* Part Songs and Christmas music	Mr S W Underwood	Church Institute
1935	February 14th	Bach's *Sleepers Wake* Wood's *Master Mariners*, miscellaneous selection	Mr S W Underwood	Stroud Subscription Rooms
1935	December 18th	Carols and Christmas Music	Mr S W Underwood	Stroud Parish Church
1936	February 6th	Handel's *Jephtha*	Mr S W Underwood	Stroud Subscription Rooms
1936	December 17th	Carols and Christmas Music	Mr S W Underwood	Stroud Parish Church
1937	March 18th	Bach's *St Matthew Passion*	Mr S W Underwood	Stroud Subscription Rooms
1937	March 23rd	Bach's *St Matthew Passion*	Mr S W Underwood	Tewkesbury Abbey
1937	December 20th	Carols and Christmas Music	Mr S W Underwood	Stroud Parish Church
1938	March 31st	Handel's *Israel in Egypt*	Mr S W Underwood	Stroud Subscription Rooms
1939	January 26th	Dyson's *The Canterbury Pilgrims*	Mr S W Underwood	Stroud Subscription Rooms
1939	March 30th	Bach's *St Matthew Passion*	Mr S W Underwood	Stroud Parish Church
1939	December 17th 3pm	Brent-Smith's *A Hymn of the Nativity*, Christmas Carols and Music	Mr A Brent-Smith, Mr S W Underwood	Stroud Parish Church

CONCERTS 1940-49

DATE		PROGRAMME	CONDUCTOR	VENUE
1940	March 10th 3pm	Dvorak's *Stabat Mater* Brent-Smith's *Elegy* (first performance) conducted by the composer	Mr S W Underwood Mr A Brent-Smith Organist Dr H Sumsion	Stroud Parish Church
1940	December 15th 3pm	Bach's *Christmas Oratorio*	Mr S W Underwood Organist Dr H Sumsion	Stroud Parish Church
1941	January 26th 3pm	Recital, Excerpts from *Elijah*, *Messiah* and Carols	Mr S W Underwood Organist Prof Bruce Davis	Stroud Parish Church
1941	February 23rd	Handel's *Elijah*	Mr S W Underwood Organist Dr H Sumsion	Stroud Parish Church
1941	April 20th 3pm	Recital, Excerpts from Mendelssohn's *Hymn of Praise*, Haydn's *Creation*	Mr S W Underwood Organist Prof Bruce Davis	Stroud Parish Church
1941	December 21st 3pm	Christmas Music and Carols	Mr S W Underwood	Stroud Parish Church
1942	January 11th 3pm	Bach's *Christmas Oratorio*	Mr S W Underwood Organist Dr H. Sumsion	Stroud Parish Church
1942	March 15th 3pm	Elgar's *The Music Makers* Vaughan Williams' *Benedicite*	Mr S W Underwood	Stroud Parish Church
1942	December 20th 3pm	Dale's *Before The Paling of the Stars* Vaughan Williams' *Five Mystical Songs* and *Fantasia on Christmas Carols*	Mr S W Underwood	Stroud Parish Church
1943	March 28th 3pm	Brahms' *Requiem*	Mr S W Underwood	Stroud Parish Church
1943	December 19th 3pm	Brahms' *Song of Destiny* Holst's *Two Psalms*	Mr S W Underwood	Stroud Parish Church
1944	March 19th 2.45pm	Bach's *Passion of Our Lord, St John*	Mr S W Underwood	Stroud Parish Church
1944	December 10th 2.45pm	Handel's *Messiah*	Mr S W Underwood	Stroud Parish Church
1945	March 11th 3pm	Wesley's *The Wilderness* Parry's *Job*	Mr S W Underwood	Stroud Parish Church
1945	December 13th 7pm	Bach's *Christmas Oratorio*	Mr S W Underwood	Stroud Parish Church
1946	April 4th	Handel's *Judas Maccabaeus*	Mr S W Underwood	Stroud Parish Church
1946	December 12th 7pm	Vaughan Williams' *Thanksgiving for Victory* (first performance in Stroud), *Five Mystical Songs* and *Fantasia on Christmas Carols* Stroud High School Choir	Mr S W Underwood Pianist Dr H Sumsion	Stroud Parish Church
1947	March 27th	Bach's *St Matthew Passion*	Mr S W Underwood	Stroud Parish Church
1947	May 10th	Solo Choir for the Gloucester Music Festival	Mr S W Underwood	Gloucester Cathedral
1947	December 11th	Fleming's *Five Psalms* Finzi's *Lo, The Full Final Sacrifice* Handel's *Coronation Anthem*	Mr S W Underwood Organist Dr H Sumsion	Stroud Parish Church
1948	March 18th	Cherubini's *Second Mass in D Minor*	Mr S W Underwood	Stroud Parish Church
1948	December 2nd	Handel's *Chandos Te Deum* Brahms' *Alto Rhapsody* Dyson's *Three Songs of Praise*	Mr S W Underwood Pianist Dr H Sumsion	Stroud Parish Church
1949	March 29th	Bach's *St Matthew Passion* Dursley Bach Choir Stroud High School Choir	Mr S W Underwood Continuo Dr H Sumsion	Stroud Parish Church
1949	December 15th	Carols and Christmas Music	Mr S W Underwood Dr H Sumsion	Stroud Parish Church

CONCERTS 1950-59

DATE		PROGRAMME	CONDUCTOR	VENUE
1950	March 30th	Elgar's *The Dream of Gerontius*	Mr S W Underwood	Stroud Parish Church
1950	December 14th	Bach's *Sleepers Wake* Handel's *Organ Concerto* Parry's *Voces Clemantium*	Mr S W Underwood Organist Dr H Sumsion	Stroud Parish Church
1951	March 15th	Elgar's *The Kingdom*	Mr S W Underwood	Stroud Parish Church
1951	December 13th	Bach's *Christmas Oratorio*	Mr S W Underwood Organist Dr H Sumsion	Stroud Parish Church
1952	March 27th	Dvorak's *Stabat Mater*	Mr S W Underwood	Stroud Parish Church
1952	May 15th	Handel's *Judas Maccabaeus*	Mr S W Underwood	Stroud Parish Church
1952	December 11th	Handel's *Messiah*	Mr S W Underwood	Stroud Parish Church
1953	March 19th	Bach's *St Matthew Passion* with the choir of the Girls' Technical School	Mr S W Underwood Mrs. Clarke	Stroud Parish Church
1953	December 10th	Haydn's *Mass in D Minor* Holst's *Two Psalms* Wesley's *The Wilderness*	Mr S W Underwood	Stroud Parish Church
1954	March 18th	Brahms' *Requiem*	Mr S W Underwood	Stroud Parish Church
1954	December 9th	Parry's *Blest Pair of Sirens* Holst's *Fantasia on Christmas Carols* Bach's *Concerto in E Minor*	Mr S W Underwood	Stroud Parish Church
1955	March 24th	Bach's *Passion of Our Lord, St John*	Mr S W Underwood	Stroud Parish Church
1955	December 8th	Bush's *Christmas Cantata* Parry's *Ode to the Nativity of Christ* Marcello's *Concerto in C Minor for Oboe*	Mr S W Underwood	Stroud Parish Church
1956	March 15th	Elgar's *Dream of Gerontius*	Mr S W Underwood	Stroud Parish Church
1956	November 18th	St Cecilia's-tide Evensong to mark approaching completion of Mr S W Underwood's 50 years as Organist and Choirmaster. Augmented choir	Organist Mr S W Underwood	Stroud Parish Church
1956	December 6th	Bach's *Come, Redeemer* Finzi's *In Terra Pax* Oldroyd's *Jhesu Christ, Saint Mary's Sone*	Mr S W Underwood	Stroud Parish Church
1957	March 21st	Verdi's *Requiem*	Mr S W Underwood MBE	Stroud Parish Church
1957	December 11th	Vaughan Williams' *Benedicite* Bush's *In Praise of Mary* Haydn's *Cello Concerto* Boccherini's *Sonata, Church Music*	Mr S W Underwood MBE	Stroud Parish Church
1958	March 26th	Bach's *St Matthew Passion* with the choir of the Girls' Technical School	Mr S W Underwood MBE	Stroud Parish Church
1958	December 12th	Fauré's *Requiem*, Dvorak's *Biblical Songs* Bush's *Christmas Cantata*	Mr R Clifford	Stroud Parish Church
1959	March 20th	Handel's *Joshua*	Mr R Clifford	Stroud Parish Church
1959	December 10th	Vivaldi's *Gloria*, Purcell's *Jubilate Deo in D* Holst's *Two Psalms*	Mr R Clifford	Stroud Parish Church

CONCERTS 1960-69

DATE		PROGRAMME	CONDUCTOR	VENUE
1960	March 24th	Verdi's *Requiem*	Mr M Foster	Stroud Parish Church
1960	December 8th	Handel's *Messiah*	Mr M Foster	Stroud Parish Church
1961	March 23rd	Brahms' *Requiem* Handel's *Concerto Grosso*	Mr M Foster	Stroud Parish Church
1961	December 7th	Bach's *Sleepers Wake* Britten's *Ceremony Carols* Kodaly's *Missa Brevis*	Mr M Foster	Stroud Parish Church
1961	December 16th	Handel's *Messiah*	Mr M Foster	Malmesbury Abbey
1962	March 22nd	Bach's *Passion of Our Lord, St John*	Mr M Foster	Stroud Parish Church
1962	March 31st	Bach's *Passion of Our Lord, St John*	Mr M Foster	Malmesbury Abbey
1962	December 13th	Fleming's *Five Psalms*, John Sanders' *Te Deum* Mozart's *Exultate Jubilate*, Holst's *Christmas Day* Bush's *In Praise of Mary*	Mr E Sanders	Stroud Parish Church
1963	March 21st	Elgar's *Dream of Gerontius*	Mr E Sanders	Stroud Parish Church
1963	December 12th	Handel's *Messiah*	Mr E Sanders	Stroud Parish Church
1964	March 19th	Mozart's *Requiem Mass*, Britten's *St. Nicolas* semi-chorus; Stroud High School and Marling School	Mr E Sanders	Stroud Parish Church
1964	December 10th	Nelson's *Christmas Story* Christmas Music and Carols	Mr E Sanders	Stroud Parish Church
1965	March 25th	Mendelssohn's *Elijah*, semi-chorus: Stroud High School, Marling School and Wycliffe College Choirs	Mr E Sanders	Stroud Parish Church
1965	December 16th	Britten's *Rejoice in The Lamb* Christmas Music and Carols	Mr E Sanders	Stroud Parish Church
1966	March 31st	Bach's *St Matthew Passion* with Stroud Girls' High School	Mr E Sanders	Stroud Parish Church
1966	December 8th	Bush's *Christmas Cantata*, Bach's *Jauchzet Gott in Alle Länder* Vivaldi's *Gloria*	Mr E Sanders	Stroud Parish Church
1967	March 16th	Handel's *Israel in Egypt* with Stroud Girls' High School	Mr E Sanders	Stroud Parish Church
1967	December 14th	Cashmore's *This Child Behold*, Christmas Carols with Stroud High School Senior Choir	Mr E Sanders Miss B Thorley	Stroud Parish Church
1968	March 28th	Verdi's *Requiem*	Mr E Sanders	Stroud Parish Church
1968	May 2nd	Elis Pehkonen's *Requiem*, first performance in Stroud, sponsored by Stroud Choral Society, with choirs of Cirencester and Westwood Schools	Mr E Sanders Elis Pehkonen Miss D Chapman	
1968	December 12th	Bach's *Sleepers Wake*, Britten's *St Nicolas* Semi-chorus; Stroud Girls' High School	Mr T Hewitt-Jones	Stroud Parish Church
1969	March 27th	Brahms' *Requiem*, Beethoven's *Overture Egmont* Thanksgiving for the life and work of Mr E Sanders	Mr T Hewitt-Jones	Stroud Parish Church
1969	December 11th	Bach's *Sing Ye to the Lord* Britten's *Ceremony of Carols*	Mr R Latham	Stroud Parish Church

CONCERTS 1970-79

DATE		PROGRAMME	CONDUCTOR	VENUE
1970	March 19th	Dvorak's *Stabat Mater*	Mr T Hewitt-Jones	Stroud Parish Church
1970	December 10th	Britten's *Festival Te Deum*, Vaughan Williams' *Fantasia on Christmas Carols*, Christmas Rounds	Mr T Hewitt-Jones	Stroud Parish Church
1971	April 1st	Haydn's *Creation*	Mr T Hewitt-Jones	Stroud Parish Church
1971	December 9th	Bach's *Christmas Oratorio*	Mr T Hewitt-Jones	Stroud Parish Church
1972	March 23rd	Handel's *The Passion of Christ*	Mr T Hewitt-Jones	Stroud Parish Church
1972	June 10th	Vaughan Williams Centenary Concert Augmented choir with members of Stroud Choral Society	Mr T Hewitt-Jones	Gloucester Cathedral
1972	October 15th	Vaughan Williams' *Mass in G Minor* as part of the service	Mr T Hewitt-Jones	Church of Immaculate Conception, Beeches Green
1972	December 7th	Handel's *Messiah*	Mr T Hewitt-Jones	Stroud Parish Church
1973	April 5th	Gabrieli's *Jubilate Deo*, Hewitt-Jones' *The Battle of Tewkesbury*, first performance in Stroud, Rose's *Three Introits*, Sumsion's *Benedicite*, Handel's *Solo Cantata Jephtha*, Adson's *Courtly Masquing Airs*	Mr T Hewitt-Jones	Stroud Parish Church
1973	December 8th	Bach's *Jesu, Priceless Treasure Motet* Byrd's *Mass for Four Voices* Carols for choir and congregation	Mr T Hewitt-Jones	Stroud Parish Church
1974	March 30th	Holst's *Two Psalms*, Purcell's *Chacony in D Minor* Tippett's *A Child of Our Time*	Mr T Hewitt-Jones	Stroud Parish Church
1974	December 14th	Bush's *Christmas Cantata* Mozart's *Exultate Jubilate*, Holst's *Christmas Day* Carols for All	Mr T Hewitt-Jones	Stroud Parish Church
1975	March 22nd	Handel's *Judas Maccabaeus*	Mr T Hewitt-Jones	Stroud Parish Church
1975	June 17th	Summer Serenade – Moeran's *Songs of Springtime* Brahms' *Songs of Love*	Mr T Hewitt-Jones	Stroud Subscription Rooms
1975	December 13th	Buxtehude's *A New Born Infant* Charpentier's *Midnight Mass*, Carols for All	Mr T Hewitt-Jones	Stroud Parish Church
1976	April 24th	Vaughan Williams' *O Clap Your Hands* Hewitt-Jones' *Return From a Far Country*, inaugural performance. Commissioned for the Society.	Mr T Hewitt-Jones	Stroud Parish Church
1976	June 29th	Summer Serenade	Mr T Hewitt-Jones	Stroud Subscription Rooms
1976	December 11th	Vivaldi's *Gloria*, Pergolesi's *Magnificat* Handel's *Messiah* (excerpts)	Mr T Hewitt-Jones	Stroud Parish Church
1977	April 2nd	Mendelssohn's *Elijah*	Mr T Hewitt-Jones	Stroud Parish Church
1977	December 8th	Concert of Christmas Music with Stroud High School Junior Choir	Mr D Fysh Mrs G Brown	Stroud Parish Church
1978	February 28th	BBC 'Songs of Praise'	Mr H Lyall	Stroud Parish Church
1978	March 16th	Bach's *Passion of our Lord, St John*	Mr D Fysh	Stroud Parish Church
1978	December 14th	Christmas Music with Stroud High School Junior Choir	Mr D Fysh Mrs G Brown	Stroud Parish Church
1979	April 7th	Brahms' *A German Requiem* in memory of Leonard Keck, Member, Secretary, President of this Society 1970–1978	Mr D Fysh	Stroud Parish Church
1979	June 30th	Leonard Stanley Festival Vivaldi's *Gloria*, Haydn's *Mass in D Minor*	Mr D Fysh	The Priory, Leonard Stanley
1979	December 8th	Handel's *Messiah*	Mr E Garrard	Stroud Parish Church

CONCERTS 1980-89

DATE		PROGRAMME	CONDUCTOR	VENUE
1980	May 10th	Purcell's *Dido and Aeneas* / Orff's *Carmina Burana*	Mr E Garrard	Stroud Subscription Rooms
1980	July 5th	Leonard Stanley Festival. Charpentier's *Messe de Minuit*, Pergolesi's *Magnificat*	Mr E Garrard	The Priory, Leonard Stanley
1980	December 13th	Bach's *Christmas Oratorio*	Mr E Garrard	Stroud Parish Church
1981	April 25th	Verdi's *Nabucco*	Mr E Garrard	Stroud Subscription Rooms
1981	June 27th	Vaughan Williams' *Mass in G Minor* / Handel's *Zadok the Priest*	Mr E Garrard	The Priory, Leonard Stanley
1981	November 28th	Rossini's *Stabat Mater*, Haydn's *Missa Sancti*	Mr E Garrard	Stroud Parish Church
1982	March 20th	Handel's *Samson*	Mr E Garrard	Stroud Subscription Rooms
1982	June 26th	German's *Merrie England*	Mr E Garrard	Stroud Subscription Rooms
1982	November 13th	Bruckner's *Mass in E Minor* / Mozart's *Mass in D Minor*	Mr E Garrard	Stroud Subscription Rooms
1983	April 16th	Haydn's *Creation*	Mr E Garrard	Stroud Subscription Rooms
1983	July 9th	Vivaldi's *Dixit*, Mozart's *Piano Duet in D Major* / Vaughan Williams' *Five Mystical Songs*	Mr E Garrard	Stroud Subscription Rooms
1983	November 12th	Brahms' *Requiem*, Fauré's *Requiem*	Mr E Garrard	Stroud Subscription Rooms
1984	April 14th	Dvorak's *Stabat Mater* / Handel's *The Passion of Christ*	Mr E Garrard	Stroud Subscription Rooms
1984	June 30th	Elgar's *Music Makers* / Coleridge-Taylor's *Hiawatha's Wedding Feast*	Mr E Garrard	Stroud Subscription Rooms
1984	September 21st	Memorial concert for Claude Allen	Mr E Garrard	Holy Trinity Church
1984	December 8th	Handel's *Ode on St Cecilia's Day* / Britten's *Ceremony of Carols*	Mr E Garrard	Stroud Subscription Rooms
1985	April 20th	Verdi's *Requiem*	Mr E Garrard	Stroud Leisure Centre
1985	December 14th	Poulenc's *Gloria* and Carols	Mr E Garrard	Stroud Parish Church
1986	May 17th	Beethoven's *Missa Solemnis*	Mr E Garrard	Stroud Leisure Centre
1986	November 15th	Purcell's *Ode on St Cecilia's Day (1692)*, Schubert's *Mass in A Flat Major*	Mr E Garrard	Stroud Subscription Rooms
1987	May 9th	Handel's *Samson* (Let The Bright Seraphim) / Brahms' *Song of Destiny* / Mozart's *Mass in C Minor K.427*	Mr E Garrard	Stroud Subscription Rooms
1987	October 4th	Stroud Festival / Vivaldi's *Gloria*, Handel's *Let The Bright Seraphim*	Mr E Garrard	Stroud Subscription Rooms
1987	December 12th	Mendelssohn's *Elijah*	Mr E Garrard	Stroud Subscription Rooms
1988	May 14th	Glinka's *Ruslan and Ludmilla Overture* / Stanford's *Songs of the Fleet*, Parry's *Blest Pair of Sirens*, Dvorak's *Carnival Overture* / Elgar's *Songs from the Bavarian Highlands*	Mr E Garrard	Stroud Subscription Rooms
1988	December 10th	Handel's *Messiah*	Mr E Garrard	Stroud Subscription Rooms
1988	December 11th	Handel's *Messiah*	Mr E Garrard	St Barnabas Church, Gloucester
1989	March 12th	Haydn's *Creation*	Mr J Lubbock	Royal Albert Hall (Royal Marsden Hospital Appeal)
1989	May 13th	Haydn's *Mass in B Flat*, Verdi's *Pezzi Sacri*	Mr E Garrard	Stroud Subscription Rooms
1989	December 9th	Rossini's *Messe Solennelle*	Mr E Garrard	Stroud Subscription Rooms

CONCERTS 1990-2000

DATE		PROGRAMME	CONDUCTOR	VENUE
1990	March 31st	Handel's *Messiah*	Mr E Garrard	St Mary's, Painswick. In aid of Mencap.
1990	May 12th	Vaughan Williams' *Sea Symphony* Brent-Smith's *Elegy*	Mr E Garrard	Stroud Subscription Rooms
1990	December 14th	Bach's *Christmas Oratorio*	Mr E Garrard	Gloucester Cathedral. In aid of Cotswold Care
1991	March 16th	Haydn's *Creation*	Mr E Garrard	Stroud Parish Church. In aid of Camphill Village
1991	May 11th	Monteverdi's *Vespers*, Mozart's *Coronation Mass*	Mr E Garrard	All Saints, Uplands
1991	December 7th	Berlioz' *The Childhood of Christ*	Mr E Garrard	Stroud Subscription Rooms
1991	December 21st	Carol Concert	Mr E Garrard	Church of the Immaculate Conception, Beeches Green
1992	May 9th	Vaughan Williams' *Dona Nobis Pacem* Mussorgsky *Missa Sancti Nicolai* Arranged by Philip Lane, present at the performance.	Mr E Garrard	Stroud Subscription Rooms
1992	November 28th	Handel's *Messiah*	Mr E Garrard	Stroud Parish Church Barnardo's Centenary Appeal.
1992	December 5th	Rossini's *Stabat Mater* Schubert's *Messe As-Dur*	Mr E Garrard	Stroud Subscription Rooms
1992	December 18th	Carol Concert Benefit Cotswold Care	Mr E Garrard	Church of the Immaculate Conception, Beeches Green
1993	March 6th	Mozart's *Requiem*, scratch performance Benefit Cystic Fibrosis	Mr E Garrard	Stroud Parish Church
1993	March 20th	Handel's *Messiah* scratch performance Benefit Malcolm Sargeant Cancer Fund	Mr E Garrard	St Matthew's Church, Cainscross
1993	May 15th	Dvorak's *Stabat Mater*	Mr E Garrard	Stroud Subscription Rooms
1993	June 12th	Brahms' *Songs of Love* Elgar's *Songs from the Bavarian Highlands*, with Stroud High School Choir	Mr E Garrard Mrs G Hale	St Matthew's Church, Cainscross
1993	December 4th	Puccini's *Messa di Gloria* Mendelssohn's *Hymn of Praise*	Mr E Garrard	Stroud Subscription Rooms
1993	December 18th	Carol Concert Including Cuthbert Webb's Christmas Carol	Mr E Garrard	Church of the Immaculate Conception, Beeches Green
1994	May 7th	Elgar's *Caractacus*	Mr E Garrard	Stroud Subscription Rooms
1994	October 8th	Handel's *Messiah* BT 'Voices for Hospices'	Mr E Garrard	Gloucester Cathedral. In aid of Cotswold Care
1994	December 10th	Haydn's *Creation*, Mozart's *Requiem*	Mr E Garrard	Stroud Subscription Rooms
1994	December 19th	Carol Concert	Mr E Garrard	Church of Immaculate Conception, Beeches Green
1995	May 13th	Mendelssohn's *Elijah*	Mr E Garrard	Stroud Leisure Centre
1995	November 2nd	Liturgical Performance, Mozart's *Requiem*	Mr E Garrard	Stroud Parish Church

1995	December 2nd	Brahms' *German Requiem*	Mr E Garrard	Stroud Parish Church
1995	December 16th	Carols for All	Mr E Garrard	All Saints Church, Uplands
1996	May 11th	Dvorak's *Requiem Mass*	Mr E Garrard	Stroud Parish Church
1996	October 5th	Opening Service, 51st Stroud Festival	Mr E Garrard	Church of Immaculate Conception, Beeches Green
1996	October 20th 50th Stroud Arts Festival	John Sanders' *The Cotswolds*, inaugural performance. Commissioned by the Society. Lennox Berkeley's *Signs in the Dark* Vaughan Williams' *Five Mystical Songs* Vivaldi's *Gloria*	Mr E Garrard	Sibley Hall, Wycliffe College
1996	December 7th	Handel's *Judas Maccabaeus*	Mr E Garrard	Holy Trinity Church
1996	December 21st	Handel's *Messiah*	Mr E Garrard	Holy Trinity Church
1997	May 10th	Verdi's *Nabucco*	Mr E Garrard	Stroud Subscription Rooms
1997	October 18th	Choruses from Oratorio BT 'Voices for Hospices'	Mr E Garrard	Cotswold Care Hospice, Minchinhampton Church
1997	December 6th	Schubert's *Mass in G*, Bach's *Magnificat* Haydn's *St Nicholas Mass*	Mr E Garrard	Stroud Subscription Rooms
1997	December 18th	Severn Sound Christmas Concert – broadcast on Christmas Morning	Mr E Garrard	Gloucester Cathedral
1997	December 20th	Carol Concert	Mr E Garrard	Church of the Immaculate Conception, Beeches Green
1998	March 28th	Orff's *Carmina Burana* Popular Opera Choruses	Mr E Garrard	Stroud Subscription Rooms
1998	May 2nd	Wotton Arts Festival. Oratorio Choruses with Rose Hill School Choir	Mr E Garrard	St Mary's Church, Wotton-under-Edge
1998	November 28th	Haydn's *Creation*	Mr E Garrard	St Matthew's Church, Cainscross
1998	December 12th	Carol Concert	Mr E Garrard	Stroud Parish Church
1999	May 8th	Verdi's *Requiem*	Mr E Garrard	Leisure Centre, Stroud
1999	December 11th	Monteverdi's *Vespers* Mozart's *Vesperae Solemnes de Confessore*	Mr E Garrard	Uplands Church, Stroud
2000	May 6th Millenium Concert	'Last Night of the Proms', with Rose Hill School Choir(*) Handel *Zadok the Priest*, *The King Shall Rejoice* Garrard *We Came Into The World** Collyer-Bristow, *When Storm Winds Blow** Verdi *Chorus of Hebrew Slaves* Strauss/Benatzky *Nuns' Chorus* Purcell *Dido's Lament* Mascagni *Easter Hymn* Verdi *Triumphal Scene* Schwartz *Children of Eden** Lloyd Webber *Loves Changes Everything** Piano Trio: E Garrard, G Fearnley-Whittingstall, A Green Borodin *Polotsvian Dances* Blake/Parry *Jerusalem* Holst *I Vow To Thee My Country* Elgar *Land of Hope and Glory*	Mr E Garrard Soloist Susan Black Leader Nigel Bowers-Broadbent	Leisure Centre, Stroud
2000	October 14th	BT 'Voices for Hospices' Concert	Mr E Garrard	Stroud Parish Church
2000	December 9th	Mendelssohn's *St Paul*	Mr E Garrard	Stroud Subscription Rooms

MEMBERS, 1897-98

Sopranos

Miss Margetson	Miss Johnson	Miss C Woodward
Miss A Okey	Mrs A H Cox	Mrs C Bennett
Miss D Clissold	Miss Barnfield	Mrs H Ferris
Miss Craddock	The Misses Gwinnell	Miss Mabbett
Miss Gardner	Miss McKellar	Miss Cox
Miss A Gardner	Miss Lewis	Miss Stone
Mrs Burford (Cainscross)	Mrs Fernley	Miss Whitmore
Miss Dore	Mrs Emerson	Master Aston
Miss B Lewis	Mrs H Norton	Master Taylor
Miss Slomas	Miss Higgins	Master Herbert
Mrs Hayward	Miss Francis	Master Lasbury
Miss Hayward	Miss Dixon	Master Furley
The Misses Stokes	Miss Hackwood	Master Hutton
Miss Whitmore	Mrs Broad	Master Cox
Miss Gillman	Miss Broad	Master Harman
Miss Reynolds	Mrs James Harper (Ebley)	Master Dommett

Contraltos

Miss A Lewis	Miss Gare	Miss R Cheriton
Miss F Woodward	Mrs Butland	Mrs W Hobbs
Mrs Aston	Miss Fluck	Miss M White
Miss Goodman	Mrs Thompson	Mrs H Erris
Miss E G Guest	Miss Wood	Mrs J White
Miss Gillman	Miss Payne	Mrs J Smith

Tenors

The Rev W H Butlin (Leonard Stanley)	Mr Fuge	Mr Rice
Mr Whiting	Mr Turner	Mr J Bennett
Mr Hoare	Mr Fitzroy Jones	Mr C Gillman
Mr Sugg	Mr A H Cox	Mr Washbourn
	Mr J Stephens	

Basses

Mr Daniels	Mr W White	Mr Browning
Mr F L Daniels	Mr Payne	Mr Nicholls
Mr Higgins	Mr H Norton	Mr A Vick
Mr F Young	Mr J Jacob	Mr F Lewis
Mr Gwinnell	Mr W Hayward	Mr S Hunt
Mr Ridson	Mr W Ridler	The Rev P Lach-Szyrina
Mr J White	Mr Redman	Mr T Knee
	Mr H Gwinnell	

101 singing members

MEMBERS, 1902-03

Sopranos

Mrs S Burford	Miss K Goodman	Mrs Solomon
Miss L Child	Miss R Hamlyn	Mrs Fred Steel
Mrs A H Cox	Miss N F Hobbs	Miss G Tarring
Miss Dorothy Cox	Miss H Hughes	Miss E Thomas
Miss M Craddock	Miss D Lewis	Miss R J Thomas
Mrs Curtis	Mrs D Noble	Mrs Truscott
Miss Darke	Mrs J H Norton	Miss E Watts
Miss Ford	Miss Emmie Nott	Miss L White
Miss F W Francis	Miss A M Okey	Miss F Wintle
Mrs C Gillman	Miss Prout	Miss I Winfield
Miss E Gould	Miss L M Reynolds	Miss E Woodward
	Miss A Rogers	

Contraltos

Mrs Bodman	Miss E Gillman	Miss E Rom
Mrs Butland	Mrs Godfrey	Miss F Tewson
Miss Byford	Miss A Guest	Mrs W Thompson
Mrs A E Chapman	Mrs Jas Harper	Mrs W I Turner
Miss A Dore	Miss M B Jefferies	Miss M White
Miss J Fluck	Miss K E Parry	Mrs J White
	Miss J Woodward	

Tenors

Mr W E Adams	Mr W Godfrey	Mr D P Rice
Mr J Bennett	Mr Wm G King	Mr H C Steele
Mr A H Cox	Miss E Malden	Mr J J Stephens
Mr J E Dyer	Mr A H Morris	Mr H W Washborne
	Mr H Whiting	

Basses

Mr Cornelius Bishop	Mr W Hayward	Mr W M Revell
Mr S H Browning	Mr John Jacob	Mr S J Reynolds
Mr Wm Browning	Mr H O Johnson	Mr E H Talbot
Mr Henry J Comley	Mr K Kempsell	Mr W Thompson
Mr George Cooke	Mr I Norton	Mr Arthur West
Mr R H Cox	Mr A J Pearce	Mr Arthur White
Mr F L Daniels	Mr A W Pearce	Mr John White
Mr J S Daniels	Mr C P Redston	

89 singing members

MEMBERS, 1955-56

Sopranos

Miss H S Archibald
Miss I V R Baker
Mrs M Baker
Mrs D Baughan
Mrs V M Beard
Mrs F Blackmore
Miss P Burghope
Miss E D Eagle
Miss B Eckardt
Miss W Estop
Mrs J D Evans
Mrs A E Forbes
Miss E Gibbons
Mrs S Giddy
Miss B A Griffith
Mrs J Hall

Mrs M Halliday
Mrs E A Hampton
Miss N Hannay
Mrs E Hatherell
Mrs T C G Hodgson
Miss M Horle
Mrs Hoskin
Mrs A J Humphreys
Mrs C Le Huray
Mrs G R Jones
Miss K L Jones
Mrs H F Mann
Miss M Mawhood
Mrs R S Meers
Mrs F E Miller
Miss E D Morris

Mrs J Perry
Mrs S Reeve
Mrs H Renes
Miss R Ricks
Mrs E M Robbins
Miss D Sansom
Mrs K P Savage
Miss E H E Senior
Mrs N E Smart
Miss J I Smith
Mrs G H Taylor
Miss N Thompson
Mrs E Tilstone
Mrs B M Wey
Miss V C White
Mrs E M Whitfield

Contraltos

Miss D Allen
Mrs W J Bashford
Mrs Bigg
Miss E K L Brinkworth
Miss E M Brinkworth
Mrs J Brooke
Mrs C H Burr
Mrs P G Cook
Miss Z Chambers
Mrs G A Davis

Mrs A M Elliott
Miss M C Fowles
Mrs K Fuller
Mrs C L Gazard
Miss J M Hampton
Mrs B Jefferies
Miss L E Johnson
Miss D Leach
Miss M Loydell
Mrs G Macrae

Mrs H B Poole
Miss E P Redman
Miss E M Robson
Miss S M Rowe
Mrs E M Slade
Mrs E M Smith
Miss E M Stephens
Miss H M Tyler
Miss K I Upham
Mrs G V Wright
Miss J M Young

Tenors

Mr F L Baker
Mr J Brooke
Mr G P Davies
Mr E Dyer

Mr D J Evans
Mr F Fuller
Mr W A Jefferies
Mr S G Sullings

Mr G H Taylor
Mr J W Vaile
Mr C W Williames

Basses

Mr G C Attwood
Mr N Bigg
Mr H Canham
Mr C P Craddock
Mr A J Evans
Mr S G Finning
Mr T C G Hodgson
Rev E Hoskin
Mr D A Malpass

Rev A F Maltin
Mr F E Miller
Mr A R G Pearce
Mr H E Norman
Mr S Reeve
Mr W S Scott
Mr W J Sellers
Mr W T Skinner

Mr G M Smith
Mr F W Smith
Mr G E Steer
Mr L J Stuart
Mr F R Theobald
Mr H E Varman
Mr C F Webb
Mr J Wilson

Semi-Chorus

Sopranos
Mrs D Adams
Mrs W Halliday
Miss M Horle
Miss Doris Leech
Mrs H Lowry
Miss Glenys Nelmes
Mrs A Steventon

Contraltos
Mrs Netlam Bigg
Mrs A Davies
Miss M C Fowles
Mrs C Laubach
Mrs J Poole
Mrs V Wright

Tenors
Mr A Elliott
Mr W E Goldthorpe
Mr M Hunt
Mr John Poole

Basses
Mr Netlam Bigg
Mr J Hodson
Mr G Mackworth-Young
Mr A Norris
Mr A J L Steventon

Orchestra

First Violins
Mr E S Brown (Leader)
Mrs H Clutton Brock
Mr L Hatfield
Mrs I Kay
Mrs R Le Noir

Cellos
Mr A Dalziel (Leader)
Mr R Bradley
Miss C Trafford
Mrs H Ashforth
Mr R H Cox
Miss M Hubert

Clarinets
Mr R Moore
Mr W Kealey

Bassoons
Miss Mary Hunt
Mr S Hatherill

Trombones
Mr J Ashby
Mr F J Brice

Bass Trombone
Mr W E Haines

Second Violins
Miss Wadna Keil (Leader)
Mr G Dixon
Mr M G Edwards
Mrs Hardy
Mrs G Mackworth-Young
Mr C Smith

Double Basses
Mr G Thompson
Mr D Brown

Flutes
Mr W H Cook
Mr W Eynon

Contra Bassoon
Mr L Reid-Baker

Horns
Mr W Burditt
Mr F Rust
Mr B Brett
Mr F Stephens

Tuba

Timpani
Mr David Hall

Bass Drum, Cymbals, etc

Violas
Miss F H C Crapton (Leader)
Mr L Franks
Mrs Watkins Shaw
Miss H Holborow
Mrs Roberts

Oboes
Miss Joy Boughton
Miss K J Stater

Cor Anglais
Mr E G Wallace

Trumpets
Mr W Stanley Smith
Mr A J Cooke
Mr A Gledstone

Harp
Miss Elizabeth Fletcher

Organ
Mr C V Allen

137 singing members

MEMBERS, 1972-73

Sopranos

Helen Archibald
Therese A Baily
May J Bailey
Elizabeth Baker
Heather R Ball
Edith M Baxter
Ena H Biella
Eleanor L Bowen
P E Baynsham
Freda Bishop
Eleanor M Boldero
Rosamund Crawford
Nancy J Evans
Janet P Evans
E Dorothy Eagle
Susan Freck

Andrea J Freeman
Marguerite Govier
Kathleen Y Garraway
Joan E Harris
Beryl R Harrold
Alison J Harrold
Sylvia J Heymans
Margaret Hannay
Heather Hayward
Ethel Hampton
Ruth Housden
Dorothy J E Jayne
Sally Jones
Jean M Le Sueur
Diana Lancaster
Barbara Leeding
Joan Miller

Rosemary E Morgan
Mary E Morse
Mary A Macer
Violet Pitkin
Maria Poldevaart
Audrey P Ray
Joyce Riddiford
Norah E Smart
Dora G Sansom
Florence Sollars
Heather Seymour
Joan A South
Pamela Watson
Barbara Whiting
Elizabeth A Webb
Margaret Wesley

Contraltos

Irene M Annis
Jean Bruce-Gardyne
Hilda Burgoyne
Winifred Bashford
Margaret Barnard
Peggy G Cook
Joyce Cordwell
Winifred Cotterill
Irene Drummond
Helen Edwards
Joan Elliott

Clarice Louise Gazard
Kathleen Henson
Nancy Harrison
Patricia A Jones
Gladys Miller
Gloria G Newton
Olive C Lyon
Carole Oosthuysen
Christine Pearce
Dora J A Paget
Betty Parker

June Ryland
Kay Sandells
Miriam J Sturm
Evelyn K Smith
Susan M Smith
Winifred Walrond
Lilian M Woodward
B Joan Wilson
Jean M Warner
Valerie M Wicks
Katherine Young

Tenors

Kenneth Burrell
Edgar A R Dyer
Anthony Franklin

John J Harrold
John P Heymans
W M A Jefferies

Leonard A Keck
Stanley G Sullings

Basses

John E Cripps
J Clifford Cotterill
H C Canham
Miles C Hayward
Timothy K Jackson

Terence D Jones
Frank E Miller
Felix B Paget
Gordon E Steer
George E Taylor
Cuthbert F Webb

R A Y Wesley
M G Whitman
James R Wilson
Robert F Wicks
Douglas J Woodward

106 singing members

MEMBERS, 1999-2000

Sopranos

Sheila Adams
Patricia Bell
Ena Biella
Joyce Bishop
Eleanor Boldero
Hilary Boorman
Jean Charles
Heather Cole
Julie Doyle
Brenda Dunn
Sue Edwards
Moyra Fozard
Ruth Frazer

Glennis Garrard
Marguerite Govier
Imogen Hartridge
Christine Headley
Alison Hesketh
Pem Hickman
Ann Horner
Margaret James
Glenys Jones
Jenny Jones
Mary King
Jackie Leake
Frankie Marsh

Barbara Moinet
Isobel Morgan
Hilary Penney
Bobbie Revell
Jennifer Salt
Frances Sinden
Mo Smith
Susan Smith
Ann Spargo
Carla Spencer
Gillian Welch
Olga Yates

Contraltos

Lesley Abraham
Elizabeth Akhurst
Brenda Banyai
Caroline Bridgens
Helen Briggs
Jean Bruce-Gardyne
Pat Burrows
Mervyn Burt
Jackie Carpenter
Sue Charlton
Anita Damsell
Naomie Dunn
Karen Fletcher
Pearl Foster
Pat Franklin

Sue Freck
Jill Goodfellow
Irene Hall
Anne Hart
Maggie Howey
Janet Jenkins
Sarah Lamerton
Heather Love
Caroline Maguire
Gweneth Martin
Jackie Martin
Mary Morse
Lindsey Murphy
Kate Page
Christine Pearce

Peggy Quelch
Ann Roberts
Audrey Roberts
Fran Russell
Janet Rutherford
Susie Salter
Kay Sandells
Sue Skeats
Deborah Smith
Rowena Stapleton
Margery van Zyl
Olivia Watkins
Jane Willmore
Marna Windeler
Margaret Wood

Tenors

Derek Cawthraw
Mark Harragin
Ian Marsh

Kenneth Morgan
Pat Robinson

Jim Shuker
Ian Stewart

Basses

Alan Bell
Brian Bolsher
Richard Bradley
Richard Burt
Peter Davies
Michael Glas
Ian Goodfellow

Kenneth Hall
Stephen Hassall (and
    guide dog Ulan)
Alan Iles
Terry Jones
Paul King
Eric Martin

Reggie Price
Tony Reeve
Graham Stanley
Michael Walker
George Warren
William Wood

109 singing members

*Verdi's Requiem April 20th 1985, Stroud Leisure Centre, celebrating 150 years of music making in Stroud.
Soloists: Frances Walker, soprano; Diana Walkley, contralto; William Kendall, tenor; Brian Rayner Cook, bass-baritone.
Conductor: Edward Garrard. Leader: Shirley Gladstone.*

Bibliography

Beard, Howard, *Around Stroud* (Tempus, 1999)
Boden, Anthony, *Three Choirs. A History of the Festival* (Alan Sutton, 1992)
Bowen, George, *Rejoice Greatly, Bristol Choral Society 1889–1989* (Bristol, 1989)
Burnett, John, *Useful Toil* (Allen Lane, 1975)
Fisher, Paul Hawkins, *Notes and Recollections of Stroud* (Alan Sutton, 1975)
Foster, Vanda, *A Visual History of Costume, 19th Century* (Batsford, 1984)
Gardiner, John, *World of Netlam Bigg* (Gloucester, 1999)
Greenfield, Edward, Editor, *Penguin Stereo Record Guide* (Penguin Books Ltd, 1975)
Harrison, Susan, Maddocks, Janet, *High Old Times* (Alan Sutton, 1994)
Hibbert, Christopher, *Social History of Victorian Britain* (Book Club Associates, 1976)
Hurd, Michael, *The Ordeal of Ivor Gurney* (OUP, 1978)
Keck, Leonard, *Stroud Choral Society* (Gloucester, 1973)
Libby, *Twenty Years History of Stroud 1870–1890*
Mahler, Oliver, *Stroudwater Valley Mills* (Bailey Litho, 1982)
Miles, Alfred, Editor, *The Family Song Book* (Hutchinson, 1897)
Mills, A D, *Dictionary of English Place Names* (OUP, 1998)
Musical Times 1959
Nolan, Ronald, *S W Underwood* (unpublished)
Open University Arts Foundation Course A102 Units 29–30 (Open University, 1987)
Pols, Robert, *Looking at Old Photographs. Their dating and interpretation* (Reading, 1998)
Smith, Adrian, Editor, *Making Music in the West Riding of Yorkshire* (R H Wood, Huddersfield, 2000)
Sollars, Jack, *Enquiry which Shocked Victorian Stroud*
Thacker, Joy, *Survival and Revival* (Alan Sutton, 1995)
Tucker, Joan, *Stroud* (Phillimore, 1991)
Victoria County History of Gloucestershire (Gloucester, 1972)
Walmsley, Philip, *Stroud* (Alan Sutton, 1994)
Wicks, Oliver, *Marling School 1887–1987* (OUP, 1986)
Ziegler, Philip, Editor, *Britain Then and Now* (Weidenfeld and Nicolson, 1999)

Stroud Choral Society Archives
Programmes 1848–2000
Minutes of meetings 1926–2000

ORATORIO.

STROUD CHORAL SOCIETY.

President:—J. E. DORINGTON, Esq.

Vice-Presidents:—REV. DR. BADCOCK and S. S. DICKINSON, Esq., M.P.

Treasurers:—E. W. WINTERBOTHAM, Esq. and S. GRIST, Esq.

Subscribers of £1 1s. each, for the Season, 1868—9:—Entitling to Two Reserved Front Seats (Dress) at each Concert.

*S. S. Marling, Esq., M.P.	A. Stanley Clarke	N. Jones	Rowland Smith
*S. S. Dickinson, Esq., M.P.	W. Dangerfield	E. Kimber	J. T. Stanton
H.S.P. Winterbotham, Esq. M.P.	*W. Davies	C. W. Kingdom	A. J. Stanton
Rev. Sir F. A. G. Ouseley, Bart.	P. H. Fisher	*A. S. Leonard	W. J. Stanton
*J. E. Dorington	A. Ford	F. Lewis	*S. S. Stephens
Rev. Dr. Badcock	W. Ford	J. Libby	G. Stevens
J. Apperly	*J. Gainer	E. C. Little	J. G. Strachan
*Rev. W. C. Baker	*R. Grist	*W. H. Marling	*Rev. W. Wheeler
J. E. Barnard	*W. C. Grist	*W. H. Paine	R. Winterbotham
R. Berry	J. W. Hallewell	W. S. Pinsent	L. Winterbotham
S. Biddell	*R. Hastings	Mrs. Power	L. W. Winterbotham
*W. Bishop	*W. Heelas	F. Roberts	A. B. Winterbotham
Jas. Bizzey	*G. Holloway	W. Roberts	E. Wise
J. R. Buckler	*H. Holloway	J. Sibree	W. H. Withey
S. Butt	F. James	S. Sims	Rev. E. Woodhouse
*W. Capel	W. Jowlings	Adolphus Smith	Mrs. Woollright
W. Chambers			

THE GENTLEMEN MARKED * ARE ALSO GUARANTEEING STEWARDS.

Subscribers of 10s. 6d. each:—Entitling to Two Reserved Second Seats at each Concert.

J. Elliott	W. Hobbs	J. W. Lewis	H. J. Poolman
W. Foster	E. Hyde	J. Norris	J. Sage
F. Hall	J. Hyde		

THE COMMITTEE HAVE MUCH PLEASURE IN ANNOUNCING A PERFORMANCE OF

MENDELSSOHN'S "ST. PAUL,"

IN THE

SUBSCRIPTION ROOMS, STROUD,

On Thursday, the 13th of May, 1869.

THE BAND AND CHORUS

WILL BE FULL AND EFFICIENT.

DOORS OPEN AT SEVEN O'CLOCK, TO COMMENCE AT HALF-PAST SEVEN.

TICKETS:—NUMBERED RESERVED SEATS, 6s.—FAMILY TICKETS to admit Five, 26s.; SECOND RESERVED SEATS, 3s.—FAMILY TICKETS to admit Five, 13s.; GALLERY (Seats not guaranteed,) 1s. 6d. —to be had at CLARK'S LIBRARY, King Street, Stroud, where Books of the Words may be had, a Plan of the Room seen, and Places secured.

Subscribers have the exclusive privilege of securing Places up to the 3rd of May, after which day the Plan will be open to the Public.

ROBERT BRAGG, Hon. Sec.

CLARK, PRINTER, KING STREET, STROUD.

Index

Page numbers for illlustrations are in *italics*. Works sung by Stroud Choral Society are listed by name.
Choir lists and works within concert listings have not been indexed.

Acis and Galatea (Handel) 25
Adams, Graham 114
Adams, Sheila 86, 87, 89, 93
Albani, Madame 126, *137*
Albert Edward, Prince of Wales 15
Albert, Prince, and Frederick Helmore 14
Alexander, Joan 63
Alexander, Maurice 51–2
All Saints, Uplands 38, 104, 113, 122
Allen, Charles 44
Allen, Claude 31, 78, 86, 91, 92, 131–2; death 93; memorial concert 96; as organist 68, 71, 77, 80, 82; retirement 90; and Songs of Praise 88; and SWU's memorial service 72
Allen, Kitty 132
Allen, Mrs Sidney 55, 64, 67, 69
Allen, Sidney 55, 56
Alto Rhapsody (Brahms) 157
Ancient Mariner, The (Barnett) 27
Angas, Richard 80
Angell, Rowena 96
Apostles, The (Elgar) 63
Archway School 91
Armiger, William 103, 106
Armstrong, Sheila 78
Arts Council of Great Britain 63, 75
As Pants the Hart (Mendelssohn) 24
Askwith, Dr W M, Bishop of Gloucester 75
Ave Verum (Mozart) 105
Axford, Eric 93, 94, 96
Ayers, Angela 109, 140; as soloist 93, 111, 115, 117, 121

Baillie, Isobel 141; sketch *136*, 138; as soloist 57, 59, 60
Baker, Dame Janet 139
Baker, Elizabeth 79
Baker, Salusbury 59
Balfe, Michael 143–4
band music, development in nineteenth century 7
Barter, A 64
Bartlett, May 62
Bashford, Robert 61
Bateman, Robert 89, 116
baton, presentation, and James Chew 11, 31, 81, 142
Batricar 99
Battle of Tewkesbury, The (Hewitt-Jones) 83
Baxter, Edith 83, 86
Baylis, Alfred 23
BBC and *Israel in Egypt* 56; question of recording 65; Songs of Praise 88; Sunday Half Hour 82, 83
BBC Choral Society 72, 127
BBC Symphony Orchestra 72, 127
Beale, Angela 132
Beale, Dorothea M 53
Beard, Ambrose 30
Beard, Howard 31
Bebb, Emlyn 58

Bedford Street Congregational Church 37, 81
Beecham, Sir Thomas 54
Before the Paling of the Stars (Dale) 157
Benedicite (Vaughan Williams) 63, 67, 71
Best, John 93
Biblical Songs (Dvorak) 73
Bigg, Margaret 62, 71, 80
Bigg, Netlam 40, 54, 61, 62, 63, 65–6, 67, 75; and Broadbent 114, 118; as committee member 83, 86; death 100; and Foster 76; and Pickled Boys 77; on Sanders 79; as Secretary 55, 64, 71, 78, 80
Birmingham Music Festival 9
Birtles, Penelope 81
Bishop, Freda 105, 106
Bishop, Mr 143
Black, Mrs V L 64
Black, Susan 120, 124, 141
Blake, Carice Elgar 67
Blake, Hilda 53, 55
Blessed Virgin's Expostulation (Purcell) 87
Blest Pair of Sirens (Parry) 63, 100
Bodey, Grace 62, 64, 71, 74
Boldero, Peter 99
Boodle, Christopher 103, 113, 117
Bordas, Pam 109
Boughton, Rutland 67
Boulanger, Nadia 81
Boult, Sir Adrian 63, 72, 127
Bourne, Iris 74, 76
Bowen, Kenneth 77
Bowen, William 111
Bowers-Broadbent, Bill 115, 119
Bowers-Broadbent, Nick 115, 117, 123, 124
Bragg, Robert 16, 23–4, 32
Bragge, W 23
Braham, Mr 143
Brandon, Thomas 20, 21, 24, 25, 26, 27
Brent-Smith, Alexander 58, 67, 103
Bretherton, David 105
Brewer, Sir Herbert 53, 126, 127
Bride of Dunkerron (Smart) 28
Bridgens, Caroline 117, 119
Brind, Edward 20, 22–3, 24
Bristol Cathedral Special Choir 72
Bristol Choral Society 52, 54, 55, 56, 64, 70, 72, 127
Bristol Philharmonic Society 64, 72
Bristol, Ronald 73
Bristol Royal Orpheus Society 64, 72
Bristol University 72
Broadbent, Maurice 5, 114, *115*, 117–18
Brockless, Pauline 71
Brooke, John 62
Brown, David 105
Brown, Edwin 71, 73
Brown, Geraldine 87, 89
Brown, Wilfred 71, 76, 77
Bruce-Gardyne, Jean 119

Bryngwyn, Owen 59
Burns, Dominic 113
Busby, May 59
Bussage House School 53, 129
Butland, W E 27
Butlin, Revd W 16
Butt, Mr 34
By the Waters of Babylon (Goetz) 54

Campbell, Susan 88–9
Campion, Joanne 103
Canada, Georgetown Choral Society 107
canals, and Stroud 6
Cantata no 51 (J S Bach) 78
Cantelo, April 73, 140; as soloist 76, 77, 87
Canterbury Pilgrims (Dyson) 56, 57
Capel, William 13
Caractacus (Elgar) 108
Carmen (Bizet) 54
Carmina Burana (Orff) 134; performances 91, 118–19; shop window 36
Carnegie Trust 60, 63
Carol Case, John 71, 76, 77, 132
carol service, arranged by SCS 55
Carpenter Turner, Robert 99
Carter, H W 51
Casualty Hospital 12, 17, *37*, 39, 40
Central School, and carol service 55
Ceremony of Carols (Britten) 81, 96, 145
Chalford Silver Band 30, 31, 113
Chambers, Elsie 53, 138
Chambers, Zoura 138
Chandos Te Deum (Handel) 157
charities, 1939 carol concert 58; Barnardo's 106; Benevolent Society 13; Camphill Village Trust 104; Casualty Hospital 12, 40; Cotswold Care 42, 103, 104, 105, 106, 108, 117; Crimean War widows and orphans 40; Cystic Fibrosis 107; elderly 40; hospices 42, 109; Leukaemia Research Fund 42; Macmillan Nurses 105; Malcolm Sargent's Cancer Fund for Children 107; Mencap 103; recent evolution 42; Stroud Baths 40; Stroud Hospital 35, 40; 'the poor' 28
charity, SCS registration as 90
charity concerts 39–42; beneficiaries 12, 13, 40–1
charity jobs 59
Chaundy, E M 43
Cheltenham Bach Choir 79, 139, 141
Cheltenham Chamber Music Group 86
Cheltenham Festival 135
Cheltenham Grammar School 83
Cheltenham Music Society 72
Cheltenham Philharmonic 127
Chetcuti, Edward 92
Chew, Caroline 89
Chew family 30

Chew, James 10, 15, 24, 28, 30, 144; and Band 23, 25; charitable fund-raising 35, 39, 40; classes 32, 142–3; commitments 26; cornet solo 16; early career 11–12; funeral 29; presentation baton 11, 31, 81, 142; and SCS 13–14; timpani 113
Chew's Band 30–1; accompaniment by 8; and *Messiah* 15; timpani, presentation to Society 74
Child of Our Time, A (Tippett) 84
Childhood of Christ, The (Berlioz) 105
Choral Class, Stroud Athanaeum 11
choral societies, growth in nineteenth century 6
Christmas Cantata (Bach) 73
Christmas Cantata (Bush) 78, 85
Christmas Day (Holst) 85
Christmas Oratorio (Bach) 122, 145; charity concert 42; performances 58, 60, 64, 81, 91, 103–4
Christmas Rounds (Hewitt-Jones) 81
Christmas Story (Nelson) 77
Church of England, nineteenth century, music in 7
Church Institute 55, 90, 92, 99
Cirencester Choral Society 14, 19, 22, 24
Cirencester Grammar School 76, 79
Clark, Leonard 114
Clark, Miss 24
Clark, Mr 16
Clarke Bros 67
Cliffe, Nigel 102
Clifford, Matthew 86
Clifford, Robert 73, 74
Coker, Revd Barry 113, 118
Cole, Heather as secretary 91, 92, 93; as soloist 96
Collman, Leonard 34
Come Let Us Sing (Psalm 195) (Mendelssohn) 149
Come Redeemer (Bach) 69
concert dress, ladies 91, 92, 100, 102, 107
concert etiquette, 1866 19
concert hall, question of Stroud's own 64, 69, 74, 83, 85, 91
concerts, and half-closing 69
Cook, Carolyn 87, 91
Cook, Kenneth 97–8
Coombe, David 108, 111
Cooper, Revd Clive 73
Cope, Mary 119, 134
Cordwell, Joyce 93, 118
Coronation Festival (1953) 65
Coronation Mass (Mozart) 104
Corp, Charles 81
Cotswold Players 85
Cotswold Savoyards 134
Cotswolds, The (Sanders) 113, 114, 123
Courtly Masquing Airs (Adson) 160
Covey-Crump, Rogers 88–9
Cox, A H 43
Cox, Lesley 99
Cox, Reginald 31, 43, 46, 74

173

Craven, A E 64
Creation Mass (Haydn) 109
Creation, The (Haydn) 24, 33–4, 145; at Royal Albert Hall 42, 101; performances 15, 25, 34, 81, 93, 104, 119–20
Cripps, John 79, 80, 82, 83
Cruickshank, Enid 54
Cubitt, Sidney 28
Curwen's Tonic Sol-fa 11

Dale, Bradley 121
Dalton, Lucinda 111
Daniels, John 56, 57, 60, 62, 64
Daniels, Lionel 64
Danks, Ysobel 81, 83, 86, 89
Davis, John 98
Davis, Mrs 71
Davis, Sue 93, 95
Davison, Debrah 107
Daw, Philip 65
de Havas, Mary Jane 93, 106, 107
Deakin, Rt Revd Robert, Bishop of Tewkesbury 96
Death of Minnehaha (Coleridge-Taylor) 155
Debenham, George 65
Deller, Mark 82
Denison, John 75
Derby, 1828 programme 143
Dickinson family 32
Dickinson, Lord 75, 85
Dickinson, Mr 16
Dickinson, Patrick 77
Dido and Aeneas (Purcell) 91
Dierck, Louis H 75
Dixit (Vivaldi) 93
Dona Nobis Pacem (Vaughan Williams) 106
Dorington family 32
Dorington, J E (father of Sir John) 16, 17
Dorington, Sir John 17, 25, 44, 45
Douglas, Andrew 120
Douse, Stephen 113
Dowd, Ronald 77
Drake, Susan 81
Dream of Gerontius, The (Elgar) 56, 145; performances 63, 77; SWU's Golden Jubilee 41, 66, 67–8, 71
Drennan, Noel 92
Ducie, Earl 13
Duckworth, Margaret 78
Dunn, Brenda 96, 101, 111
Dunn, Brian 75, 93
Dursley Bach Choir 62
Dursley Operatic Society 134, 135

early closing, for Society concerts 32, 69
Edmunds, Janet 78
Edwards, Sue 104–5, 108, 116–17, 119
Elegy in Memory of Edward Elgar (Brent-Smith) 58, 103
Elgar, Sir Edward 58, 95–6, 103
Elijah (Mendelssohn) 12, 38, 107, 145; performances 20, 21, 25, 28, 43, 77, 87; and EG 99, 110–11, 112; and SWU 46–7, 50, 59
Elliott, Mr 15
Ellis, Kenneth 53
English, Mr 34
Eric Sanders Memorial Prize 80
Erlam, Denys 53
Evans, John F 77
Evans, Nancy 68
evening classes 83
Everall, Shelley 121
Ex-Impresario 20–1, 142

Exeter Hall, London 10, 11, 143–4
Exultate Jubilate (Mozart) 76, 85

Fairy Queen, The (Purcell) 54
Fantasia on Christmas Carols (Vaughan Williams) 60, 61, 81, 89
Fawdon, Benjamin 103
Fearnley-Whittingstall, Gail 93, 107, 111, 116, 119, 133–34; and concerts 97, 102, 110, 113, 119, 120, 124
Fearnley-Whittingstall, George 133, 134
Festival Benedicite (Sumsion) 83
Festival of Britain concert 63–4
Festival Chimes (Holst) 155
Festival Te Deum (Britten) 81
fire regulations, and Parish Church 81
First Philharmonic, print 67, 130, 143
Fitzwater, Mrs 62
Five English Folk Songs (Vaughan Williams) 86
Five Mystical Songs (Vaughan Williams) 60, 61, 93, 114, 145
Five Psalms (Fleming) 76
Flag of England (Bridge) 45–6
Fletcher, Liz 96
Foli, Signor 20
Foote, Miss E 21
For the Fallen (Elgar) 155
Forbes, Garrick 116
Fortin, Neil 96, 116, 117
Foster family 32–3
Foster, Mark 108; as Conductor 73, 74, 75, 76
Foster, Murial 126
Four Sacred Pieces (Verdi) 101
Fowler, Madeleine 101
Fox, Ian 102
Fox, Revd Cannon 28
Fraser, Ruth 117, 119
Friedhoff, Andrew 109
fuel crisis, effect on concert 84
fund-raising 101
Fysh, David 86–7, 90

Garrard, Edward (EG) 115, 123, 124, 134–5; twentieth anniversary 38, 122; 1980s 93, 97, 98, 99, 100–1; 1990s 103, 104, 107, 108, 109, 111, 113, 119, 120; as Conductor 90
Garrard, Glennis 93, 134
George, Michael 88–9
Georgetown Choral Society 107
German Requiem (Brahms) 110, 145; Keck memorial performance 89, 131; performances 51, 60, 80, 93–4, 113
Gibbs, Colonel M St J V (Lord Lieutenant of Gloucestershire) 96, 97
Gibbs, Rt Revd John 105
Gilchrist, James 103
Girls' Technical School 71
Gladstone, Shirley 122; as orchestra leader 92, 93, 97, 99, 100, 104
Gloria (Poulenc) 97
Gloria (Vivaldi) 145; performances 74, 78, 86, 87, 96, 99, 114
Glories of Our Blood and State, The (Parry) 155
Gloucester Cathedral 38, 42, 53, 61, 103
Gloucester Choral Society 15, 64, 70, 72
Gloucester Cooperative choir 127
Gloucester Festival Choir 127
Gloucester Orchestral Society 70, 72

Gloucester Orpheus Society 70, 72, 127
Gloucester Prison 128
Gloucester Regiment 25
Gloucestershire Concert Orchestra 85, 86, 87, 89
Gloucestershire Education Committee 64, 83
Gloucestershire Organists Association 72
Gloucestershire Youth Orchestra 82
God Thou Art Great (Spohr) 149
Godley, Margaret 58
Godsell, Major K B 57
Golden Legend, The (Hodson) 45
Göttingen Choir 98–9
Govier, Marguerite 91, 96
Gray, Joyce 111
Gray, Michael 101, 105, 106, 107, 108, 111, 116; and award from Performing Rights Society 115, 116
Greaves brothers 80
Green, Alison 124
Greenaway, Helen 113
Greene, Eric 60
Greener, Helen 80
Greenhill, Hilary 100
Gregory family 32
Griffel, Clare 91
Griffin, Elizabeth 91
Griffiths, Heulwen 91
Grist, W 16
Gulliver, David 74
Gurney, Ivor 114, 126

Hackwood, Thomas 27, 28, 43, 55
Hale, Gillian 107
Halifax Choral Society 8
Hallelujah for Hospices 42, 109
Hallewell, E G 10
Hallewell family 32
Hallewell, J Watts 10, 15
Halliday, Maude 62, 63, 67, 71
Hamilton, Alex 111
Hancock, Margaret 24
Harbridge, Adrian 31
Harding, Victor 58
Harper, Heather 74, 139
Harradine, Philip 106, 107
Harrold, John 83, 86
Hartley, Michael 87
Hassell, Stephen 111
Helmore, Frederick 14, 15, 16, 22, 129, 142
Henderson, Roy 55, 60, 136
Henriques, Kate 109
Herbert, William 68
Hewetson, Roger 100, 101, 105, 108
Hewitt-Jones, Anita 78
Hewitt-Jones, Tony 31, 77, 78, 101; as conductor 81, 82, 83; retirement 86, 87; and SCS 79–80
Hewlett, John 34
Heymans, Philip 83, 86, 98, 114
Heymans, Sylvia 93, 95, 97, 98, 121
Hiawatha's Wedding Feast (Coleridge-Taylor) 46, 95, 145
Higgs, W 13
Hildick-Smith, Frankie 124
Hildick-Smith, Georgina 119
Hill, Mona 55
Hill, Mr 16
Hiller, Peter 70
Hodges, Anne 89
Hodgson, Mr 63
Holden, Elizabeth 77
Holland, Michael, poem 118
Hollyman, Nicola 108, 111, 113

Holmes, C 20
Holmes, Laurence 62
Holst, Gustavus Mattias von 15
Holy Trinity, Stroud 38, 96, 115, 126
Honour and Arms 24
Horle, Mabel 71, 87
Horner, Ann 108, 119
Hoskin, Niall 105, 108, 111, 114, 140
Huddersfield Choral Society 8, 107
Hudson, Alison 98, 100, 102, 103
Hulbert, Joan 90, 96
Hullah, John 11, 12
Hunt, J 25
Hyde, Mabel 122
Hymn on the Nativity, A (Brent-Smith) 58
Hymn of Praise (Mendelssohn) 15, 28, 45, 108, 145
Hymns Ancient and Modern 7
Hymns from Rig Veda (Holst) 155

Immaculate Conception, Church of the, Beeches Green 38, 82, 106, 109, 117
In Praise of Mary (Bush) 71
In Terra Pax (Finzi) 69
Ineson, Mr 25
instruments, lent to exhibition 67
Israel in Egypt (Handel) 56, 78
Ivor, Ben 47

Jackdaw of Rheims, The (Lang) 55
Jackman, Jeremy 119
Jackson, Craig 87
Jackson, Revd Peter 117
Jacob, John 56, 57, 60, 75, 129–30
Jauchzet Gott in Alle Länder (Bach) 159
Jenkins, Neil 83, 86
Jephtha (Handel) 155; solo cantata 160
Jesu, Priceless Treasure (Bach) 84
Jhesu Christ, Saint Mary's Sone (Oldroyd) 69
Job (Parry) 157
John, Thomas 75
Johnston, David 79
Jones, Darren 122
Jones, Glenys see Nelmes, Glenys
Jones, Hirwen 28
Jones, Nicki 103
Jones, Mr R 83
Jones, Terence 86
Joshua (Handel) 24–5, 73–4
Joyce, Kathleen 73
Joynt, Scott 68
Jubilate Deo in D (Purcell) 158
Jubilate Deo (Gabrieli) 160
Judas Maccabaeus (Handel) 130, 145; performances 17, 24, 57, 60, 86, 115

Kane, Laura 78
Kay, Kathleen 60
Kearton, Harper 28
Keck, Leonard 86, 87, 89, 99, 124, 131; hospitality 82, 84, 85; as President 85, 86; as secretary 82, 83; and Society history 81, 83, 84, 122
Kempster, Stewart 107
Kendall, William 97
Kennedy, Nicki 105, 109
Kern, Patricia 74
Keyte, Christopher 79
Kiddle, Marjorie 53
King Arthur (Purcell) 155
Kingdom, The (Elgar) 158
Kinsey, A 93
Kok, Alexander 81, 83, 86

INDEX

Labbette, Dora 54
Lake, Mary 60
Lamerton, Sally 117, 119, 122
Lancaster, Maria 119
Lancia, Mlle 20
Lane, Mrs John 28
Lane, Philip 106
Langford, Margaret 101
Last Judgement (Spohr) 28, 152
'Last Night of the Proms' 38, *120*, 123–4
Latham, Richard 80, 81
Laubach, Cecil 61
Lavy, Clare 91, 93
lawnmowers, and Stroud 5
Lay of the Bell (Romberg) 151
Lea, Jean 87
Lee, Laurie 114
Leonard Stanley Festival 92
Leonard Stanley Priory 38, 91, 92
Let the Bright Seraphim (Handel) 99
Let Their Celestial Concerts (Handel) 99
Let us now go even unto Bethlehem 20
Leukaemia Research Fund, and Albert Hall Verdi *Requiem* 119
Lewis, Miss 59
libretti, availability 14
Liebeslieder (Brahms) 86, 107
life membership 97
Lloyd, Gareth 102
Lloyd, Mr *137*
Lo, the Full Final Sacrifice (Finzi) 157
logo competition 120, 122
London, c. 1830 programmes in SCS' possession 143
London Handel Festival Choir 20
Lort Phillips, Mrs 47
Lott, Dame Felicity 139–40
Lowis, Denise 105
Lullaby of Life, The (Leslie) 44
Lyall, Harry 88

McCarney, Kate 99
MacDonald, Robert 108
McDowell, Kathryn 115, *116*
Machin, Mr 10, 143
McKerracher, Colin 98
Maden, Andrew 99, 101, 105, 106, 108, 112
Magnificat (Bach) 117
Magnificat (Pergolesi) 86, 91
Maguire, Margaret 98
Malet, Kathleen 85
Malmesbury Abbey 38, 76
Maltin, Revd Arthur F, and Underwood's memorial service 71, 72
Maltman, Christopher 106, 141
Mann, Richard 16, 17, 19, 20–1, 22
Mansell, Frank 114
Marchant, Sir Stanley 132
Marling family 25, 60
Marling, Sir John 83
Marling School 53, 55, 77, 98, 106; song 51, *52*
Marson, Robert 115
Martin, Eric 117, 119
Martin, Jackie 108
Mass in A Flat Major (Schubert) 98, 106
Mass in B Flat (Haydn) 101
Mass in C Minor (Mozart) 99
Mass, Coronation (Mozart) 104
Mass, Creation (Haydn) 109
Mass in D Minor (Haydn) 158, 160
Mass in D Minor (Mozart) 161
Mass in D Minor, Second (Cherubini) 62

Mass for Four Voices (Byrd) 84
Mass in G Minor (Vaughan Williams) 82, 92
Mass in G (Schubert) 117
Mass, Midnight (Charpentier) 86
Mass No 2 in E minor (Bruckner) 93
Mass, St Nicholas (Haydn) 92, 117
Mass, Twelfth (Mozart) 19–20, 34
Massochi, Jeanette 101
Master Mariners (Wood) 55
Matthews, Basil 92
Maunsell, T A K 75
Maw & Sons 34
May Queen, The (Sterndale Bennett) 24, 25, 43
Mayhew, Delyth 105
Meiner, Sian 106
Mencap, charity supported 103
Mendelssohn, Felix 12, 20
Merrett, Jean 114
Merrie England (German) 93
Merry, Revd Tom 96
Messe de Minuit (Charpentier) 91
Messe Solonelle (Gounod) 24
Messe Solonelle (Rossini) 102–3
Messiah (Handel) 27, 66, 86; 1863 hall decoration 33; 1960–78 75, 76, 77, 82; charity concert 40, 42; and EG 90, 100–1, 103, 105, 106, 107, 115; Hallelujah for Hospices 109; popularity 145; and SWU 50, 53, 55; to 1914 15, 23, 24, 25, 26, 44, 46, 129
Midnight Mass (Charpentier) 86
Milhofer, Mark 108
Millennium 123
Millennium Book 122
Miller, Frank 31, 38, 71, 81–2, 85, 86; as president 69, 72, 76, 78, 80, 83
Miller, Joan 71, 86
Mills, Bronwyn 113
Minall, Revd Peter 81
Minty, Shirley 87
Missa Brevis (Kodaly) 159
Missa de Gloria (Puccini) 108
Missa Sancti Nicolai (Haydn) 92
Missa Sancti Nicolai (Mussorgsky, arr Lane) 106, 107
Missa Solemnis (Beethoven) 38, 98
Mitchells, Edna 73
Moayedi, Farhad 82
modern music, SCS as innovator 71
money, comparative value 14–15
Moore, Kenneth 87
Moore, Mary 93
Morgan, Kate 105
Morgan, Mr 12
Morris, R O 66
Morrison, Elsie 139
Moses (Capes) 14, 143
Museum in the Park 31, 66
Music Makers, The (Elgar) 95
Mussorgsky concert, recording 106, 107
mutual societies, development in nineteenth century 7

Nabucco (Verdi) 91, 115
Nash, Heddle 63, 138
National Federation of Music Societies 57, 63, 64, 75, 85
Nelmes, Glenys 87, 105, 108, 122; committee member 71; sketch 141; as soloist 75, 77, 80, 81, 82; soloist for EG 93, 94, 96, 97, 108; soloist for SWU 62, 64, 71; on SWU 128
New-Born Infant, A (Buxtehude) 86, 87

Newman, H 10
Nicklin, Celia 81
Noble, Denis 63
Noel Davies, Martin 115
Non Nobis Domine (Quilter) 63
Norris, Mr 9
Nowakowski, Marian 74
Nuclear Electric, donation 109

O Clap Your Hands (Vaughan Williams) 86
O Gladsome Light (Sullivan) 63
O Sacred Head Surrounded (*St Matthew Passion*) 72
Ode on St Cecilia's Day (Handel) 96
Ode on St Cecilia's Day (Purcell) 98
Ode to the Nativity of Christ (Parry) 158
Odoardo, Barri 136
Oliver, W M F 83
opera choruses, performance 118
Oram, Martin 81
Original Holloway Society 96, 99, 103, 105
Orr, C W 67
Ouseley, Sir F A Gore 22

Page, Kenneth 80
Painswick Music Society 72
Parish Church 66; applause in 80; organ fund 41; organ improvements 74, 75; separate search for organist 73; and SWU 126; SWU as organist 69, 70; as venue 36–7, 54, 58, 62, 86
Park, James 105
Parks, Michael 108, 109, 111
parliament, and Stroud 6, 44
Parry, Sir Hubert 24, 45, 67
Parry, Richard 108
Parsons, David 93, 94
Parsons, William 60
Pashley, Mr 59
Passion of Christ (Handel) 82, 94
Paterson Zachonis, donation 99
Patey, Mrs *137*
Paul, Sir John Dean, and SCS 13
Pearce, Christine 91, 93, 111, 116, 119, 122
Peasant Cantata (Bach) 155
Penney, Hilary 93, 95, 116, 119
Performing Rights Society 87–8, 115
Perkins, Mr 95
Petit, Marie-Louise 103
Petite Messe Solonelle (Rossini) 102–3
Pezzi Sacri (Verdi) 101
Pfeiffer, Herr 15
Philomusica of Gloucestershire 139, 141
Plaice, Ken 91
Plank, W J 51
podium, disappearance 95
Poole, John 62, 70, 71, 73, 75
Portbury, James 105
Power, Michael 105, 108, 109
Power, Tina 105, 108, 109, 114, 115
Price, Christopher 98, 100, 105
Price, Vivien 87
Prince of Wales, later Edward VII 15
printing, expansion 7
Prodigal Son (Sullivan) 24
programmes, old, of other societies' concerts 143–4
Promenade Concert, 1887 25
Proms, Last Night of the 38
Prout, Mrs 60
Psalms (Holst) 75
Purcell, David 79

Queen of My Soul 9, 143

Quelch, Margaret 108

railways, expansion 6
Ransome, Antony 87
Rayner Cook, Brian 97, 132, 140
Read, David 84–5
recording, Mussorgsky mass 106, 107
Regency Percussion Ensemble 119
Rejoice in the Lamb (Britten) 77
Religious Drama Festival 67, 114
Requiem (Dvorak) 113
Requiem (Fauré) 73, 93
Requiem (Mozart) 77, 93, 107, 109, 113
Requiem (Pehkonen) 79
Requiem (Verdi) 36, 38, 42, 74–75, 145; performances 71, 79, 96–97, 120–21, 122
Return From a Far Country (Hewitt-Jones) 86
Revenge, The (Stanford) 152
Richards, Anthony 83, 86
Ricketts, Jenifer 99–100, 101
Ricketts, Keith 77
Ridout, Isobel 79
Ritz Cinema, wartime use 58–9
roads, expansion 6, 7
Robinson, Pat 108, 112, 117, 119, 122
Robinson, Wilf, life membership 108; and Social Committee 93
Robotham, Barbara 77
Rodborough Fort 15
Rolf, Muriel 60
Roocroft, Amanda 98, 99, 108, 141
Rose Hill School 134, *135*; participation 111, 114, 119, 123, 124
Rose Maiden, The (Cowen) 25
Rouse, Mr 34
Rowlands-Pritchard, John 103, 109, 115
Russell, Fran 93, 101
Ryland, June 83

St John Passion (Bach) 65, 76, 88–9, 145
St Laurence Hall (Church Institute) 55, 90, 91, 92, 99
St Mary's, Frampton-on-Severn 105
St Mary's, Painswick 38, 103
St Matthew Passion (Bach) 145; performance 56, 57, 62, 71, 77
St Matthew's, Cainscross 38, 107, 119
St Nicolas (Britten) 77, 80,159
St Nicholas Mass (Haydn) 92, 117
St Paul (Mendelssohn) 22–3, 27, 34, 36, 163
St Sepulchre's, Holborn 129
Salter, Susie 117, 119, 120
Samson (Handel) 19, 24, 145
Sandells, Kay 106, *111*; as committee member 83, 86, 91, 93, 108, 117, 119
Sandells, Leon 114
Sanders, Eric 76, 77, 79, 80
Sanders, John 114, *115*
Sanders, Myra 79, 80
Sansom, Dora 62, 63
Santley, Sir Charles 20, 136, *137*
Sapio, Mr 10, 143
scores, availability 14
Scott, William 62
Scrope, P G 10
Sea Symphony (Vaughan Williams) 103
Seacome, Diggory 119
Seasons, The (Haydn) 149
Second World War, impact 57–8

175

Senior, Miss E 64, 71
Severn Sound, performance on 117
Seymour, Jack 89
Shepherd Boy's Song (Parry) 59
Sheppard, Honor 77
Sheppard, Miss 55
Sherriff, Jane 123
Shilham, K J 51
Shirley-Quirk, John 77
shop window decorations 36, 115–16, 117, 118, 120, *120*
Sibley Hall, Wycliffe College 38, 114
Sibree, J 129
Siege of Rochelle (Balfe) 144
Signs in the Dark (Lennox Berkeley) 114
Simon, Elizabeth 77, 79
Sinden, Frances 108
Sing Ye to the Lord (Bach) 81
Sir Patrick Spens (Brewer) 153
Sleepers Wake (Bach) 55, 80, 145
Sleeping Beauty (Cowen) 27
Sloan, Iain 111, 120
smallpox, effect on 1896 concert 28
Smart, Christopher 77
Smart, Sir George 10
Smith, Adam 110, 111, 116
Smith, Douglas 86
Smith, E S 55
Smith, Malcolm 78
Smith, Mary 91
Soames, René 62, 64, 138
Social Committee 93
social events 91, 98, 131
Sollars, Jack 128
soloists, shared between Stroud and Gloucester 70–1
Solomon (Handel) 78
Song of Destiny (Brahms) 60, 99
Song of Hiawatha (Coleridge-Taylor) 155, see also Hiawatha's Wedding Feast
Songs of the Fleet (Stanford) 63, 100
Songs from the Bavarian Highlands (Elgar) 86, 100, 107
Songs of Love (Brahms) 86, 107
Songs of Springtime (Moeran) 86
Spargo, Ann 116
Sparkhall, Christopher 115
Stabat Mater (Dvorak) 58, 81, 84–5, 94, 107, 145
Stabat Mater (Rossini) 28, 92, 106
Stalman, Roger 77
Standen, Richard 71, 73
Stanton family 32
Stanton, W H 10
Steel, John 84–5
Steer, Canon R P 55, 57, 58, 60, 61
Sterndale Bennett, William 43

Stinchcombe Hill Festival Choir 56, 57, 72
Stone, Mr 47, 48–9
Stonehouse, and *The Rose Maiden* 25
Stonehouse Choral Society 24
Stotesbury, Marcia 59
Strange, Sylvia 93, 94, 114
Stratford Park 47, 66, 67; Leisure Centre as venue 38, 96, 98, 120, 123, 124
street lighting1865 17; 1866 20
Stroud Athanaeum, Choral Class, programme 11
Stroud, Australia, recipient of recording of excerpts from *St John Passion* 65
Stroud Choral Society (SCS)125th anniversary 75–6; 1867 finances 19; 1907 photo 47, 48–9; 1948 finances 63; 2001 photo *123*; Christmas cards *102*; demise and reconstitution 23, 24; foundation 9; logo 89; as permanent rather than seasonal society 17–18; photo 94, *104*; question of independence 85–6
Stroud Choral Society (Keck) 83, 84
Stroud College 74
Stroud Dispensary *37*, 40
Stroud and District Band 72
Stroud District Centre Feasibility Study 83, 85
Stroud Festival 81, 117
Stroud Festival Choir 79
Stroud First Philharmonic, picture 75
Stroud Glee Club 16
Stroud High School 55, 72, 77, 78, 80; participation in carol concerts 79, 88, 89; participation for EG 106, 107; participation for SWU 61, 62
Stroud Hospital 35, *39*, 40
Stroud Museum, Lansdown 67
Stroud Music Festival, 1875 24
Stroud Music Society 72
Stroud, nineteenth century, background 5–8; Borough 6
Stroud Oratorio Society 144
Stroud Parish Church see Parish Church
Stroud Philharmonic Society 9
Stroud Religious Drama Festival 72
Stroud Rugby Football Club 98
Stroud Subscription Rooms 35, *37*; 1869 renovation 22, 23, 34; 1998–2000 renovation 119; booking priorities 98; building 7; decoration 32–3; opening 32; quirks 36; return to 92;

shortcomings 103, 110; as venue 8, 54, 116, 144
Stroud Technical School 72
Suddaby, Elsie 60, 136
sugar bowl, and society finances 64
Sullings, Stanley 62, 63, 75, 80, 99, 103; as committee member 86; as NFMS representative 93; as treasurer 64–5, 71, 74, 77, 78, 83
Sumsion, Herbert 53, 60, 75, 84; and SWU 70, 71, 72, 127–8
Sutton, Joyce 58
Swain, Christopher 96
Swan, Sylvia 84–5
Swindon Choral Society 70, 72, 127

T L Chew & Sons 31, *33*, 34
Tarlton, Revd T H 16
Taylor, George 55, 63, 83
Te Deum (Sanders) 159
Tear, Robert 77, 78, 139
teatowels, and fund-raising 112
Telford, Andrew 101, 103
Tewkesbury Abbey 38, 83, 105, 108
Thanksgiving for Victory (Vaughan Williams) 61
Thayer, Rosemary 78
Theatre Royal, Drury Lane, c. 1830 programmes 143
These Things Shall Be (Ireland) 63
This Child Behold (Cashmore) 79
Thomas Keble School, and logo competition 122
Thompson, Barrie 80, 89
Thorley, Barbara 77, 79
Three Choirs Festival 52, 58, 126, 127
Three Introits (Rose) 160
Three Songs of Praise (Dyson) 157
Tidman, J Edis 44, 45–6
timpani, from Chew's Band 31, 74, 113
Tippett, Michael 84
Titus, Graham 88–9
tonic sol-fa 7, 11
Toole, Jack 132
Towards the Unknown Region (Vaughan Williams) 155
transport *152, 154*
travel arrangements, 1865 17
Tregenza, Mrs 51, 53
Trent, Miss 65
Trotter, Paul 98, 99, 100
Tucker, Canon Ernest 86, 95, 105, 132; ill health 99, 101, 103; as president 92, 93, 100; as soloist 91, 93
Tucker, Robert 103
Turner, P 67
Turri, Ida-Maria 102
Twelfth Mass (Mozart) 19–20, 34
twinning, and Göttingen Choir 98–9
Two Psalms (Holst) 145, 158

Underwood, Miss 86
Underwood, Percy 47, 48, 55, 61, 62, 70
Underwood, Samuel (SWU) 29, 37, 46–56, *51*, 62, 63, 64–5, 70, 125–9; anniversary 66, 67–9; as conductor 60–1, 71; death 72; MBE 69; memorial plaque *129*; and Netlam Bigg 80; timetable 69–70
Unilever, donation 99
Uplands Church 38, 104, 113, 122

van Zyl, Margery 98, 107, 116
Vaughan Williams, Ralph 71, 72, 82, 132

Vaughan Williams, Ursula 132
venues, various 38
Vesperae Solemnes (Mozart) 122–3
Vespers (Monteverdi) 104, 105, 122–3
Victoria (Hackwood) 28
Victoria, Queen 28, 43
Voces Clementium (Parry) 45, 145
Voices for Hospices 117; SCS participation in 42
Vyvyan, Jennifer 139

Wagner, Siegfried 127
Walker, Doreen 88–9
Walker, Frances 92, 97, 116
Walker, James 64
Walker, Penelope 114
Walker, Sarah 81, 139
Walkley, Diana 92, 97
Walkley, James 90, 91, 94, 138–9
Wall, Joshua 33, 34
Walrond, Lionel 67
Ward-Davies, Ivor 77
Watkin Mills, Robert 136
Watkins, Olivia 105, 106, *111*, 116, 119
Watkins Shaw, Harold 65, 66, 82
Watts, J 10
Weaver, Dennis 79, 82, 90, 91, 96
weaving, and Stroud 5
Webb, Cuthbert 106, 108, 113
Webb, Mr 16
Webb, Philip 105, 113
Webster, J 69
Wesley, Margaret 89
Wesley, R A Y 86, 89, 91, 92
Westbrook, Cecilia 20, 21
Weston, Richard 117, 120, 121
Westonbirt Society 72
Westwood's School, Northleach 79
Wheatley, P 55
Whiley, Geoffrey 105
White, Mr 46
Whitehead, Jillian 90, 91, 94, 106
Whiting, B 93
Whiting, Mrs M 83
Wicks, R 86
Wicks, Valerie 87
Wilderness, The (Wesley) 157, 158
Williames, E 71
Williams, Revd Kenneth 61
Williams, Leslie 92
Williams, Misses A and M 9, *10*, 12, 25
Willink, Simon 93
Wilson, Jim 62, 86, 103, 119
Wilson, Joan 83, 86
Wilson, Sir Steuart 69
Winterbotham, Edward 16
Winterbotham family 32
Witchell, E Northam 26
Wood, Ann 60
Wood, Peter 59
Woodchester Pianos 119, 134
Woodward, Mr 33
Woodyatt, Miss 10, 143
Woollam, Kenneth 80
Worth, Mary 58
Wright, Mrs G 63
Wright, Helen 116, 117
Wycliffe College 38, 77, 114, 132; Junior School 87

Yates, Barbara 84–5
Yates, Rt Revd John, Bishop of Gloucester 105
Yates, Tony 119
Young, Phillip 91
Young, Vanessa 98

SCS logo designed by Darren Jones, 1999.